Katharina Grosse

LUND HUMPHRIES | CONTEMPORARY PAINTERS

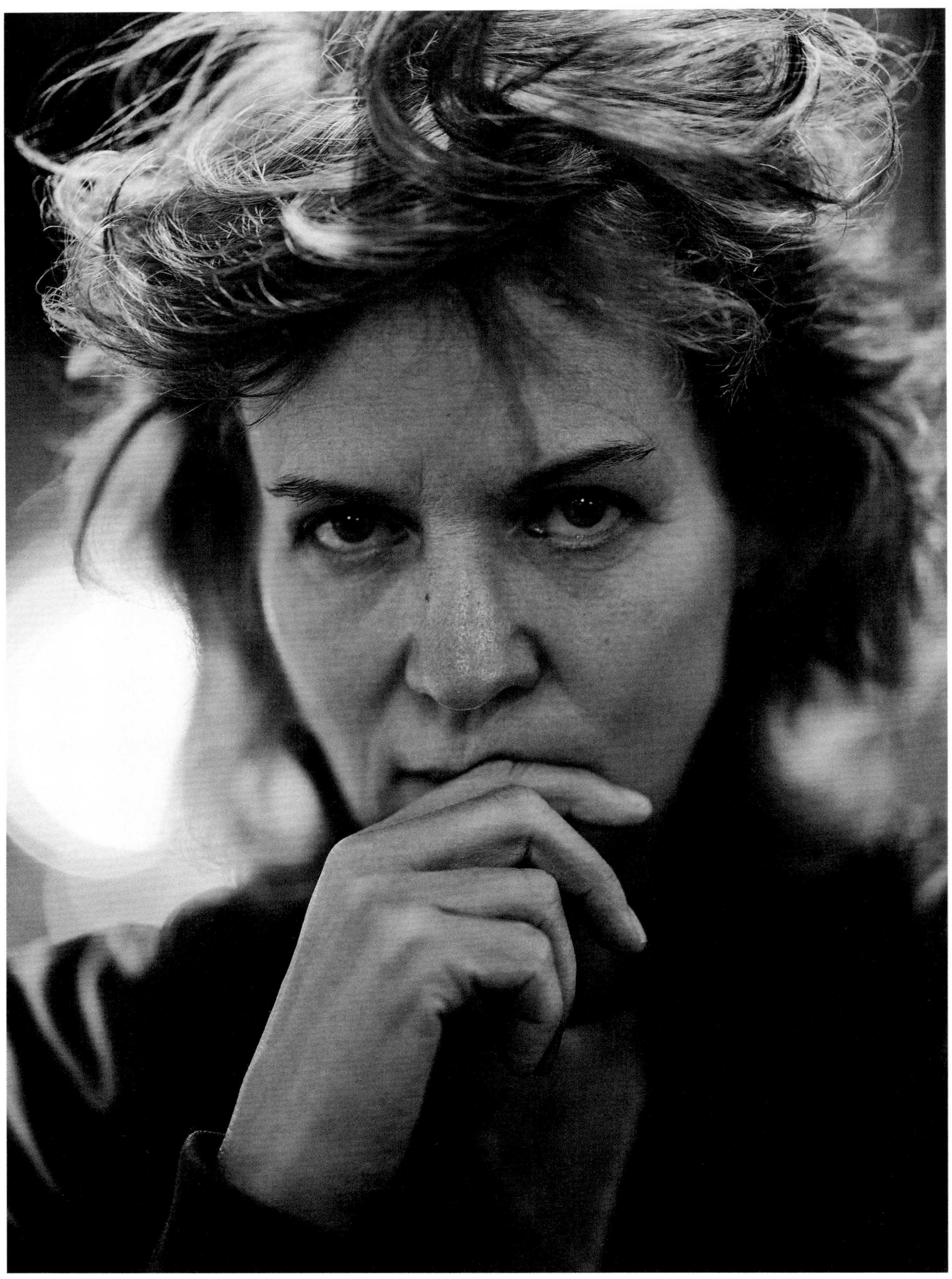

Gregory Volk

Katharina Grosse

LUND HUMPHRIES | CONTEMPORARY PAINTERS

Contemporary Painters Series
Series Editor: Barry Schwabsky

The Contemporary Painters Series is a new, curated series of accessible, authoritative and highly illustrated monographs on the world's leading living painters, which locates painting as a vibrant and vital part of contemporary art.

The series is edited by American art critic Barry Schwabsky, supported by an international advisory board with a specialist interest in contemporary painting. It aims to redefine 'painting' in the contemporary context as work which is done within the conventions and history of painting, but which may incorporate other materials or techniques.

Advisory Board
Paco Barragán, independent curator and arts writer and Contributing Editor of *ARTPULSE*
Tony Godfrey, freelance writer and curator based in the Philippines
David Pagel, Los Angeles-based art critic, curator and writer
Ida Panicelli, former Editor-in-Chief of *Artforum*
Simon Rees, former Director of the Govett-Brewster Art Gallery/Len Lye Centre, New Zealand
Beatrix Ruf, former Director of the Stedelijk Museum, Amsterdam
Philip Tinari, Director of the Ullens Center for Contemporary Art, Beijing
Gilda Williams, art critic, writer, lecturer and London correspondent for *Artforum*
John Yau, poet, art critic and curator

Contents

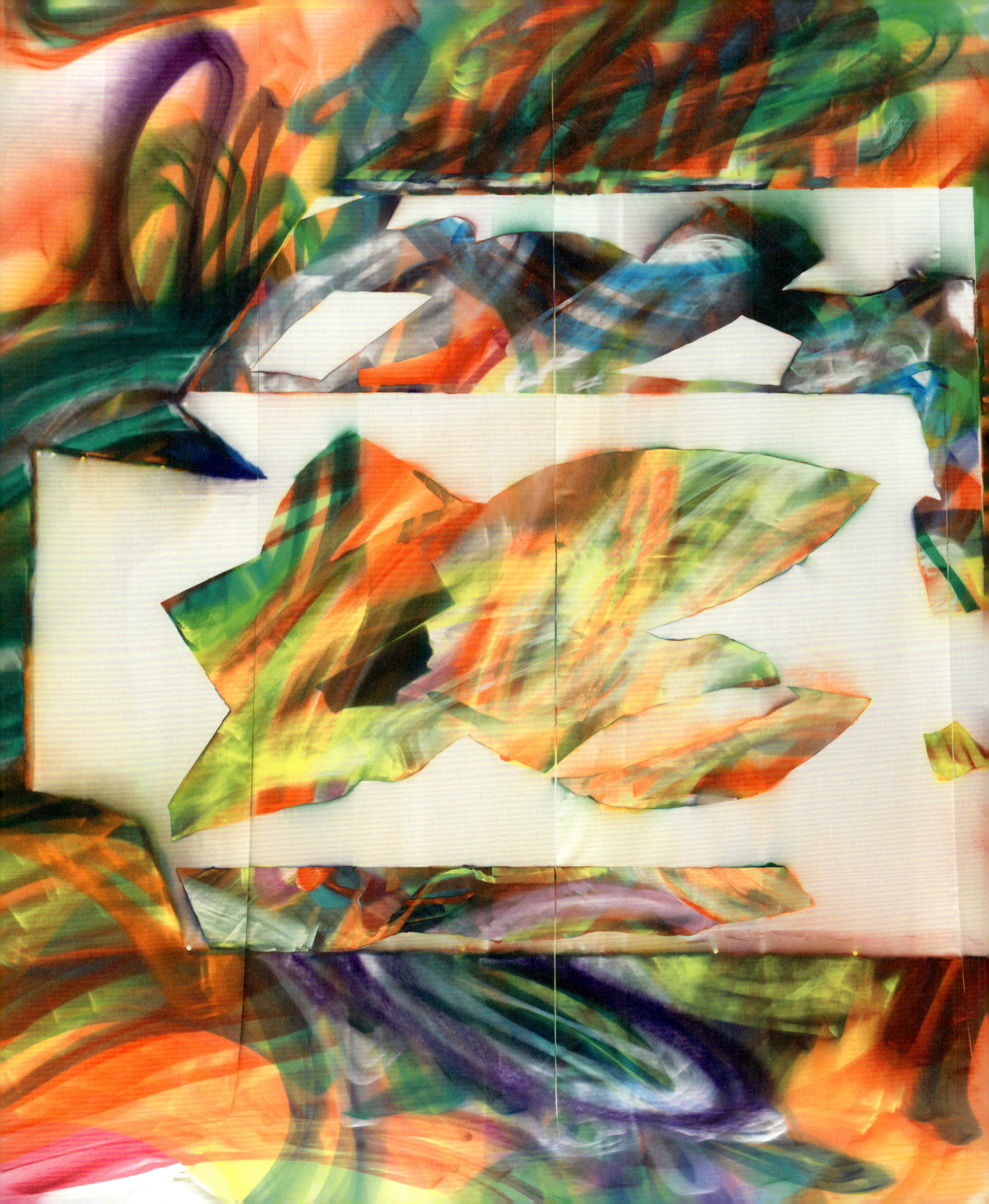

Foreword

Katharina Grosse's work asks us to revise our understanding of what painting is
or can be. Often made on an environmental scale such as one rarely encounters, it
tolerates no preconceptions about what can count as a surface for painting – her
clouds of color occupy not only canvas; not only walls, floors, and ceilings; but also
trees, soil, Styrofoam, furniture, sculptural objects, or whatever: in fact anything,
natural or artificial, that one might encounter in the course of making one's way
through the everyday world of contemporary life. For example, one recent work
incorporated, as Gregory Volk explains, '[p]iles of dirt seeded with rocks and stones,
crates, stacks of sections of drywall, panels, industrial tubing, the floor, walls and
other materials . . . spray-painted blue, orange, yellow, purple, and many colors
more.' In the end, what brings all this into the specific realm of painting is Grosse's
extraordinary abstract use of color. With their shifts in scale and viewpoint, their
strange overturning of spatial distinctions such as inside and out, front and back,
the experience of such works can be disorienting, and deliberately so: the viewer can
hardly find a stable perspective. 'It is very important for me to show there is no one
vantage point from which you can see the work', Grosse has said. 'Every corner, every
bit of the painting that you see will move and change your understanding of what you
see.' But this disorientation need not be alienating – far from it. It means that every
moment in which one interacts with the work can offer new revelations, new pleasure.
This overturning of boundaries, this openness to the unexpected, underlies Volk's
intuition that Grosse's art can best be explicated by way of the idea of carnival, for,
as the Russian thinker Mikhail Bakhtin once said, 'Carnival brings together, unifies,
weds, and combines the sacred with the profane, the lofty with the low, the great
with the insignificant', destabilizing hierarchies and social conventions and thereby
refreshing people's perception of things and of each other. Here, in the most thorough
account yet given of the whole of Grosse's career as an artist, Volk conveys the gist
of Grosse's all-encompassing art with an infectious enthusiasm that will make readers
want to join the carnival.

Barry Schwabsky

1. Wunderbild (detail) 2018
National Gallery in Prague

Acrylic on fabric
1450 × 5620 × 670 cm and 1450 × 5490 × 690 cm
(571 × 2213 × 264 in and 571 × 2161 × 272 in)

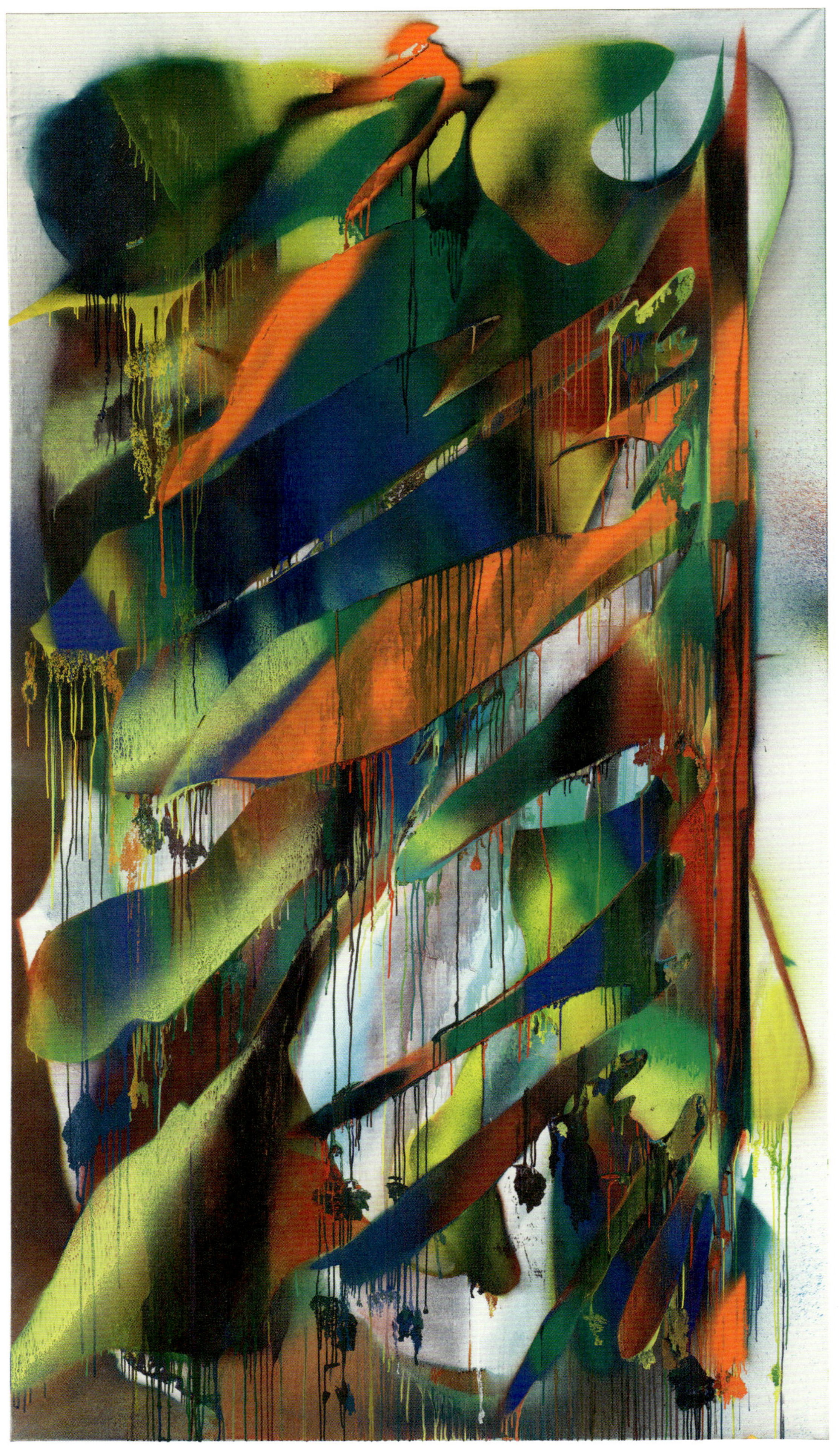

1   Toward a Carnival Art

*Friday I tasted life. It was a vast morsel. A circus passed the house –
still I feel the red in my mind though the drums are out.*[1]
Emily Dickinson, Letter to Elizabeth Holland, May 1866

In May 1866 a traveling circus arrived in Amherst, Massachusetts, the sedate western Massachusetts university town, steeped in Protestant orthodoxy, where the great poet Emily Dickinson lived her entire life, largely as a recluse. Such circuses, bringing colorful excitement and entertainment, bright costumes and garish posters to far-flung small towns, were common and beloved in that era – and they were also sometimes controversial, railed against by clergymen and other upstanding citizens as an affront to morals and civic virtue. According to one account, the circus in Emily Dickinson's Amherst 'paraded through the streets . . . with spangled costumes, gilded chariots, and shiny brass trumpets' temporarily turning the town (including Dickinson's lawn right on Main Street) into 'a magical landscape'.[2]

It is fascinating how Dickinson wrote about the circus parade that passed before her eyes, just outside her house. She didn't write about the exotic animals and costumes but instead about the color red, in a very specific way and as a noun: 'still I feel the red in my mind'. For her, this predominant color was a thing, a thing with presence, and it obviously affected her enormously. It changed Amherst (not at all identified with vibrant colors) and it changed her. In a mere eight words she fused color, thought, and feeling – and she understood that color is a force, not a decoration, that it affects your thoughts and emotions, that it can be powerful and transformative. She also understood that this ephemeral 'morsel' – this raucous circus, this colorful rift in the town's routine – was 'vast', and had vast implications that went far beyond momentary entertainment. For Dickinson, this circus had so much to do with life – with life transformed, with life intensified – however temporarily.

With Katharina Grosse's works, made with her signature spray gun and air compressor on architectural surfaces and sundry objects as well as on canvases, you also feel the red in your mind – along with the orange, yellow, blue, green, purple, and many others. Color is the first and most prominent aspect of what I call Grosse's carnival aesthetic: brazen, rampant colors straight out of the Golden Paints buckets. She uses color in this way not because it refers to an object in the world or something she recalls, but precisely because it does not. According to her, color is 'unreliable and versatile' because 'you think about it differently every time you see it'. It is 'independent from time and location', 'never refers to the past', and 'can appear anywhere'. It is 'very appropriate' to the 'notion of where am I *now* (my emphasis)'.[3]

2. Untitled   2016

Acrylic on canvas
375 × 216 cm (148 × 85 in)

Grosse's large, distinctly carnivalesque paintings on canvas or fabric of the past few years – which have been shown in recent exhibitions at the Gagosian Gallery in New York and London, Berlin's König Galerie and Galerie nächst St. Stephan Rosemarie Schwarzwälder in Vienna – push excessive color almost to breaking point. Using spray-painting and her unusual, irregularly shaped stencils, which she adjusts on the surface to both block and layer paint, Grosse constructs these paintings out of twining and interlacing color-shapes – many angular and jagged, others more rounded and organic.

Some parts are opaque, others are semi-transparent. Parts of underlying background forms advance while parts of foreground forms recede, or half-dissolve. The layered stencil forms abut one another, overlap, pull apart, and morph into new structures. Color is not just pronounced, it's everywhere: sometimes harsh and jarring, sometimes subtle and inviting, and always shifting. 'What you see is what you see', Frank Stella famously declared, but with Grosse's recent paintings, many of which are huge, that is not at all the case.[4] Instead, the more and longer you look, the more you really open yourself to the paintings with all their chromatic shifts and surprises, the more you see and discover – even things you hardly noticed at first. *Untitled* (2016) from Grosse's first exhibition at Gagosian in New York in 2017 (fig.2) is more than 3.7 meters (12 feet) high and 2.1 meters (7 feet) wide. Irregular forms, some with straight lines and pointed tips and made from Grosse's stencils, slant across diagonally; multicolored drips dangle down, almost like swaying tendrils. There are glaring colors – for instance, sharp reds, deep blues, and yellows – but also feathery, soft purples and barely visible aquas. It's a sublime work (some of Grosse's works may recall the emotional intensity and visual grandeur of certain Romantic paintings, although in decidedly fresh ways) and that sublimity was also apparent in Grosse's 2017 exhibition of three large paintings in the chapel at the former church of St. Agnes, one of König Galerie's Berlin exhibition sites. Towering above viewers in the contemplative and meditative space, Grosse's multitudinous, color-packed paintings, each with glowing white bands at the left and top borders, were immersive and overwhelming.

For *Wunderbild* (2018) at the National Gallery in Prague (figs 1 and 4), Grosse took her spray-painting and stencil aesthetic to staggering proportions: two approximately 20 by 50 meter (66 by 167 foot) acrylic on fabric paintings (which she composed in sections) removed from the walls and facing each other on either side of the great hall, with their excess bottom sections spilling onto the floor. These giant-size paintings also functioned as soft walls, and suggested both theater curtains and projection screens. The title, which can be translated as 'wonder picture' or 'miracle picture', has distinctly carnivalesque connotations. It also refers to Sigmund Freud's famous paper on the Wunderblock, a children's writing toy in which two thin sheets, one celluloid and one waxed paper, upon which to draw or write, cover a wax tablet; when the sheets are removed the writing or drawing mostly disappears, leaving only faint traces on the wax. Freud likens this toy to how stimuli received by the conscious mind are stored as memories in the unconscious; the toy is his metaphor for complex psychological processes.[5]

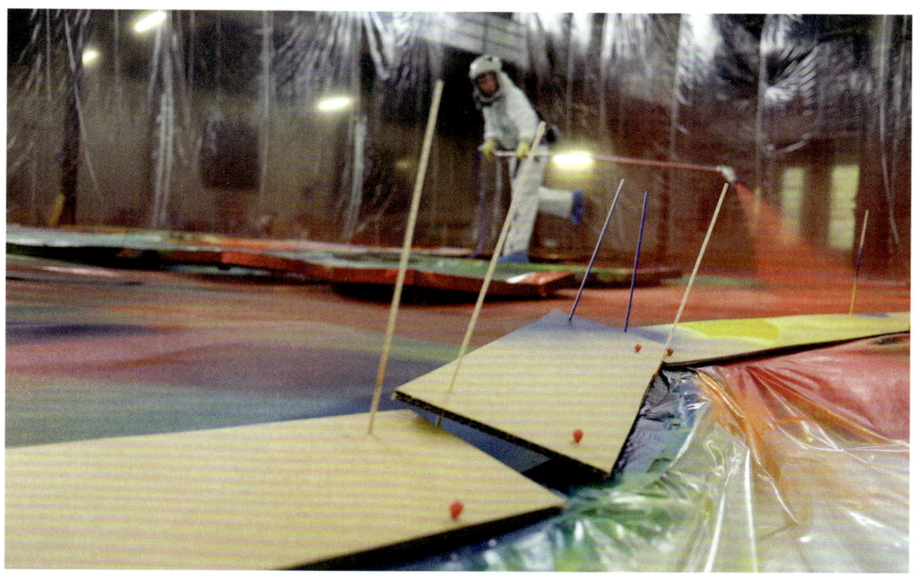

On display for more than a year, the exhibition began outdoors with four chunky parts of trees, liberally painted with Grosse's radiant colors, in a pile atop the gallery's concrete walkway, which was also streaked with colors – an eccentric and dramatic introduction. The colors continued into the museum, covering more tree parts, making a section of the cafe's floor especially eventful and the stairs resplendent.

Grosse's dual paintings in the grand hall coupled rampant colors and free-form shapes with angular forms (made from stencils) and numerous, irregularly shaped blank white areas. Some parts were atmospheric – soft mists billowing on the fabric. Others were clotted and layered, dense with multiple colors and forms, with some areas looking downright sculptural and also architectural. Positive and negative (all those blank areas) space elided, while the white forms were also jarring, interrupting and blotting out the color flow. Moving through the space, you were quite literally inside Grosse's work – sandwiched between the two massive paintings. Her work was simultaneously in front of and behind you, overhead and almost underfoot because of how the fabric sloped across part of the floor. Grosse's outrageous exaggeration of a painting – and I'll have more to say about exaggeration and excess a bit later – filled, even overwhelmed, your entire field of vision and seemed more like a dynamic event than a static painting: a parade of color events.

Also, when you looked closely at what was right in front of you it was as if two dimensions were bending into three. You almost felt you could enter this painted surface, merge with this variegated world, while remaining aware of the surrounding imposing architecture. Everything also changed, constantly. No matter how many times you traversed the whole work, taking in as much as you could and trying to remember what you had seen, there were always new discoveries – a delicate spray of

following spread

4. Wunderbild   2018
National Gallery in Prague

Acrylic on fabric
1450 × 5620 × 670 cm and 1450 × 5490 × 690 cm
(571 × 2213 × 264 in and 571 × 2161 × 272 in)

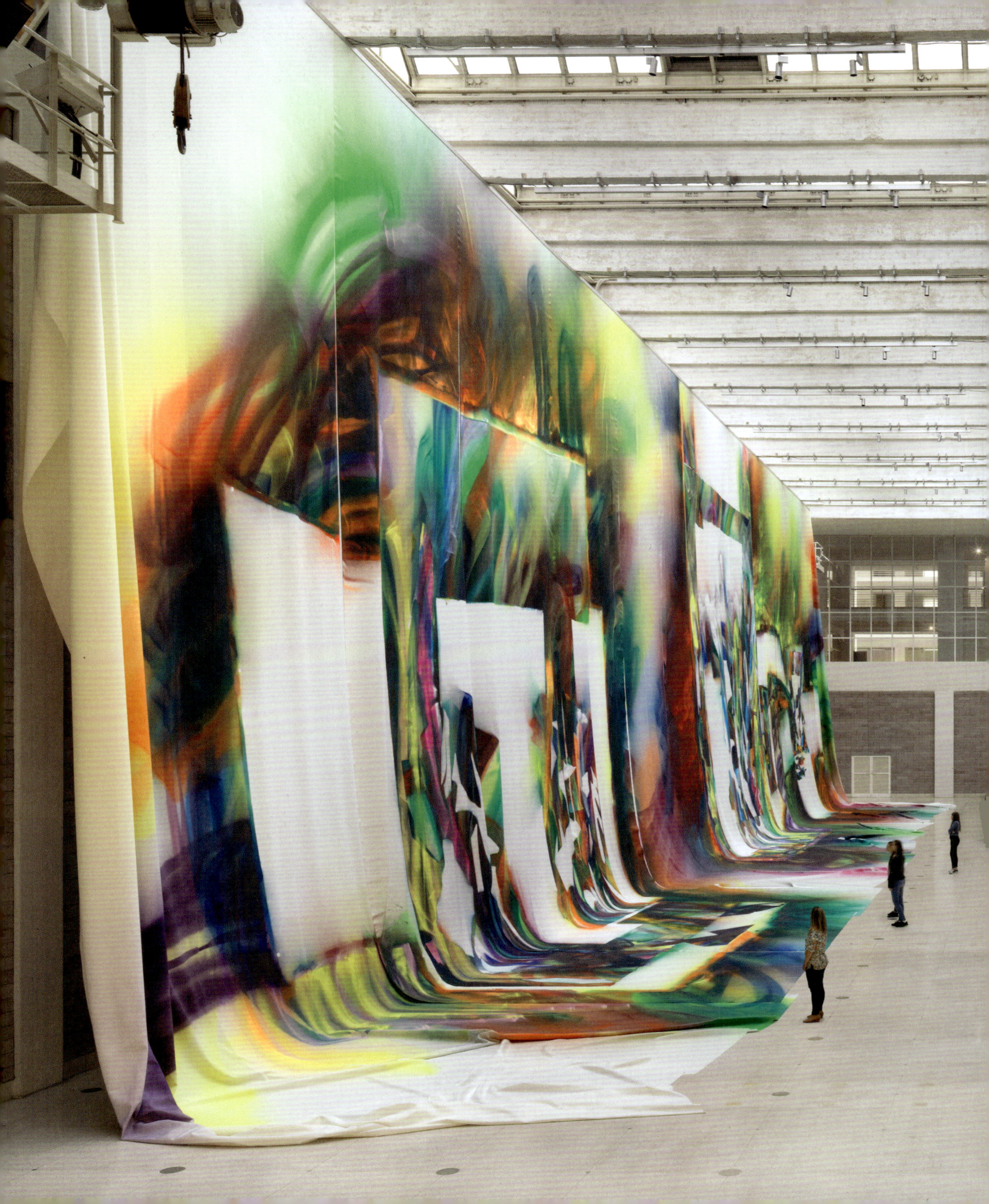

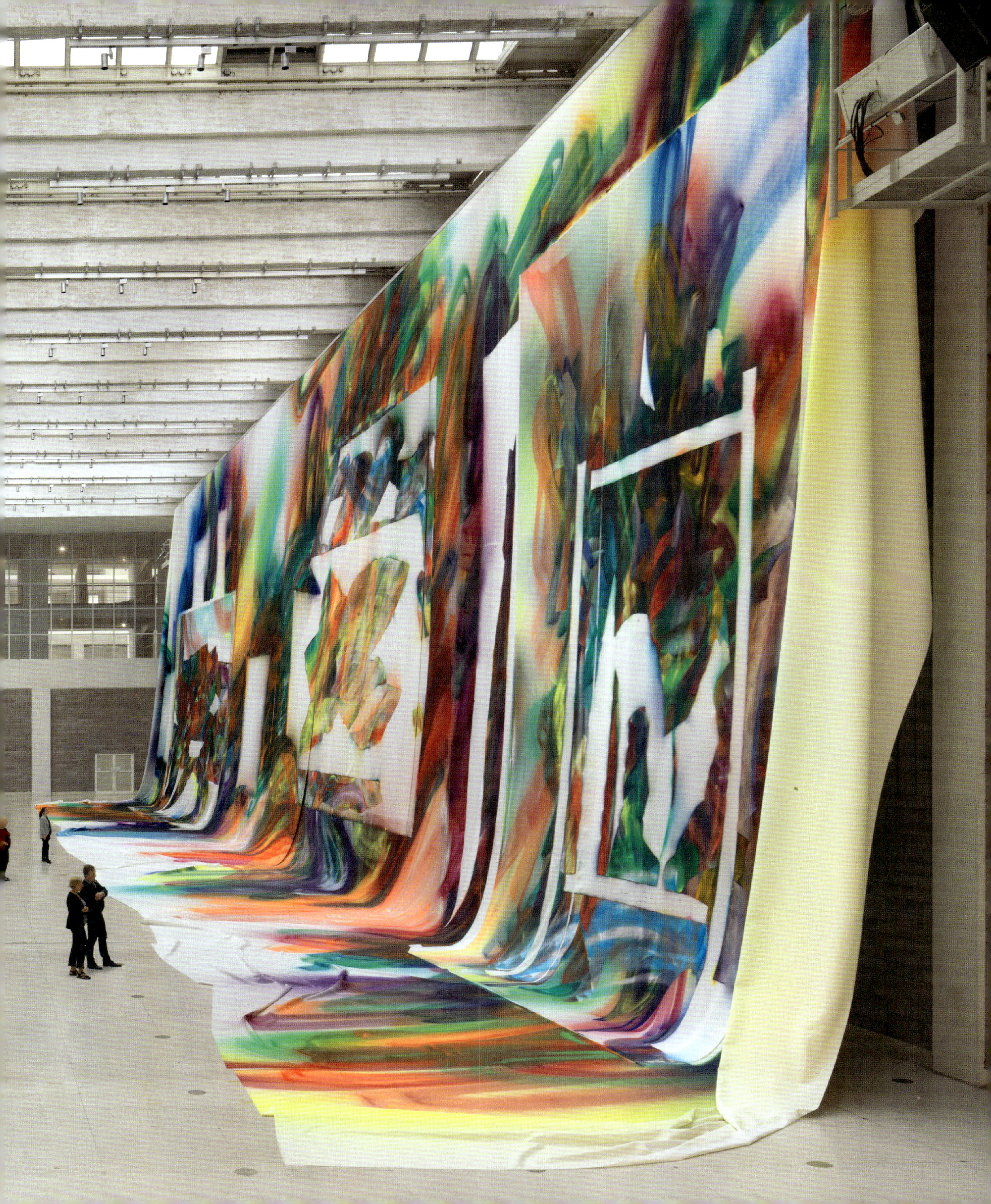

yellow dots; a chunky, multicolored form with a hurtling-asteroid look; abstract forms that just barely hinted at human figures; a magenta-and-orange section that really seemed like an opening, inviting you in. Every now and then a Minimalist, electronic-music sound piece by Grosse and Stefan Schneider commenced, the music responding to and washing over the immersive paintings. Towering over viewers and evoking wonder and awe, this was painting for a new era marked by multiple viewpoints and constantly shifting information.

Like Dickinson's circus, Grosse's full-on painting installations – and *Wunderbild* is one of them – often have an air of the marvelous. They can stun you from the outset and overwhelm you from up close – for instance, her painting installation atop an undulating floor, commissioned for the exhibition *Berlin–Tokyo/Tokyo–Berlin* by noted Japanese architect Toyo Ito, in the Ludwig Mies van der Rohe-designed Neue Nationalgalerie in Berlin, in 2006. With Ito's floor transformed by multiple colors, some vivid and others diffuse and withdrawing, and with circular painted canvases scattered about, Grosse's work looked downright otherworldly (*Untitled*, 2006) (figs 5 and 6). The same goes for Grosse's only work to date made of painted foam, which also doubled as the stage for another of her performances with Stefan Schneider – this time in Austria's spectacular and biomorphic Kunsthaus Graz, designed by British architects Peter Cook and Colin Fournier (*Who, I? Whom, You?*, 2014) (fig.7). The foam – in an expansive pile, with all its swollen mounds, folds, and crevasses – was covered in multiple colors, as was the floor.

But there are other carnival aspects to Katharina Grosse's unprecedented art which, for me, get to the core of exactly why it is so transformative, consequential, and also so exceedingly unusual. Each of her projects begins with a clear-headed appraisal of the site in question, taking into account sight lines, specific structures, architectural details, history, and materials. A fundamental empiricism is a large part of her process, and her paintings clarify and accentuate what is already there – the 'roomness' of the room, so to speak.

However, Grosse's works rarely amount to comprehensive, space-changing installations because they typically involve painting parts of a room (or building, or landscape) but leaving other parts untouched. What occurs represents a fascinating principle of simultaneity, in which the space as it normally is coexists with the same space reconfigured as an artwork. It is for the viewer to constantly shuttle between the familiar and the magical, between the normal life (and look) of a space and its new incarnation as a vehicle for aggressive, mind-bending beauty. Grosse's kind of fractious splendor emerges not from elsewhere, not from an autonomous artwork per se, but instead from the very midst of the normal and known.

In 2002, for the 25 Bienal de São Paulo in Brazil, Katharina Grosse made her first wall painting in an iconic building, the famous Oscar Niemeyer pavilion. She settled on a long wall that most artists would have avoided at all costs, since it features two slots for the bathrooms and corrugated roller doors for the delivery dock. Spanning the whole

right

5. and 6. Untitled   2006
Berlin–Tokyo / Tokyo–Berlin: The Art of Two Cities, Neue Nationalgalerie, Berlin

Acrylic on floor and canvas
170 × 2160 × 1440 cm (67 × 850 × 567 in)

following spread

7. Wer, ich? Wen, du? (Who, I? Whom, You?)   2014
Kunsthaus Graz

Acrylic on foam and floor
691 × 3400 × 5500 cm (272 × 1339 × 2165 in)

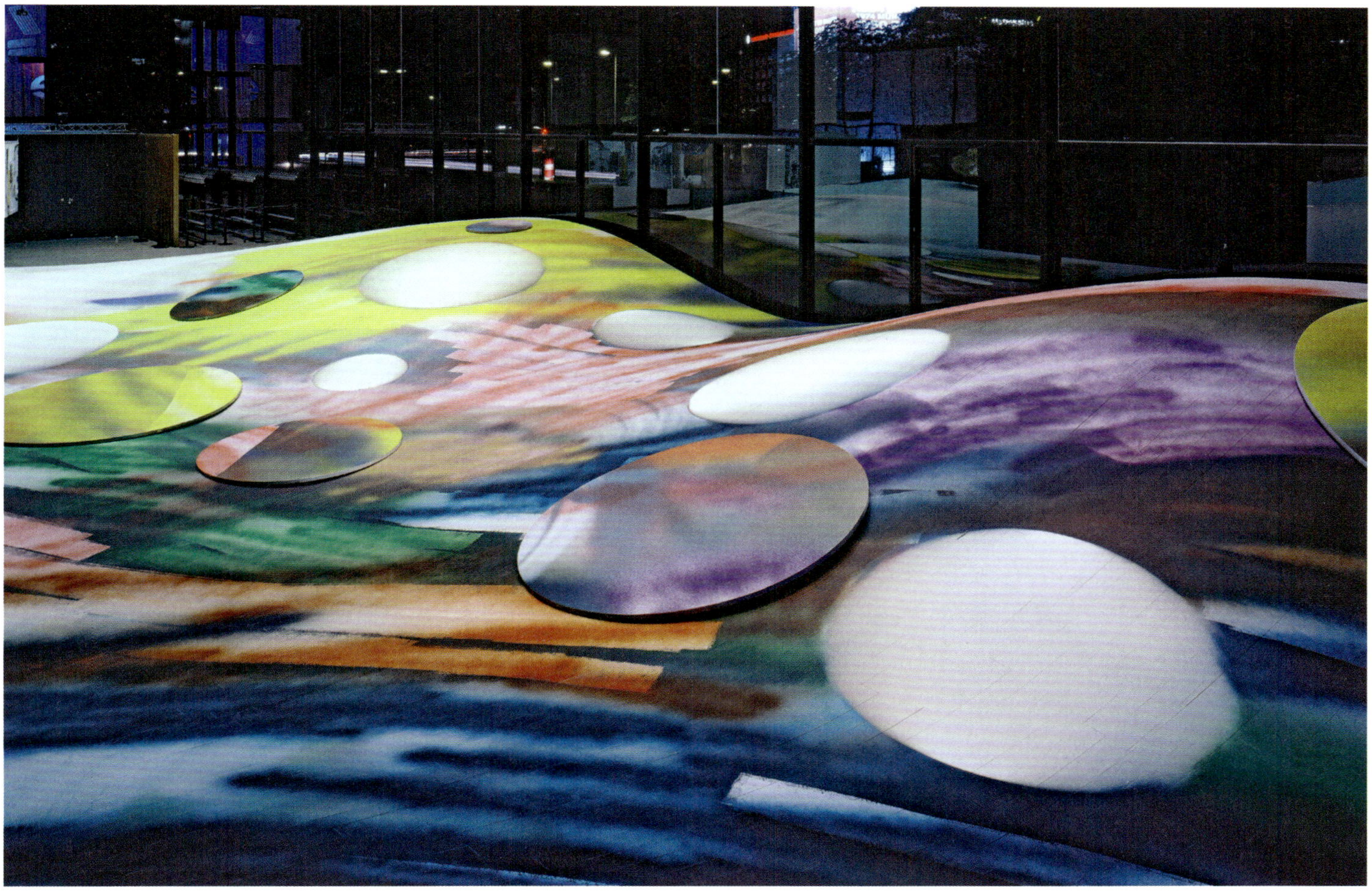

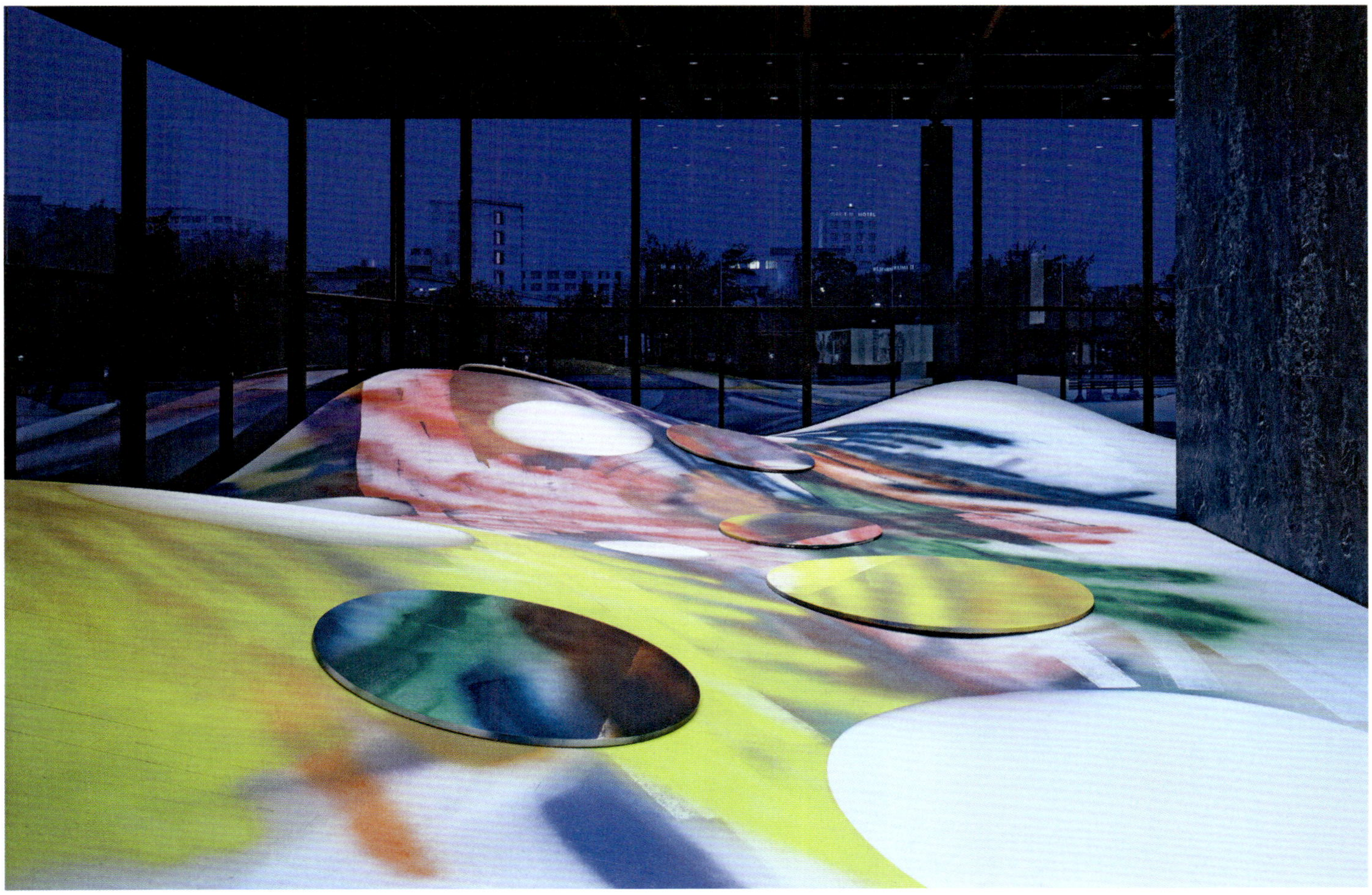

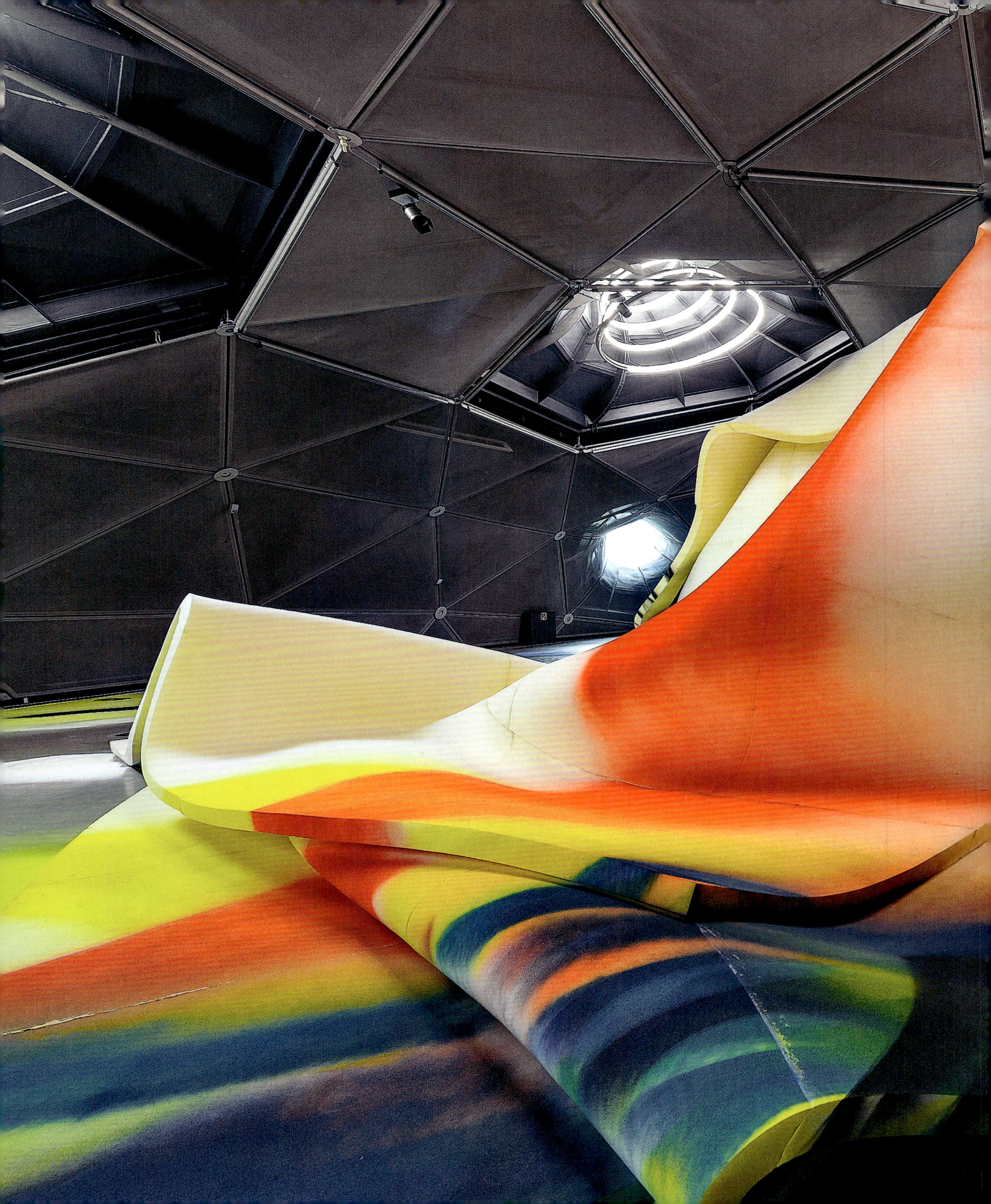

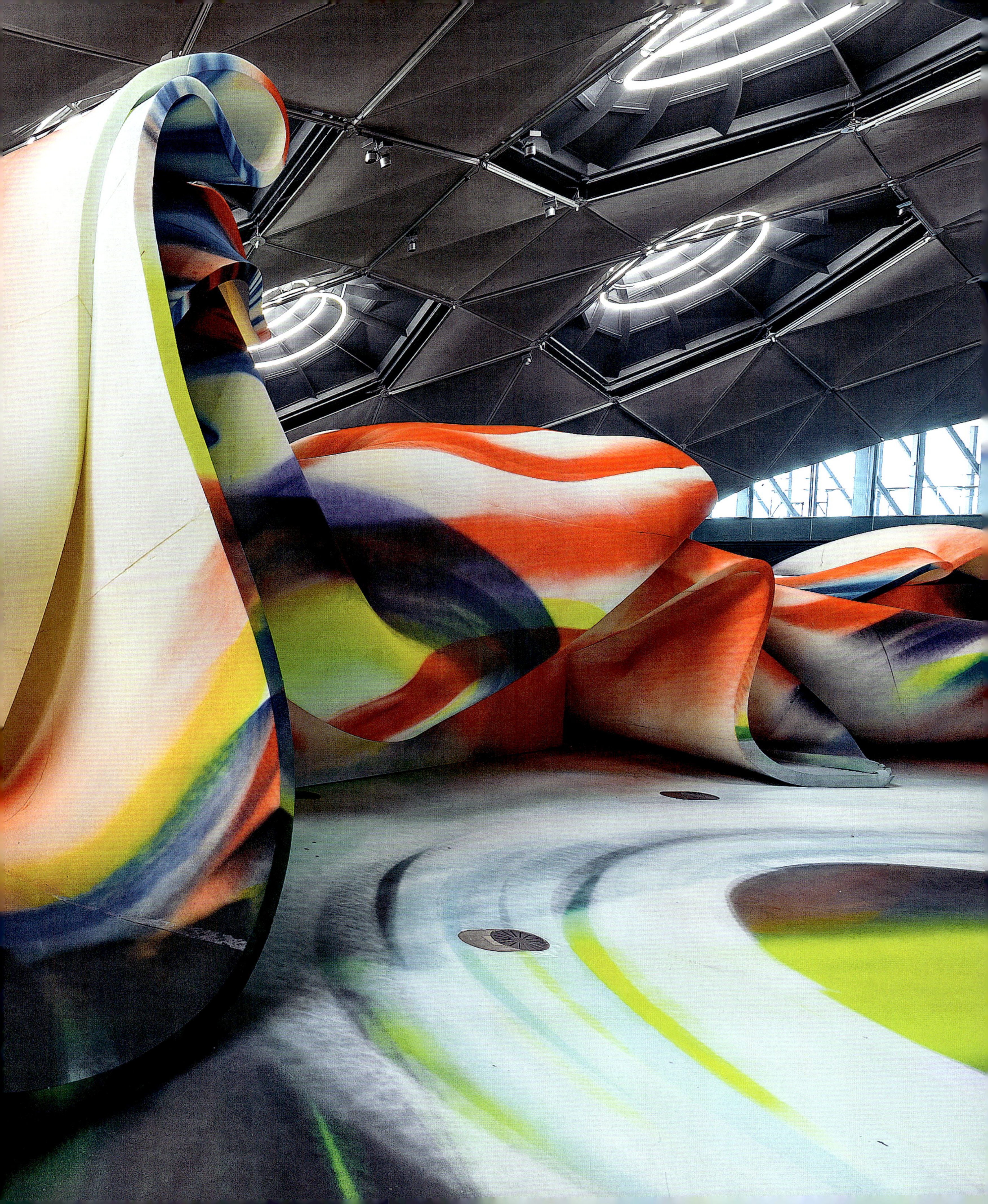

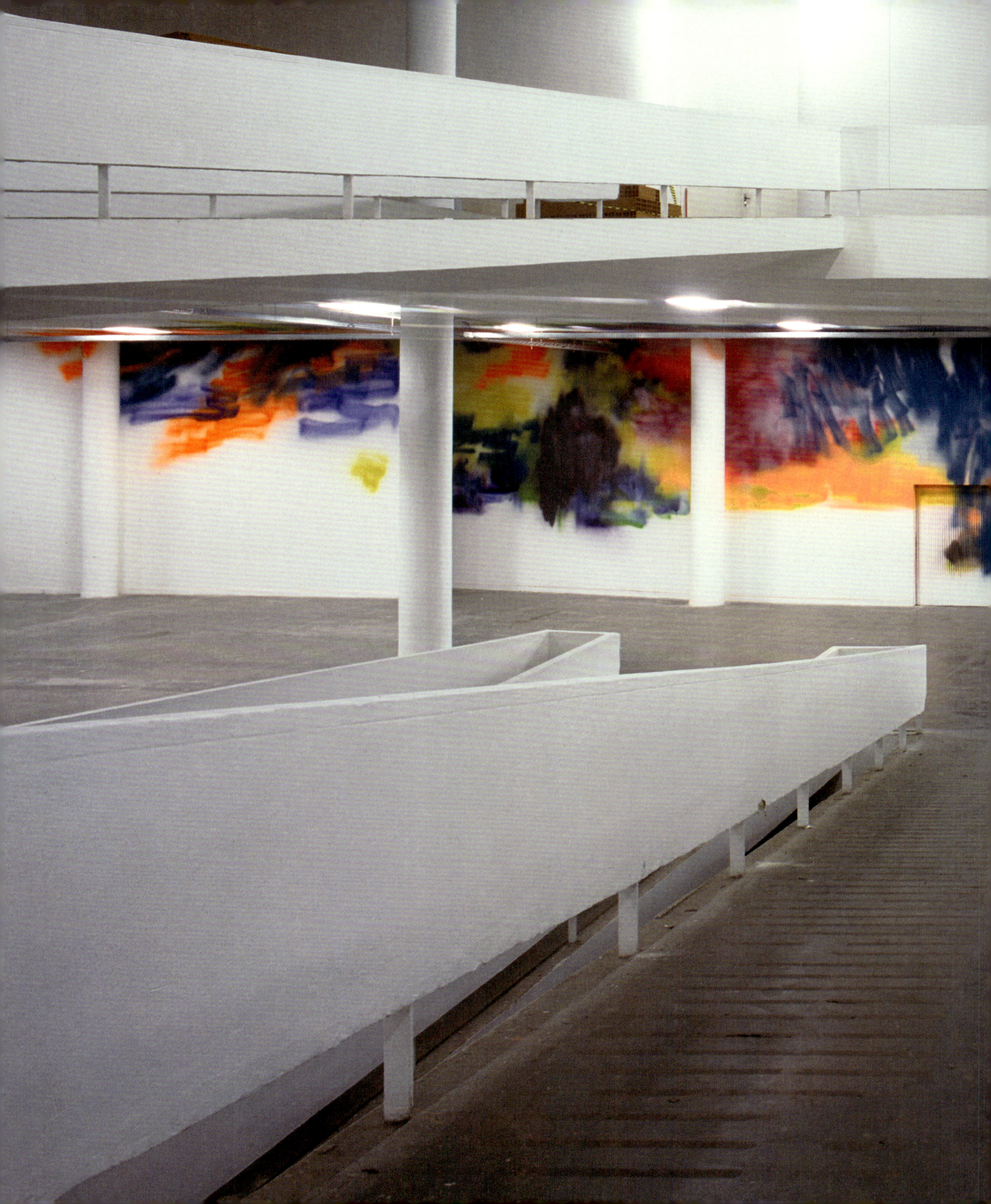

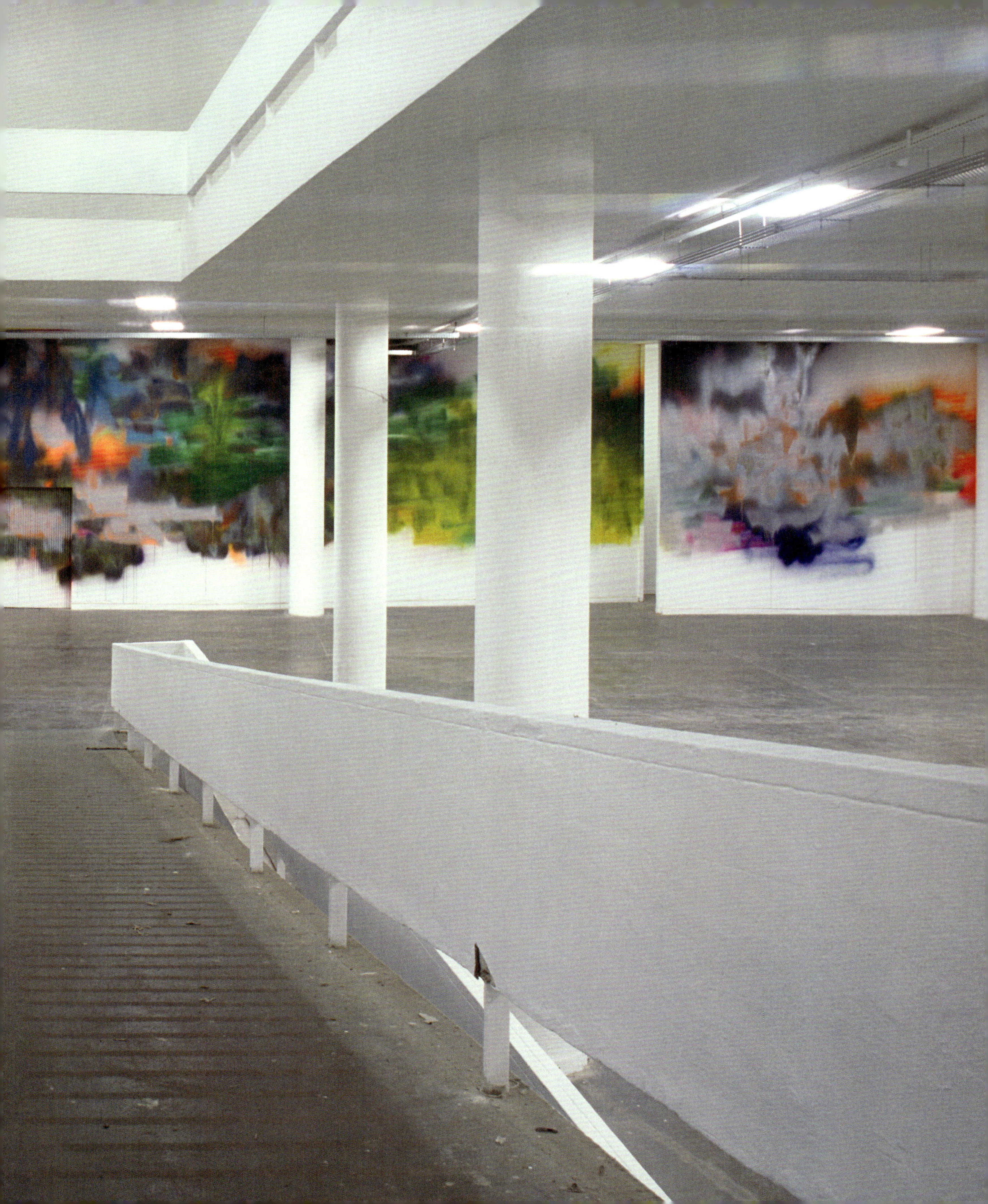

wall and spreading onto the ceiling, Grosse's gigantic painting with its jagged teals, fuzzy yellows, glowing oranges and reds, descending purples, and many, many others invested this workaday part of the space with spectacle and splendor (*Untitled*, 2002) (fig.8).

Speaking of historic structures, Grosse's *Another Man Who Has Dropped His Paintbrush* (2008) was in the seventeenth-century Palazzina dei Giardini in Modena, Italy. In the numerous rooms of the symmetrical building, Grosse presented an emphatically asymmetrical installation with large, colorful paintings leaning against ornate walls, their colors repeating on walls and floor in new configurations; with out-of-the-way sites also painted (closets in gold streaks, a bathroom with a purple mist); with red marks seemingly flying off a painting to land on the ceiling, and a big mound of multicolored soil outside. As viewers moved through the rooms, they encountered, simultaneously, the famous Baroque building with all its underpinning logic and Grosse's chromatic interventions with all their decidedly alternative logic. Of particular interest to Grosse was how the pavilion, in a garden, is a miniature version of a much larger palazzo – according to her, 'a transformed echo of another building'.

In London Grosse made a room painting with a significant surprise, given how much she is identified with vibrant colors (*This Drove my Mother up the Wall*, 2017) (fig.10). She installed a white floor and used a foam stencil to block paint during the spray-painting process. When the stencils were removed, white void areas – which were actually the most prominent parts of the work – remained on the floor and walls. Around them colors climbed up the walls from the edges of the white floor, clustered in a corner, spread across the door, drifted from the top of the walls over the moldings. Most viewers have entrenched expectations of how a painting exhibition might look, and how the paintings in it will 'behave'. Grosse's exhibition thoroughly challenged such expectations – in fact, it broke with them altogether. The whole work circulated in the space, it seemed to be sliding around the room and across the door, always changing, always offering new perspectives, at once rising and descending while the room remained intact. 'It is very important for me to show there is no one vantage point from which you can see the work', Grosse said. 'Every corner, every bit of the painting that you see will move and change your understanding of what you see.'[6]

With these works in mind, it is worth considering the great Russian literary critic and philosopher Mikhail Bakhtin and, specifically, his understanding of the carnival derived from his investigation of pre-Lenten celebrations in Europe, which he applied to literature (especially to Dostoevsky's novels) but which can also be fruitfully applied elsewhere, including to certain kinds of visual art – for instance Grosse's.

In Bakhtin's terms, the 'carnivalized moment' or the 'carnivalized situation' are those times when the normal rules, values, hierarchies, and modes of apprehension are temporarily suspended in favor of a brand-new freedom, which can be at once exhilarating and ungainly, liberating and bewildering; according to him, 'carnivalistic

previous spread

8. Untitled   2002
Bienal de São Paulo

Acrylic on wall
500 × 5000 cm (197 × 1969 in)

life is life drawn out of its usual rut'. Excess, exaggeration, hyperbole, exuberance and parody (all essential, by the way, in Grosse's art) are intrinsic to these carnival moments or situations, which, however, do not seek to transcend normal life; they don't try to substitute a keen new consciousness for an enervated or outdated one. Instead, both routine and carnivalized life exist together and we move between the two, entering the carnivalized situation in order to be tested and transformed and then returning to our normal lives – perhaps shaken, perhaps deepened, perhaps extended – with some of the wisdom that we gained.[7]

I am not suggesting that Katharina Grosse is beholden to Bakhtin, or even that she has read him. I am suggesting that an eccentric, disorienting, carnival under-standing, not just of art but also of the world – which temporarily replaces normal life with all its rules, categories, hierarchies, and endless stratification – permeates her works. And then there is the fact that many of Grosse's artworks really do have a carnivalesque look and appeal, an air of roisterous showmanship and razzle-dazzle spectacle.

In Stockholm, visitors to Katharina Grosse's wonderfully titled, multipart *Wizz Eyelashes* (2014) at Magasin III encountered painted 'balloons', acrylic on PVC spheres several times a person's height, installed indoors in an industrial warehouse (Magasin 6) and outdoors at Nybroplan (fig.9). It was as if a flock of mysterious, colorful, spherical, and maybe even magical objects had suddenly alighted in the city. The same exhibition also featured what Grosse calls a 'resurrection' of one of her ephemeral wall paintings previously exhibited at Magasin III, presented as a life-size print on fabric and

9. Wizz Eyelashes 2014
Nybroplan, Magasin III Museum and Foundation for Contemporary Art, Stockholm

Acrylic on PVC
335 × 1,980 × 300 cm (131 × 779 × 118 in)

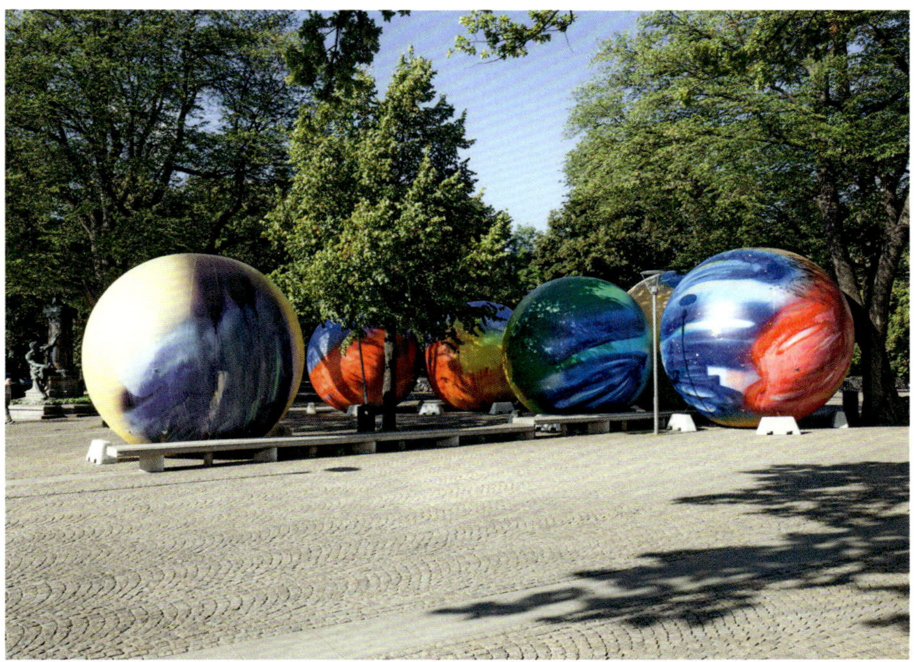

following spread

10. This Drove my Mother up the Wall 2017
South London Gallery

Acrylic on wall and floor
700 × 2100 × 1000 cm (276 × 827 × 394 in)

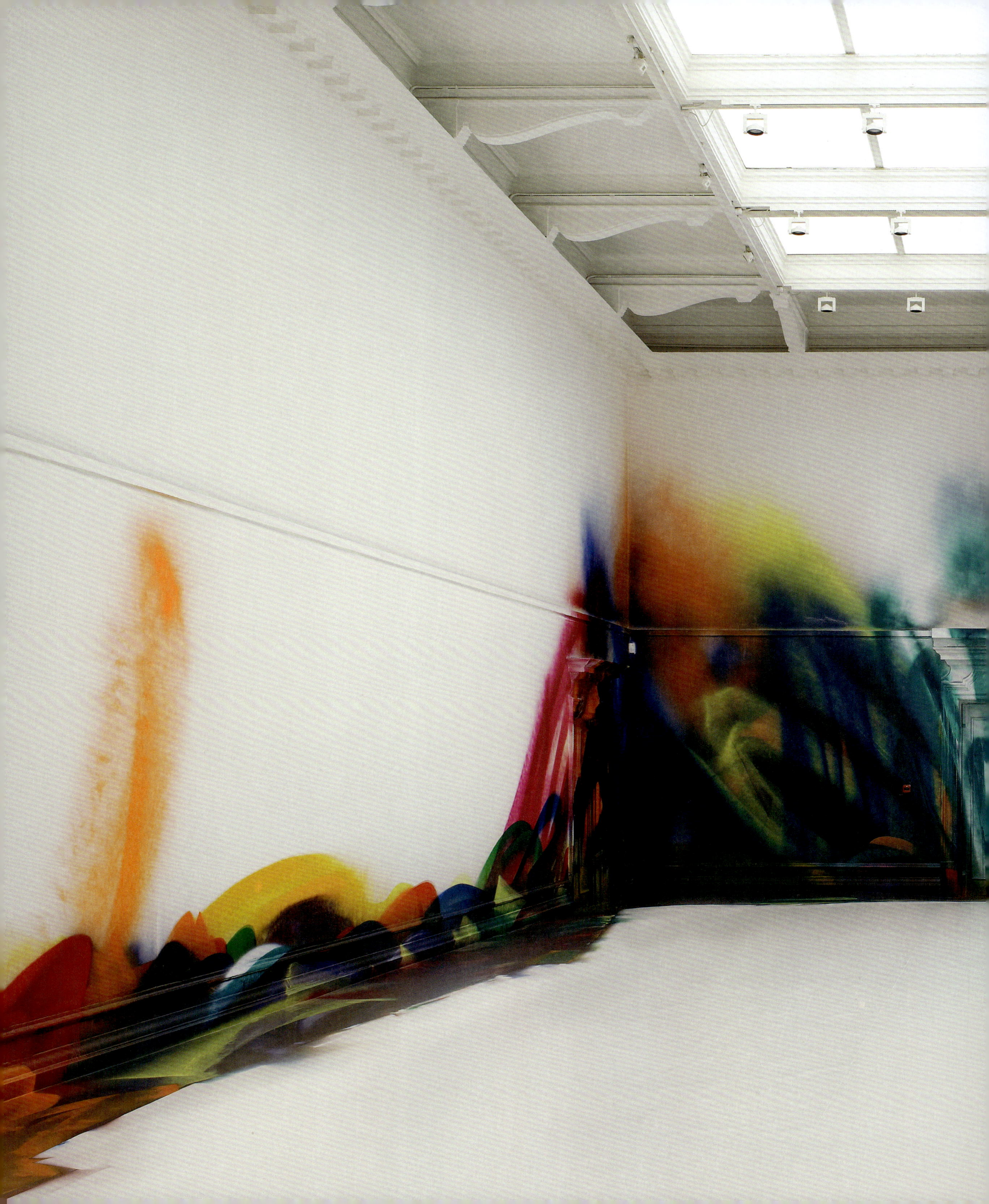

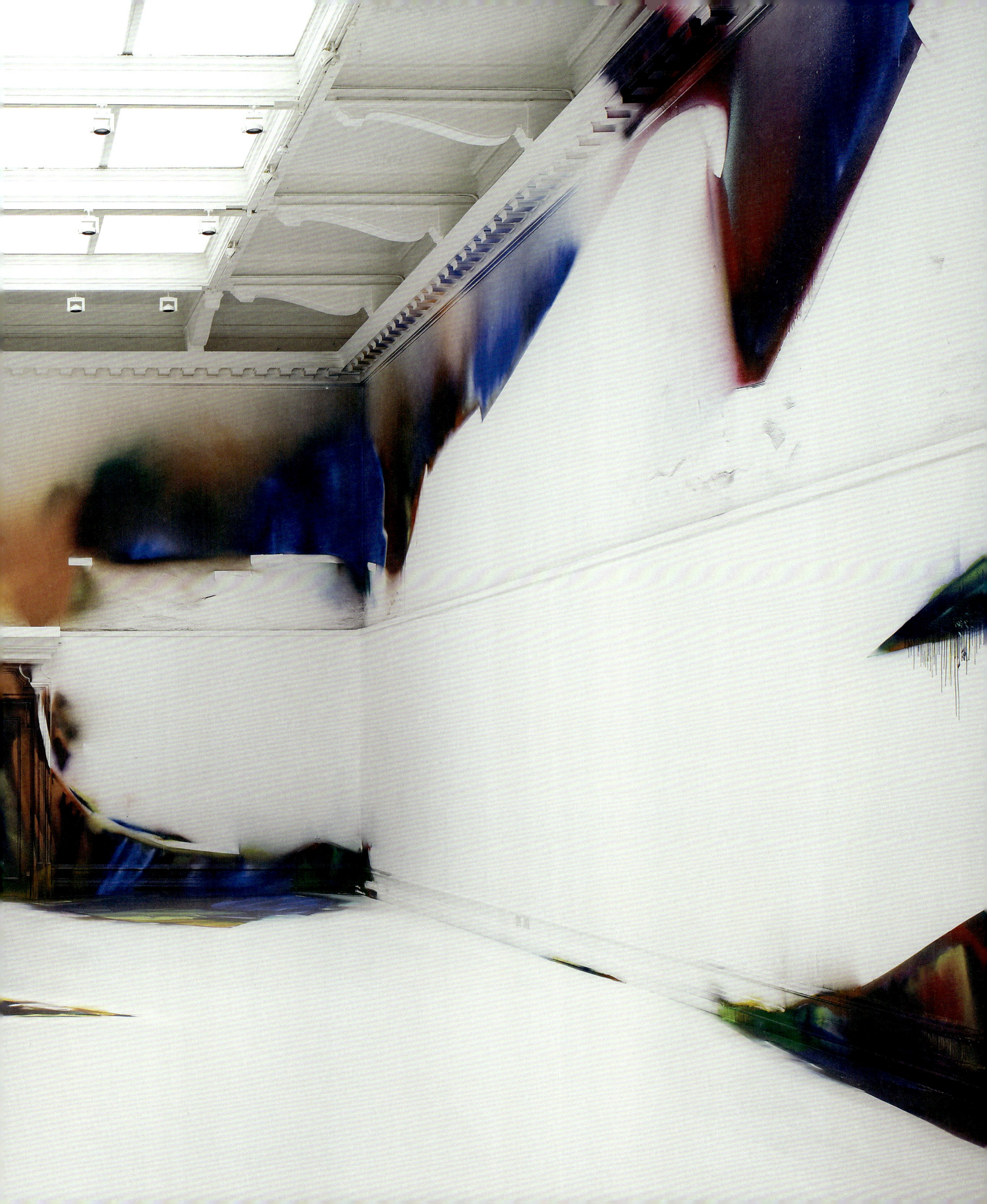

installed in relation to Walter De Maria's stainless-steel *Large Rod Series: Circle/Rectangle 13*, part of which rested on Grosse's print. In Brisbane, at the Queensland Art Gallery, painted balloons floated in mid-air (previously Grosse had incorporated balloons in her 2006 exhibition at Galería Helga de Alvear in Madrid and her 2007 exhibition at the Serralves Museum in Porto), propped up paintings protruded from mounds of painted soil and bright colors gathered on and spread across the walls (*Picture Park*, 2007) (fig.11). This was one of Grosse's most festive works, and it really had the visual sizzle that Emily Dickinson noted in that Amherst circus many years ago.

At the Renaissance Society in Chicago Grosse exhibited floating, giant-size, deliriously painted balloons above a floor streaked with multiple colors and next to walls streaked with the same (*Atoms Inside Balloons*, 2007) (fig.12). Grosse's balloon constellation suggested a really gargantuan atom or molecule, cosmic bodies like planets and moons, and maybe also exaggerated party decorations. It was no matter to her that the balloons sagged and deflated over time. This was an exhibition that kept changing from beginning to end.

Grosse's 2009 exhibition *Shadowbox* at the Temporäre Kunsthalle in Berlin featured four huge, carved structures, made of glass-fiber-reinforced foam leaning against the walls; with a vaguely science-fiction look they are among the most unusual paintings you are ever likely to see (fig.13). Grosse painted the outside surfaces of these warped structures with markedly differing colors and gestures: cloud-like purples and reds, jagged yellows, swooping greens; blank white areas mix with these colors. She left the inside surfaces (which you can duck around to see) unpainted and white. Holes and carved gaps allow you to look at but also right through these works, which, while massive, seem precarious: just barely balancing. In a way they seem like physical mist and you could imagine them easing off the floor, floating in the space. They are really heavy paintings that want to levitate.

Some of Grosse's architectural works are permanent, a large, overhead painting on two upper walls in Toronto's Pearson International Airport, for instance, that she once likened to 'a child [who] has gone mad with a felt pen'.[8] *Untitled* (2003) in Terminal 1, and still going strong, is a bold array of jagged oranges and yellows, diagonal reddish-pink streaks that swarm around a cluster of blue and green stains, a section in which horizontal reds merge with greens and soft purples, among many others, and it courses and swirls above ticket counters and lines of passengers, directing people's attention up toward the ceiling and, implicitly, toward the sky, where they will soon be anyway (fig.14).

In the Menlo Park, California headquarters of Facebook, designed by Frank Gehry, there is another permanent work by Grosse. In the glass-and-steel foyer Grosse's dramatic work on one wall, part of the ceiling and metal beams measures more than 20 meters (65 feet) high and 17.5 meters (57 feet) wide (*Untitled*, 2015) (fig.15). Long, curving blue strands interact with yellow, green, and red diagonals while multiple colors spread across metal beams and gather on the ceiling; in the headquarters of one of the most prominent corporations of this era Grosse's painting is decidedly non-corporate art.

right

11. Picture Park   2007
Queensland Art Gallery, Brisbane

Acrylic on wall, soil, latex balloons, and canvas
1540 × 4895 × 855 cm (606 × 1927 × 337 in)

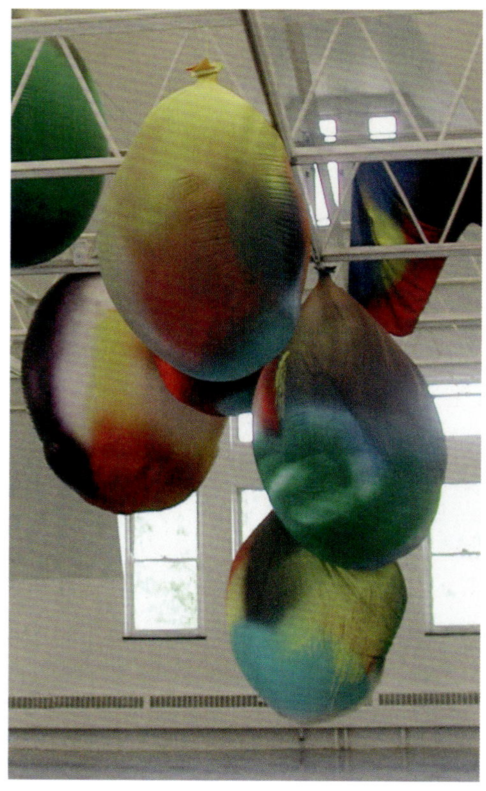

above and following spread

12. Atoms Inside Balloons   2007
Renaissance Society, Chicago

Acrylic on wall, floor, and latex balloons
900 × 2438 × 1219 cm (354 × 960 × 480 in)

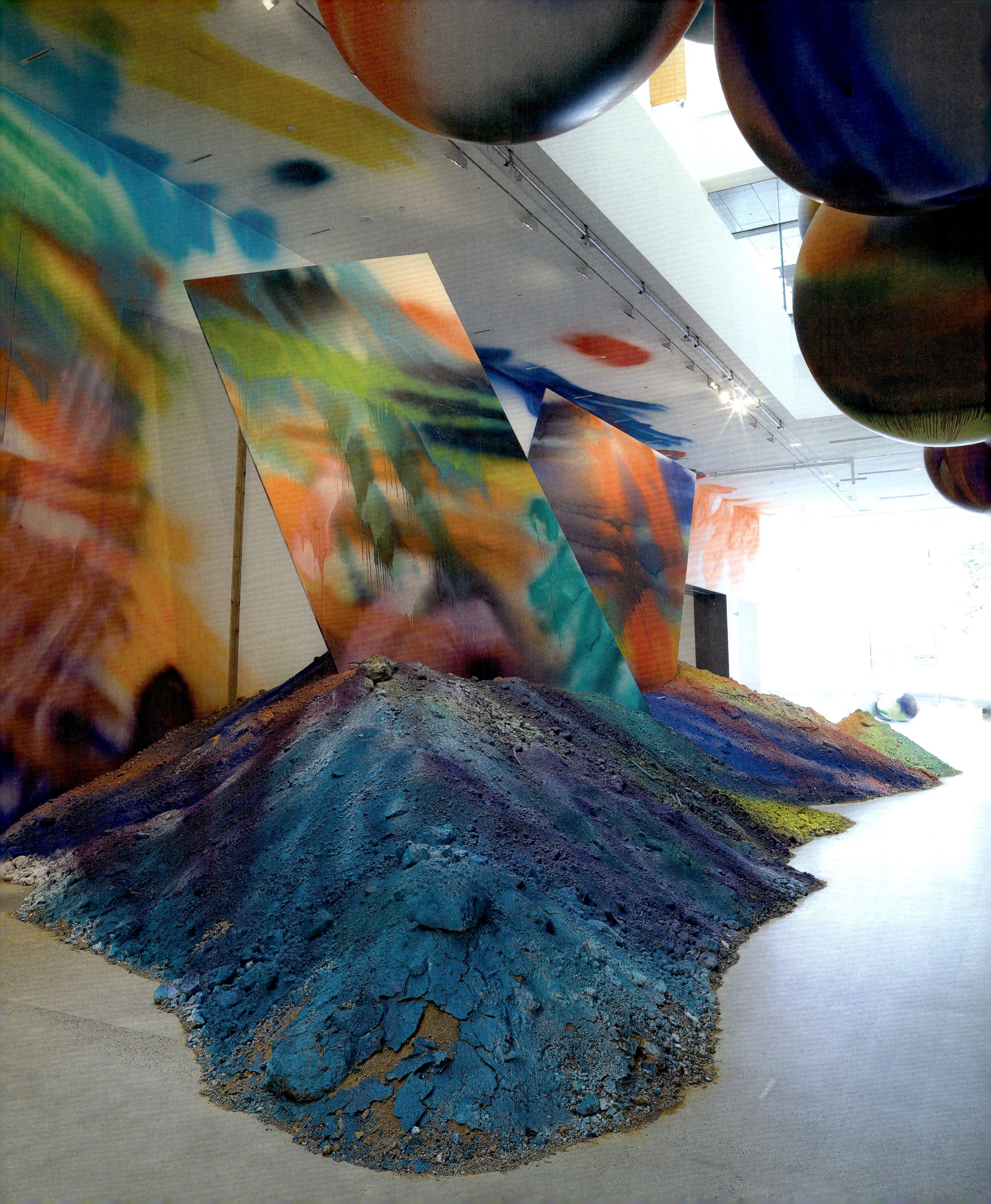

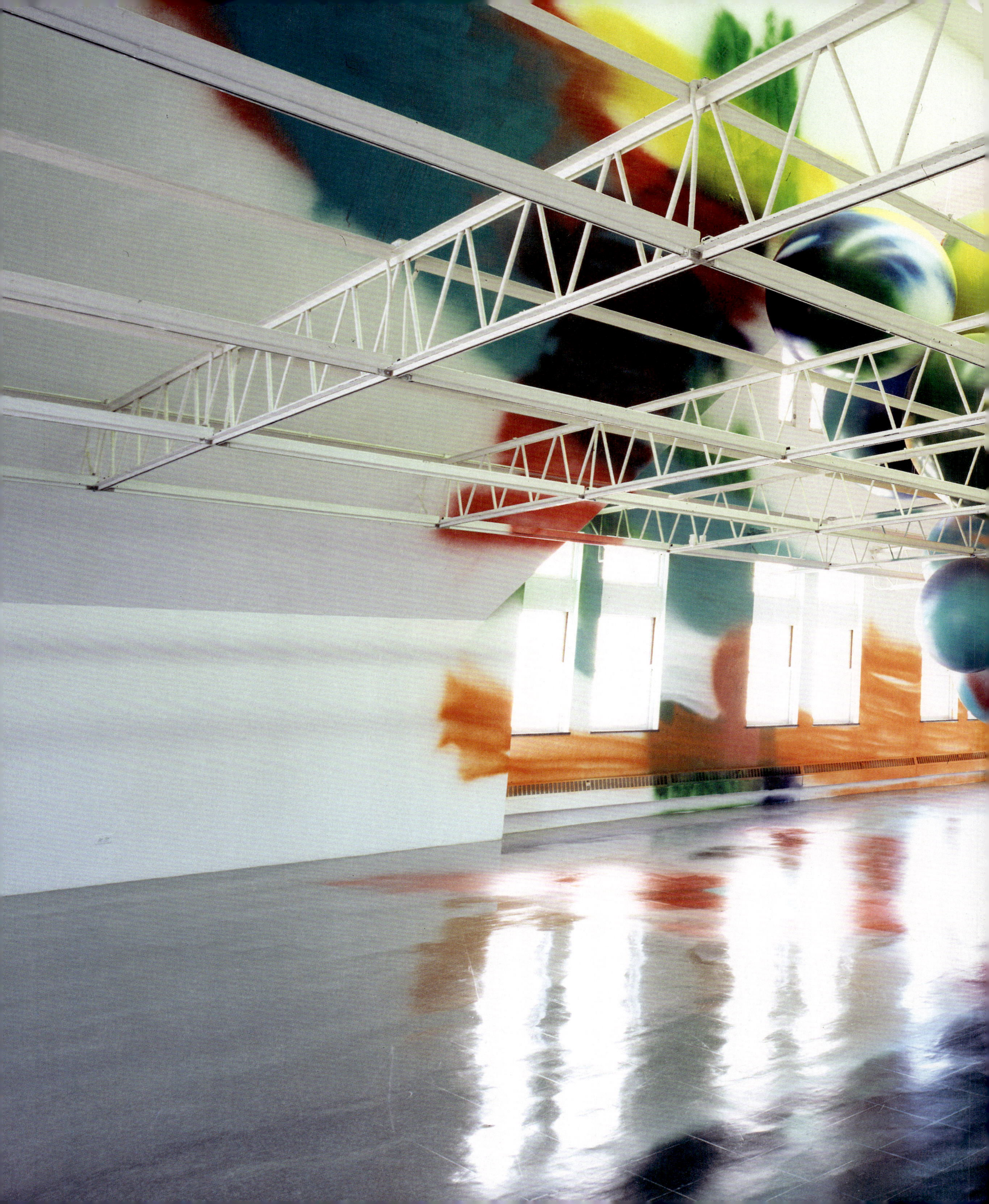

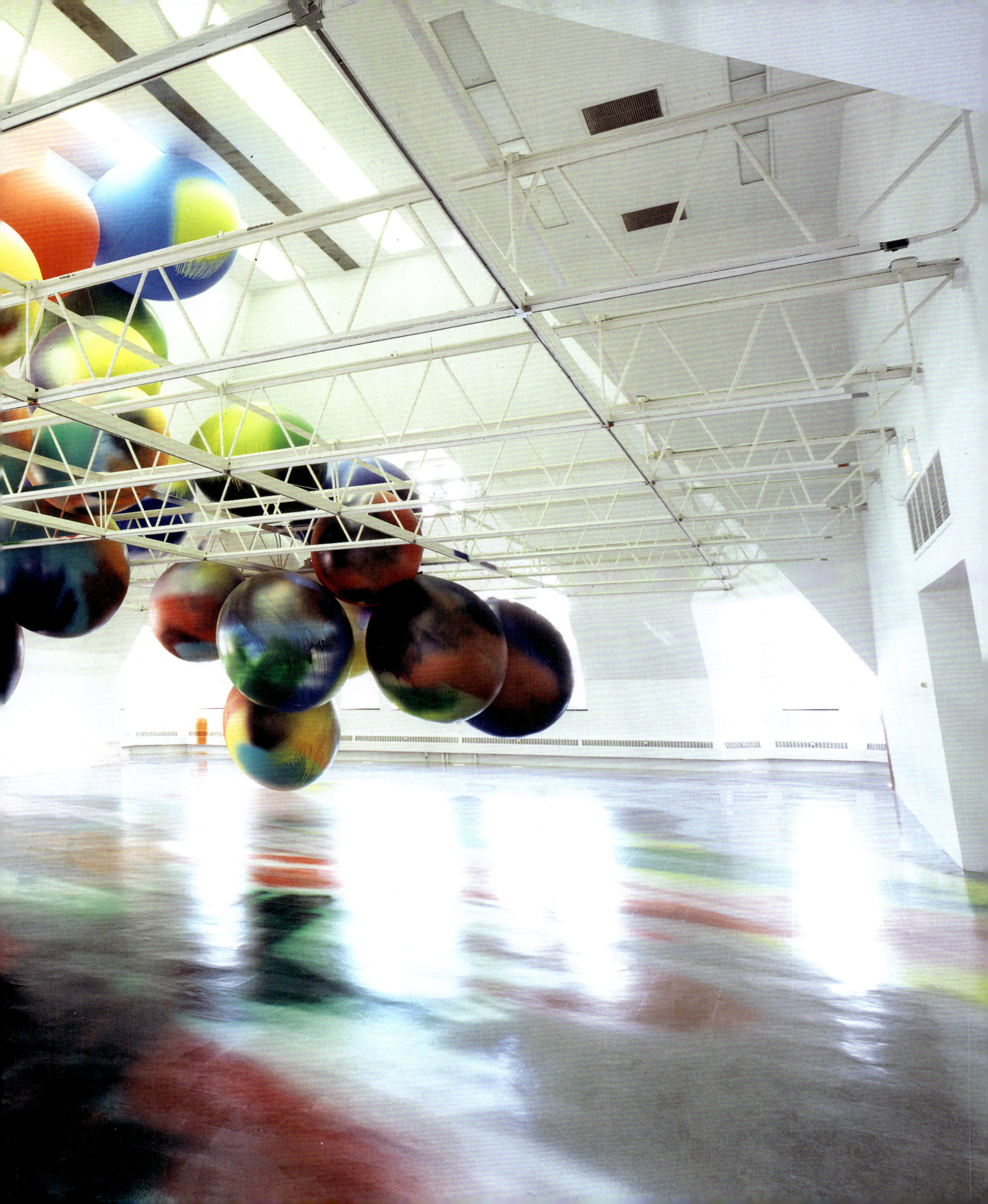

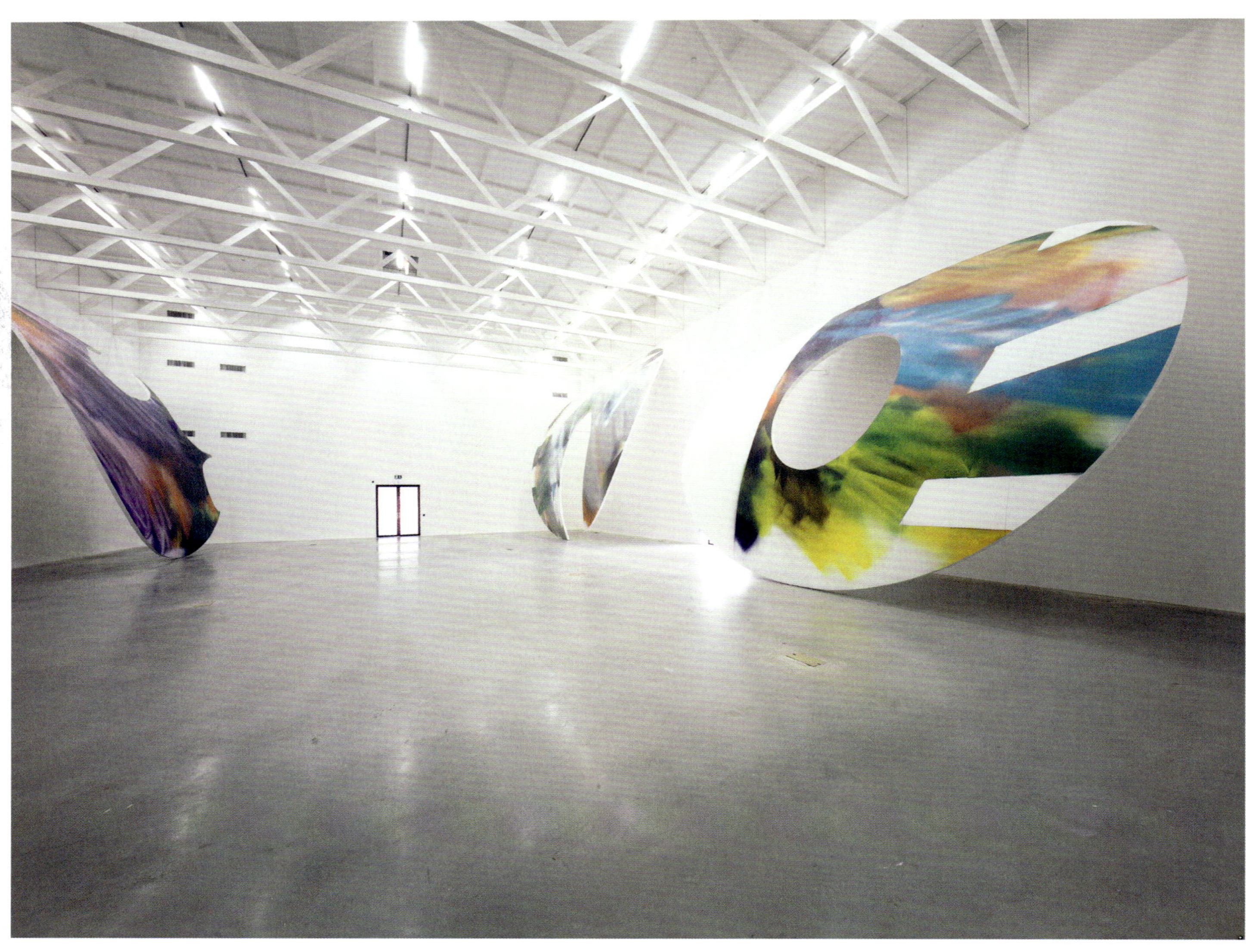

above and right

13. Shadowbox   2009
Temporäre Kunsthalle, Berlin

Acrylic on glass-fiber-reinforced plastic
800 × 1150 × 10 cm (315 × 453 × 4 in)

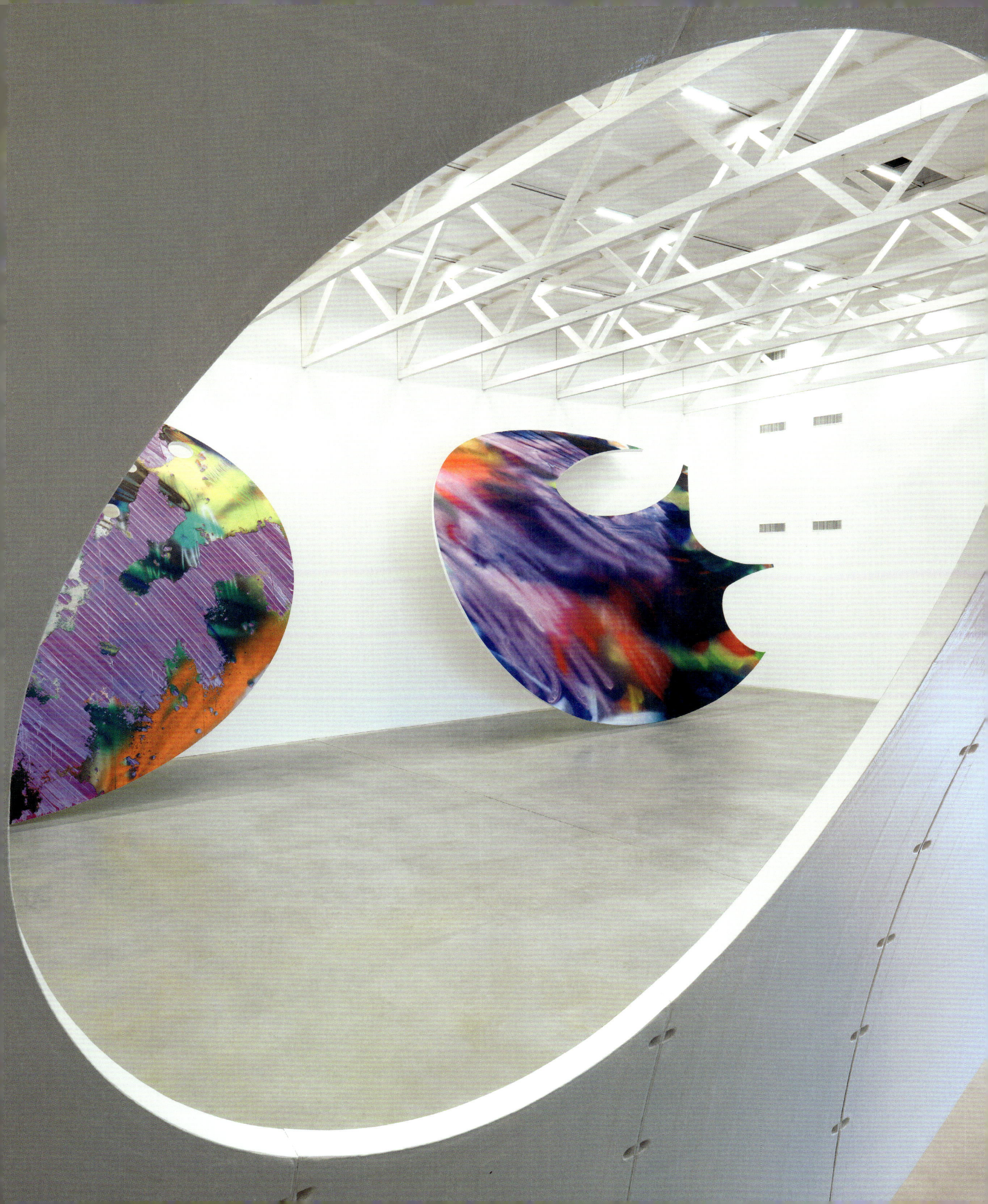

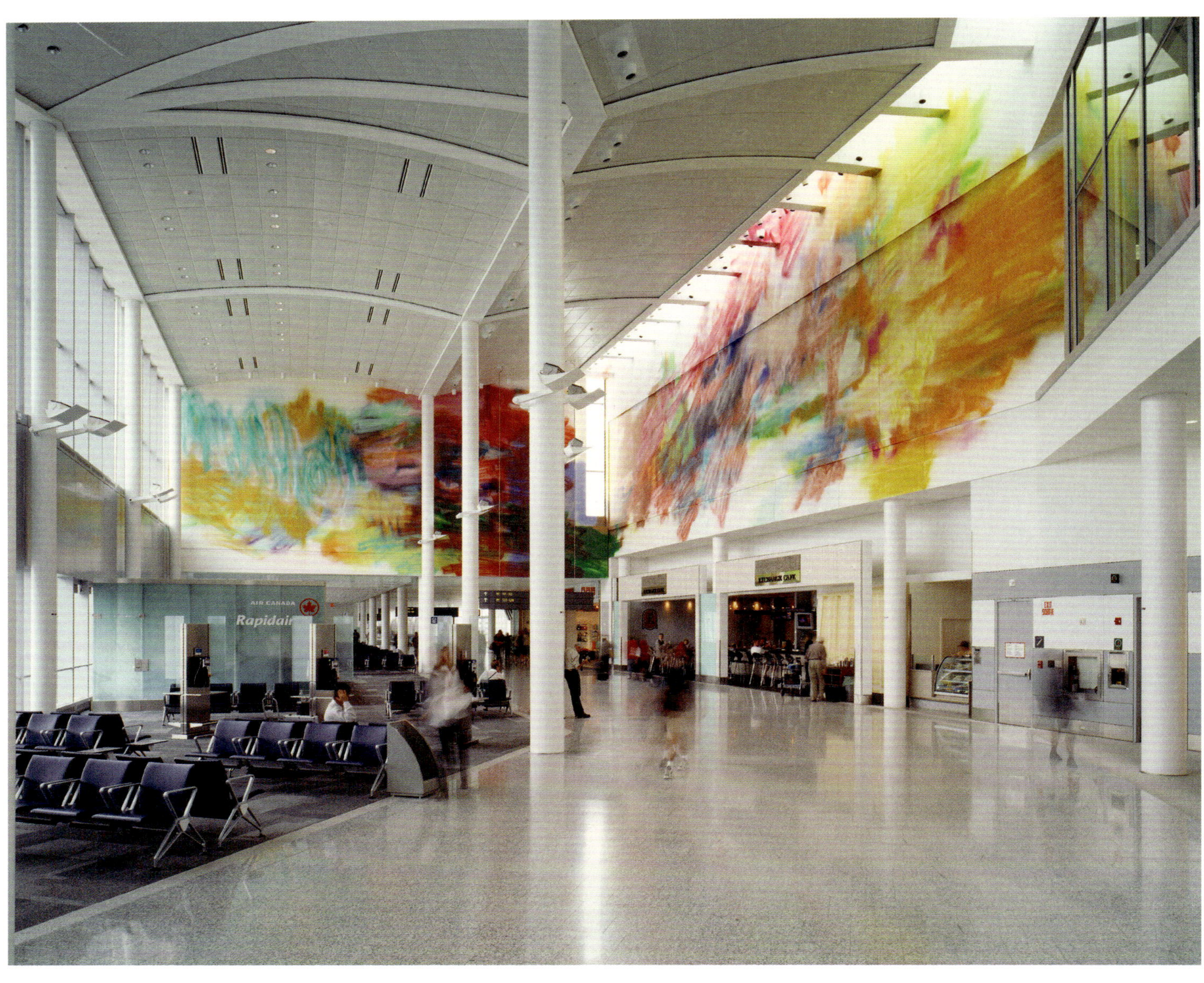

14. Untitled   2003
Pearson International Airport, Toronto

Acrylic on wall
885 × 1750 × 2350 cm (348 × 689 × 925 in)

right

15. Untitled   2015
Facebook Headquarters in Menlo Park, California

Acrylic on wall and steel beams
2000 × 1750 cm (780 × 689)

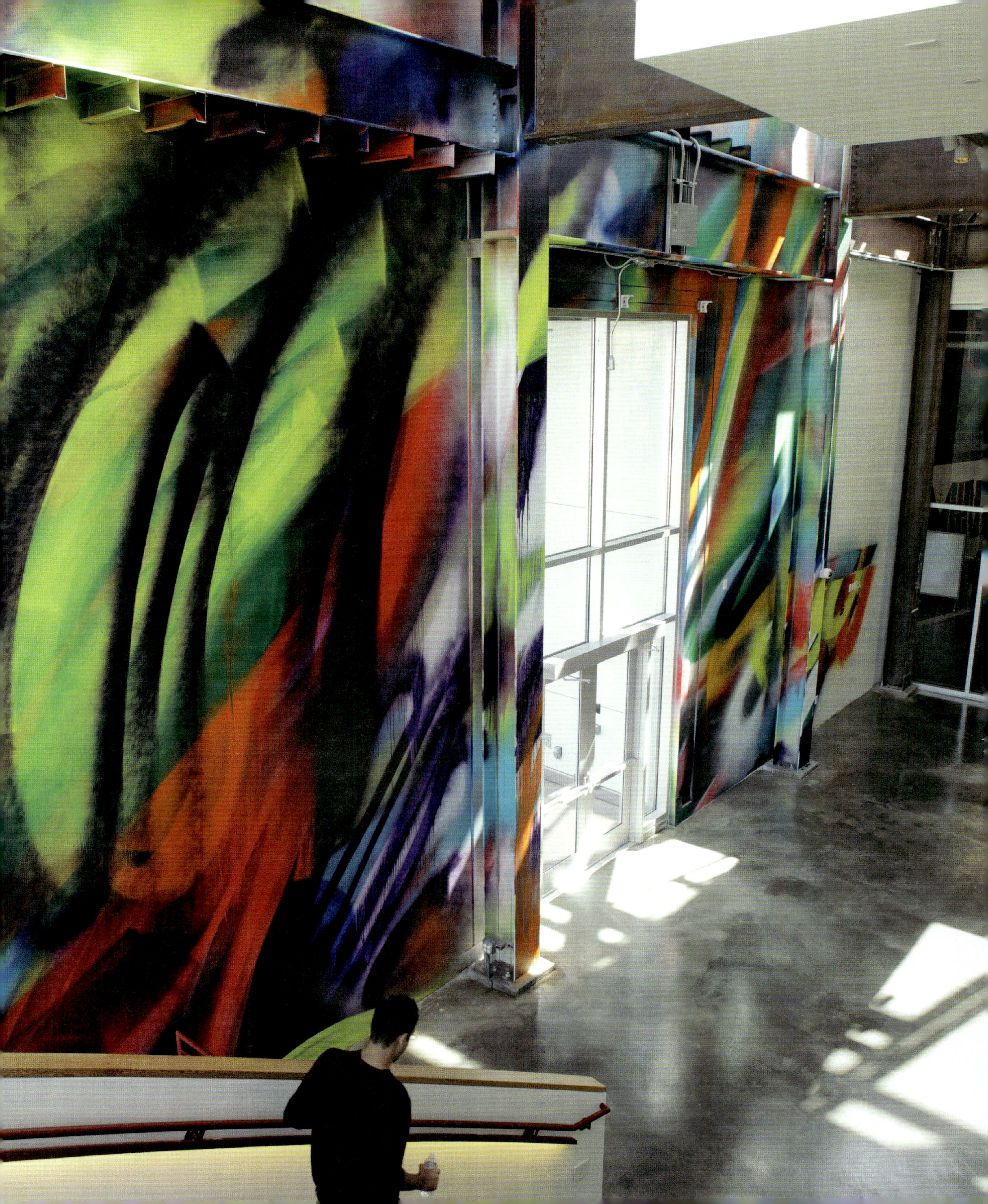

Leaning against the outside wall of the Kunstmuseum Bonn is a warped and elliptical painting on both sides of a glass-fiber-reinforced structure (*In Seven Days Time*, 2011) (fig.16). The 'outside' is a riot of colors while the 'inside' is comparatively subdued, with interlacing white and purple bands. Shifting sunlight and cast shadows are important components of this work, which, while massive, leans precariously against the museum as if it had been inexplicably left there during a delivery. It also looks a little like a chunk of some twenty-fifth-century spaceship.

Still, most of Grosse's painting installations are not permanent. Most have vanished. They are made for specific sites and have limited durations, and when the exhibition concludes they are summarily overpainted, removed, and sometimes destroyed. Grosse makes brilliant works that disappear as a matter of course; however, that very temporariness only adds to their carnival impact. Like Dickinson's circus, annual carnivals when people dress in outlandish costumes and go wild, and the Hindu festival of Holi (often called the 'festival of love' and the 'festival of colors') when people fling powdered colors at one another, turning their bodies, the surroundings, and the very air pink, orange, red, blue, and yellow, Grosse's works arrive to affect their decisive, consciousness-altering transformations and then they are gone.

Excess, for Bakhtin, as I mentioned, is a crucial part of carnival; think of wild costumes, copious alcohol, sexual freedom, and unfettered emotions – all of which undermine restrictions often placed on the body and pleasure. Excess is a crucial part of Grosse's works as well, with their over-the-top colors and often considerable dimensions. In fact, she may well be the most excess-prone major painter of this era. Exaggeration and parody, for Bakhtin, are likewise fundamental; think of mock speeches by buffoonish dignitaries, kings presented as fools, clerics who are silly. Several of Grosse's works are absurdly exaggerated versions of basic painting tools like paintbrushes, canvases, and pigments – workaday tools for a painter but also symbols of artistic authority, mastery and history.

Consider Grosse's two-person exhibition (with French artist Tatiana Trouvé) in 2018 at Villa Medici in Rome, as part of the institution's exhibition series *Le numerose irregolarità* (The Many Irregularities). Her response to this historic building, which dates back to 1540, was riotous, calamitous, oddly meditative; and, again, sublime. The basic physical components of most paintings are a piece of fabric, usually canvas; wood stretcher bars; and paint. For Grosse's *Ingres Wood* (2018), the principal work in her multipart installation, she presented outsize, exaggerated versions of all three (fig.17). Instead of stretcher bars, at the base of the stairs were rough logs, haphazardly piled as if heaped up by a flood; raw nature invaded this building so steeped in history and culture. Instead of a taut piece of canvas, a huge swathe of loose fabric spilled and rippled down the stairs of the former horse ramp and swept across the floor; the log pile was installed on top of it.

Grosse painted (more like saturated) both fabric and logs with a stunning array of colors and shapes. Orange-red streaks angled across a light-orange expanse.

right

16. In Seven Days Time   2011
permanent outdoor installation at Kunstmuseum Bonn

Acrylic on glass-fiber-reinforced plastic
920 × 1950 × 12 cm (362 × 768 × 5 in)

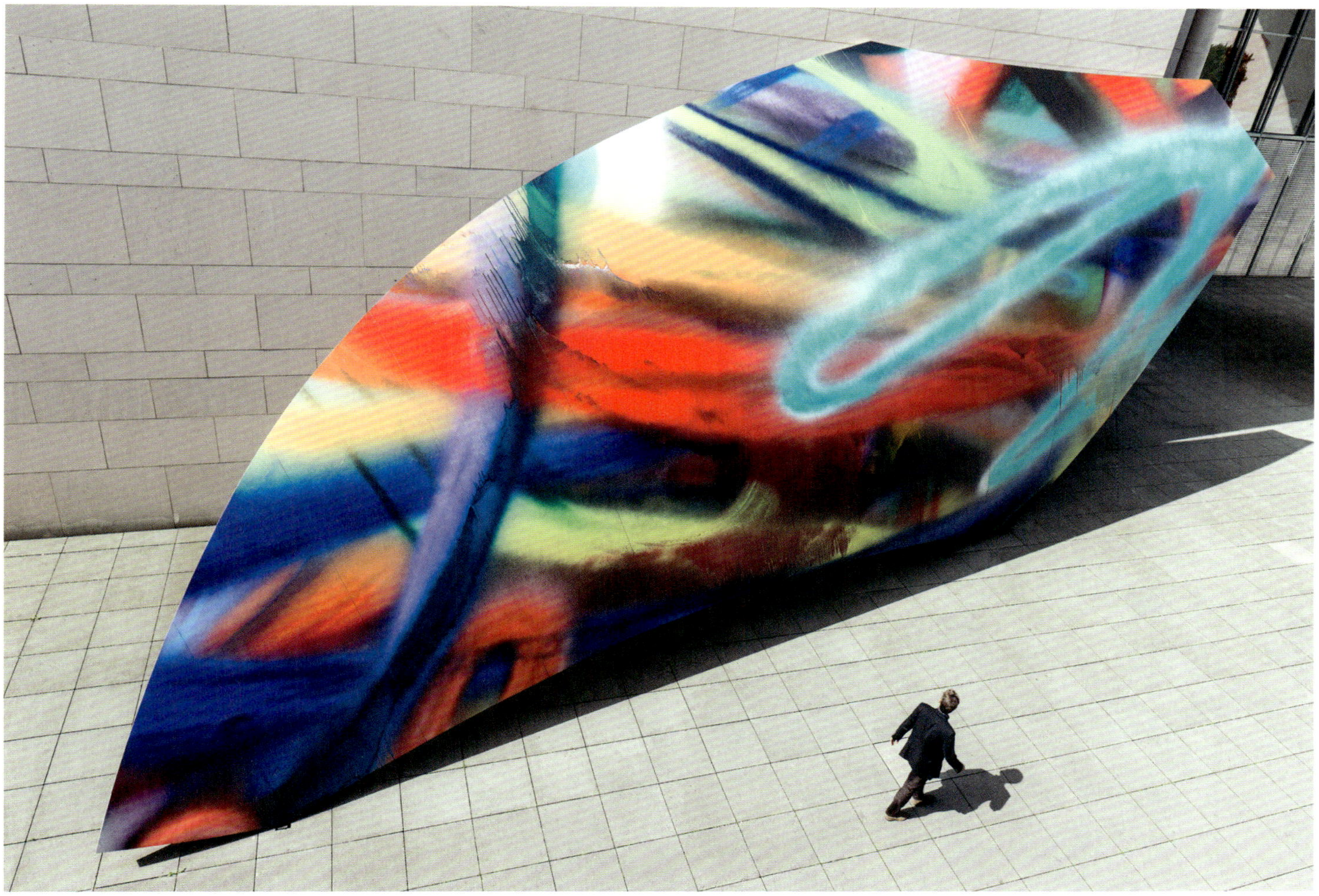

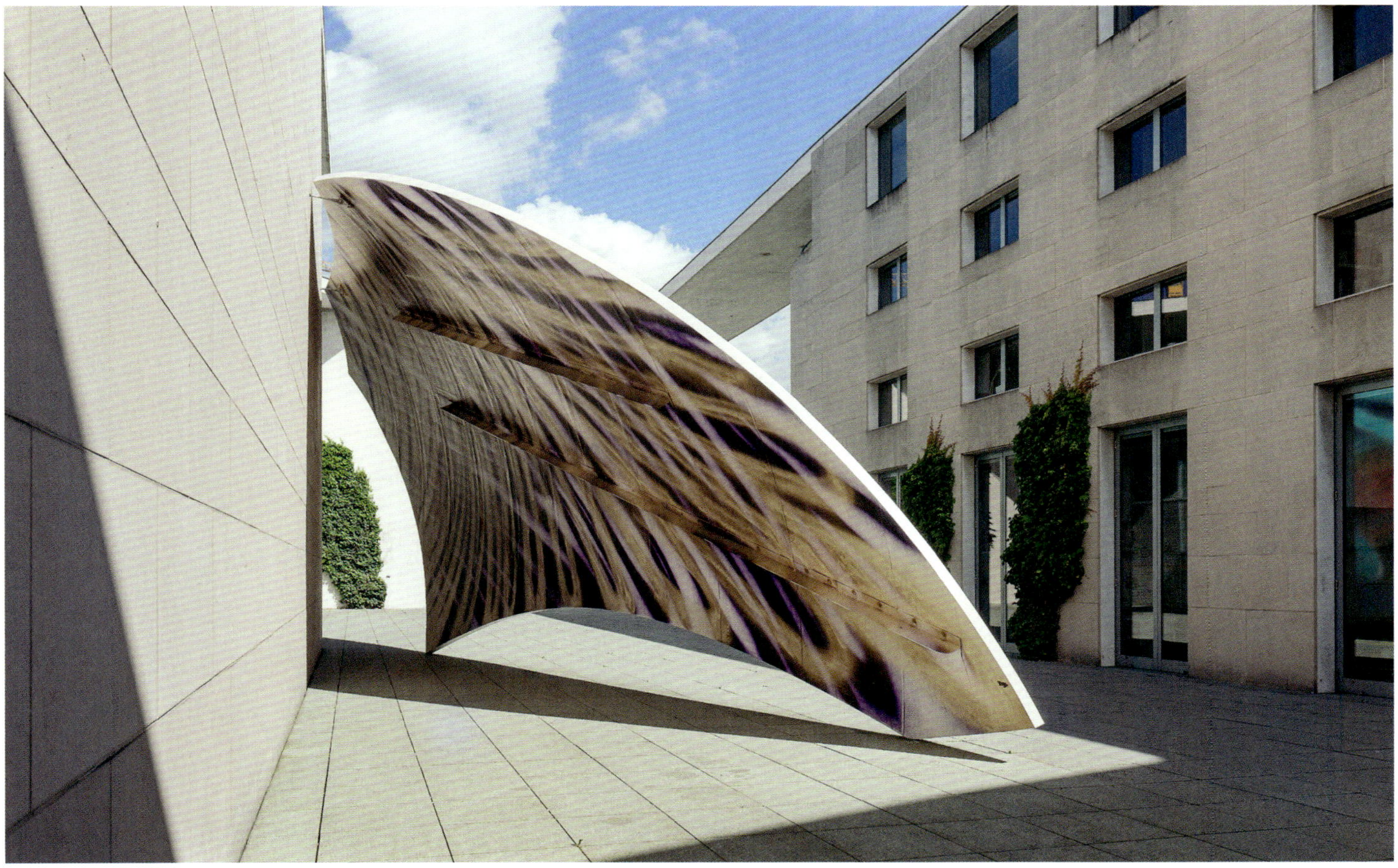

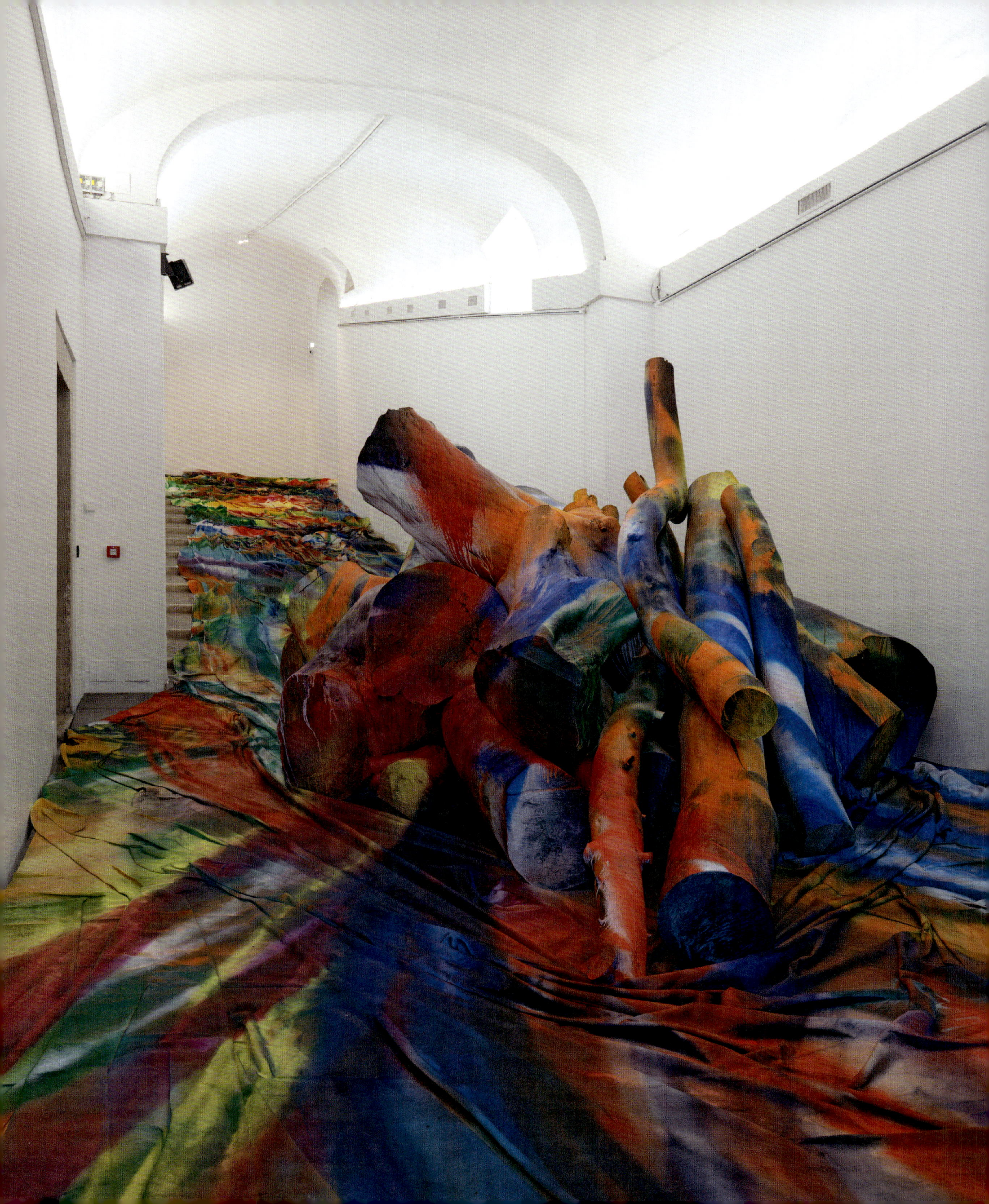

Crimson and purple forms and areas merged on the logs, mixing with deep blues and yellow-greens. Multicolored curves abounded on the fabric and there were drips and smears of cobalt blue, glowing patches of pure white, elongated green curves atop fuzzy chartreuse bands.

Grosse's huge work on fabric again challenged what we expect from paintings and rearranged how we apprehend and interact with them. You could climb up the stairs on Grosse's painting. You could sit on her painting and lounge on it (which I did, for a long time) – not exactly the most normal behavior in a museum. From the top of the stairs you could especially see how important the folds in the fabric were: all those ridges and indentations, which contributed to the rippling effect. You could also see the exchange occurring between fabric and log pile. Vibrant colors seemed to flow down the stairs and gather on the logs; the logs seemed to project colors back at the fabric. The whole installation was rugged (with the logs) and sullied (from all the climbing and footprints). It was also luscious and bedazzling. In the meantime, Grosse incorporated, highlighted and transformed a functional part of the building – the stairs – which in most cases would be ignored and which very possibly had never been used before as a site for artworks.

Then there is the matter, in Grosse's art, not merely of viewership but of full-on experience and participation – and here, too, she connects with Bakhtin and the carnival. Bakhtin well understood the social, political and communal importance of both carnival celebrations and 'carnivalized situations' in societies inevitably bound up with hierarchies and restriction. They offer the exact opposite: freedom, license, adventure, unfettered consciousness, unbridled emotions. Here is how Bakhtin explores these social and political dimensions:

> The laws, prohibitions, and restrictions that determine the structure and order of ordinary, that is noncarnival, life are suspended during carnival: what is suspended first of all is hierarchical structure and all the forms of terror, reverence, piety, and etiquette connected with it – that is, everything resulting from socio-hierarchical inequality or any other form of inequality among people (including age). All *distance* between people is suspended, and a special carnival category goes into effect: *free and familiar contact among people.* This is a very important aspect of a carnival sense of the world. People who in life are separated by impenetrable hierarchical barriers enter into free familiar contact on the carnival square.

Something quite similar happens with Grosse's installations. They almost magnetically attract viewers, in part because of their sheer dynamism but also because viewers tend to gather in them and stay for a long time to commune. They uncommonly become communal experiences, unsteadying new zones of perception and inquiry. Even when a work by Grosse is very large, this is still a very small part of the world that she has transformed – but that small part looks wondrous,

17. Ingres Wood   2018
Villa Medici, Rome

Acrylic on tree trunk and fabric
260 × 560 × 2360 cm (102 × 220 × 929 in)

unprecedented, never seen before, full of unexpected possibilities. What Grosse really deals in, and what she offers to viewers, are 'new thresholds' and 'new anatomies', as the American poet Hart Crane put things in his excellent poem *The Wine Menagerie*. Her works involve not only intensified visual and spatial experiences but also intensified life and consciousness altogether.

All of which brings me to Katharina Grosse's huge painting installation/architectural construction with the enigmatic, humorous, seemingly nonsensical title, *The Horse Trotted Another Couple of Metres, Then It Stopped* (2018) in Sydney, Australia (fig.18).

This work was at Carriageworks, housed in a cavernous industrial building that dates back to the late nineteenth century when it was a repair facility for trams. The building is immense, rigid, industrial; and, on the face of it, inhospitable to painting. Needing to create a space fit for her kind of painting, Grosse came up with an idiosyncratic, in some ways outrageous, solution: a huge, soft room with an exposed top so that visitors could see the surrounding industrial architecture – a room within a room made of more than 2,500 square meters (27,000 square feet) of fabric. This was the 'canvas' that she spray-painted with her flamboyant colors.

Voluminous, sloping and draped white fabric, knotted at the top, was suspended from the industrial rafters; it didn't just hang down but seemed to be cascading down and coursing across the floor. From the outside this structure was largely white, luminously white, icily white with a smattering of brilliant colors. Once you slipped inside everything changed, and shockingly so: a colorful, fabulous elsewhere in the middle of right here. Colors and shapes coursed everywhere, up and down, horizontally and diagonally, all over the soft walls and the floor: deep, sweeping blues leading to both light and dark greens, green squiggles merging with oranges and magentas, rich reds flowing down to pool on the floor, yellows merging with purples. From some perspectives the fabric looked like giant figures: an angel with extended wings; a hooded creature in a multicolored robe; a mythic spirit from Europe's deep, pagan past – although this was probably unintentional. There were shifting colors and also shifting moods or states of being: whimsy, ardor, excitation, thoughtfulness, joy. There was no point in trying to 'read' or decipher this work, in breaking it down into parts, in attempting to understand how those parts related to one another. Much better was to temporarily shut down your rational mind altogether, to dispense with expectations and eliminate words and instead become all eyes and feeling.

There was a steady stream of visitors during the several hours when I was with and in Grosse's Sydney artwork over two days. Visitors were uncommonly hushed and meditative, even reverential, like they might be in a tremendous cathedral or beholding some wonder of nature – a towering mountain in the Rockies, perhaps, or one in the Dolomites; a rocky outcrop in Australia with its colors and striations; or a staggering waterfall in Iceland. People stayed for a long time – sometimes sitting or lying down, sometimes walking slowly about. A young mother waited respectfully behind her son, who was likely three years old. He just stood there, all on his own, with his head tilted all the way back, looking up and sometimes craning his neck to gaze left and right. Then he started gasping with pleasure and delight.

right and following spread

18. The Horse Trotted Another Couple of Metres, Then It Stopped   2018
Carriageworks, Sydney

Acrylic on fabric
1000 × 4600 × 1500 cm (394 × 1810 × 590 in)

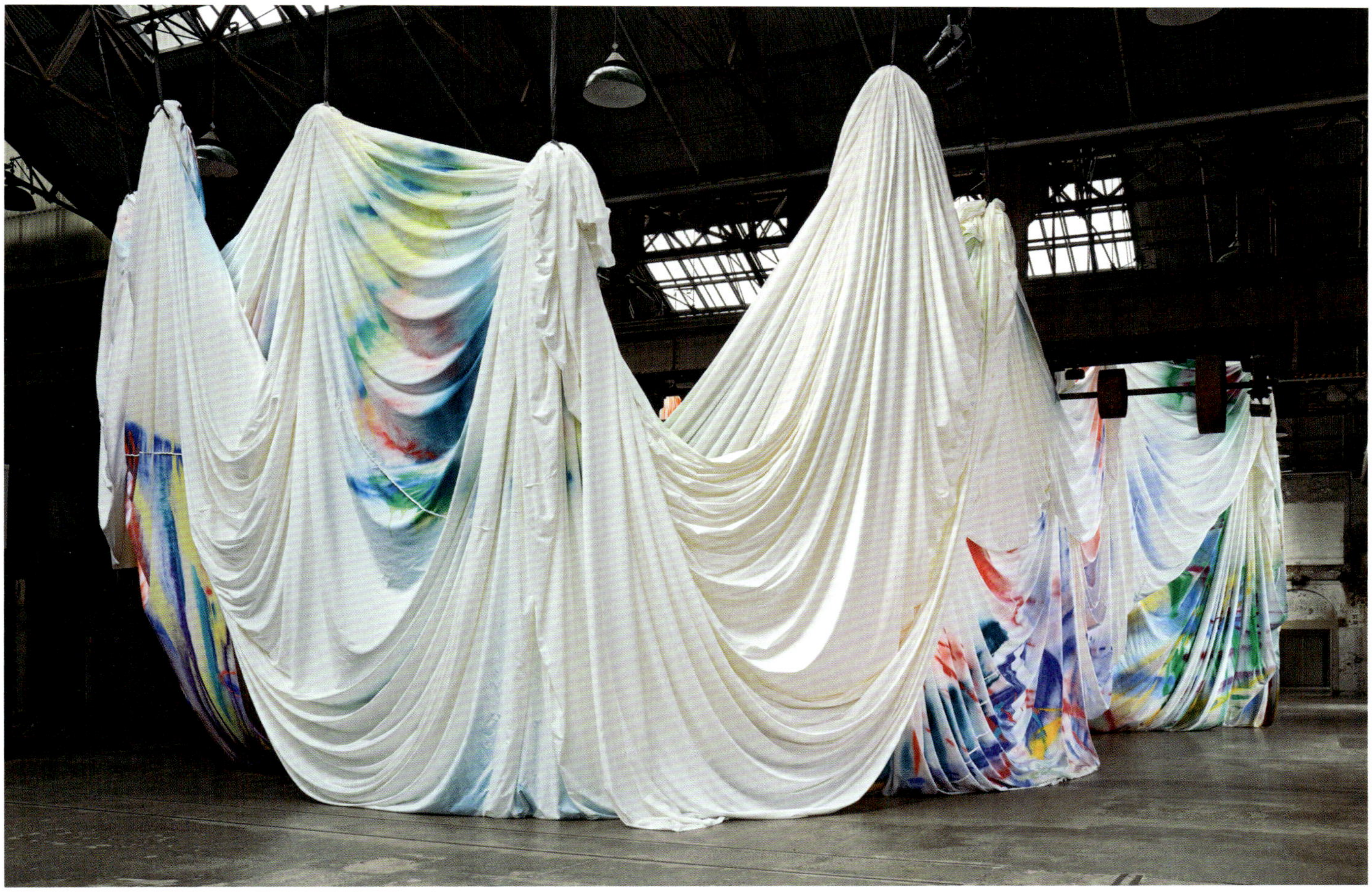

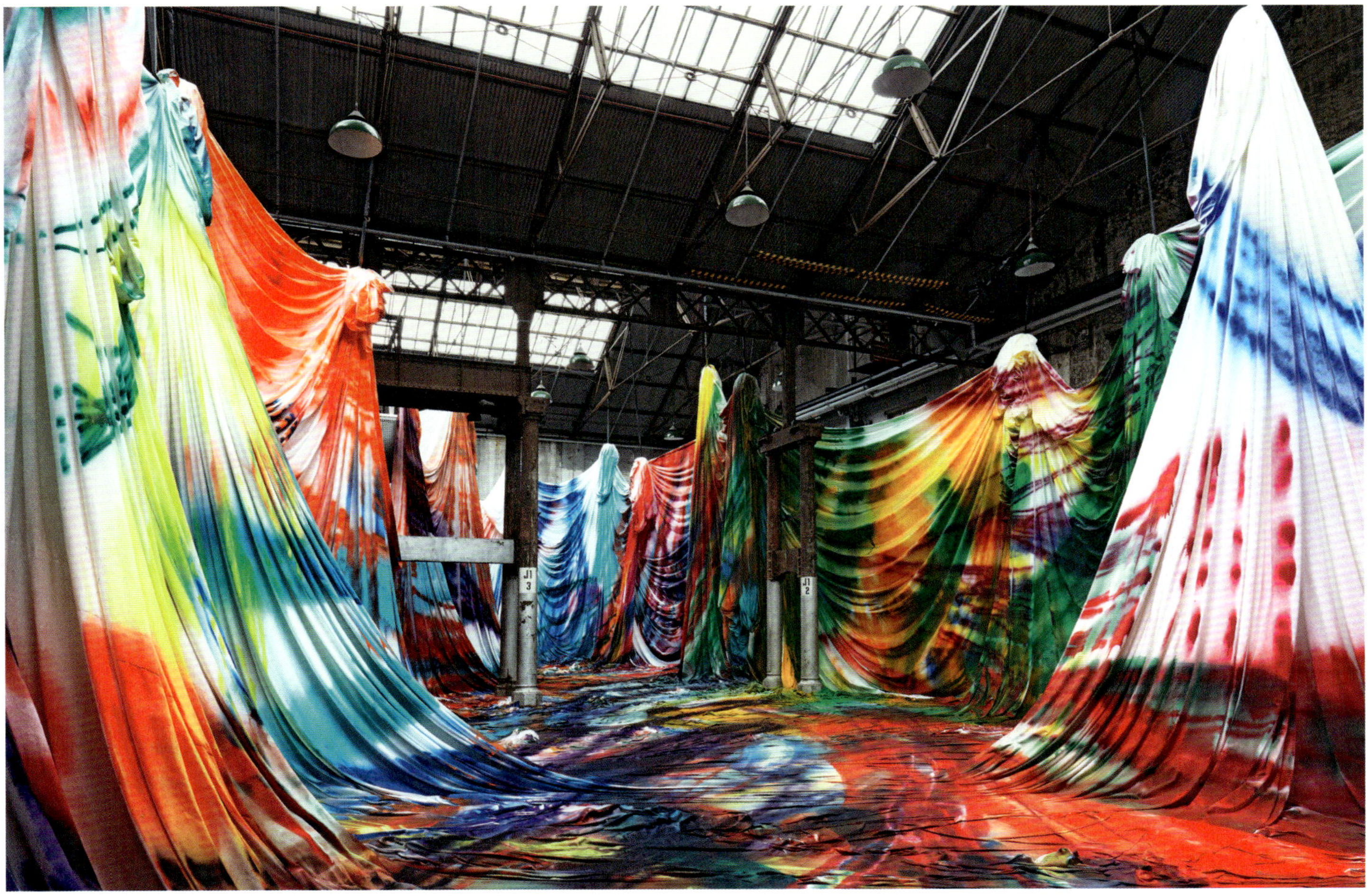

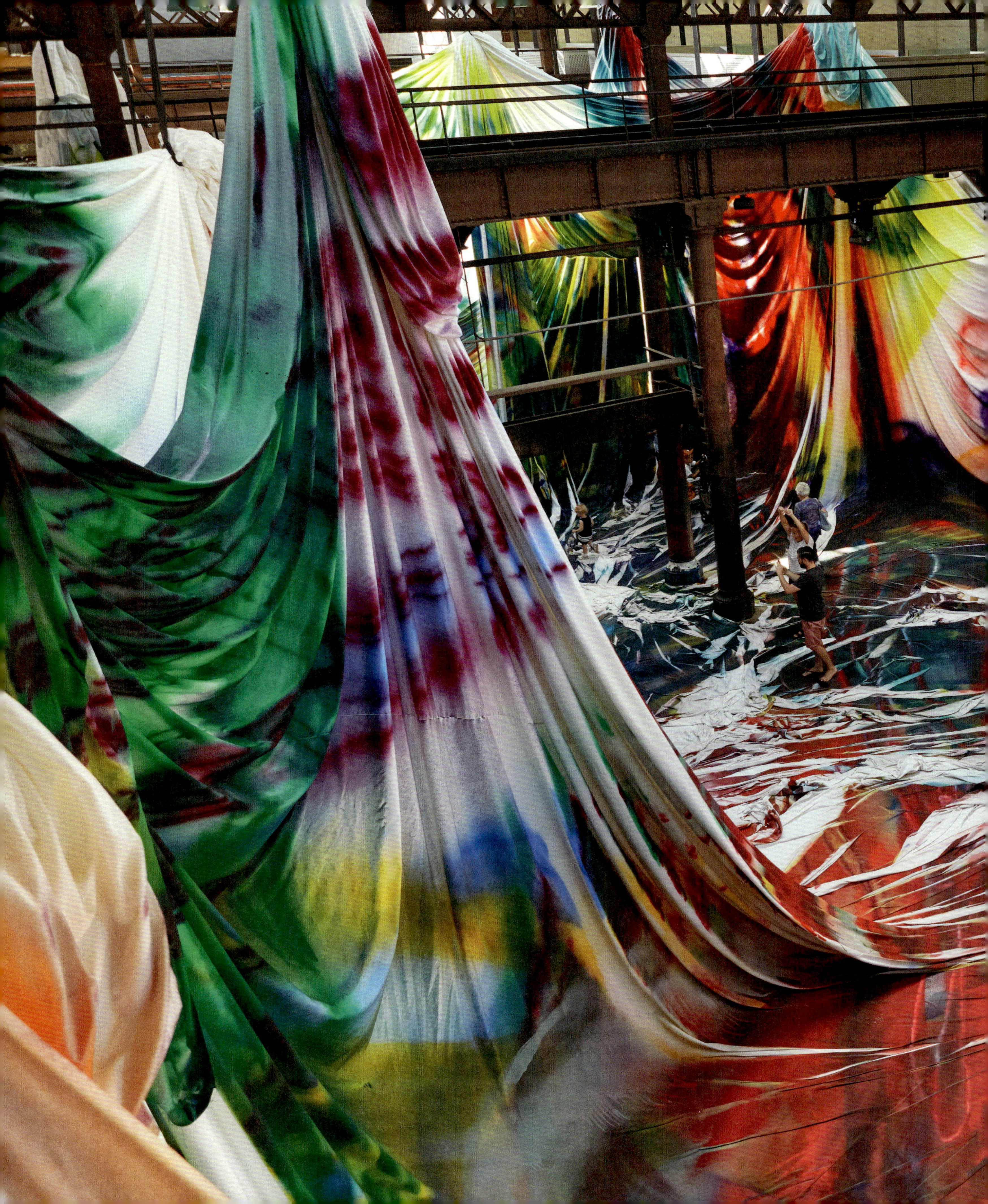

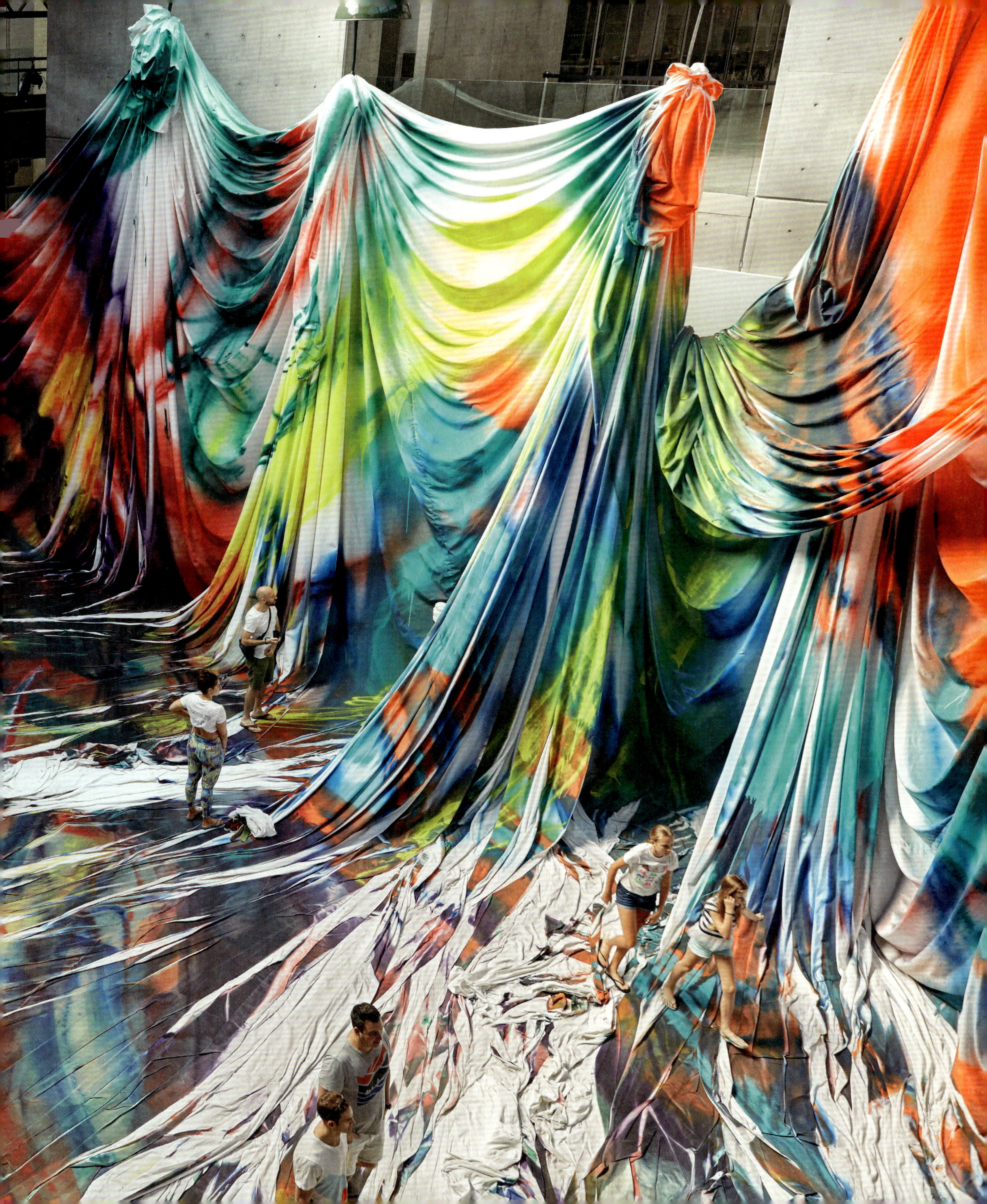

2   Carnival Origins

19. Untitled   1998
Project Space, Kunsthalle Bern

Acrylic on wall and ceilling
450 × 1250 × 400 cm (177 × 492 × 157 in)

20. Untitled   2013
Museum für Gegenwartskunst Siegen, Germany

Digital print on silk
450 × 1250 × 400 cm (177 × 492 × 157 in)

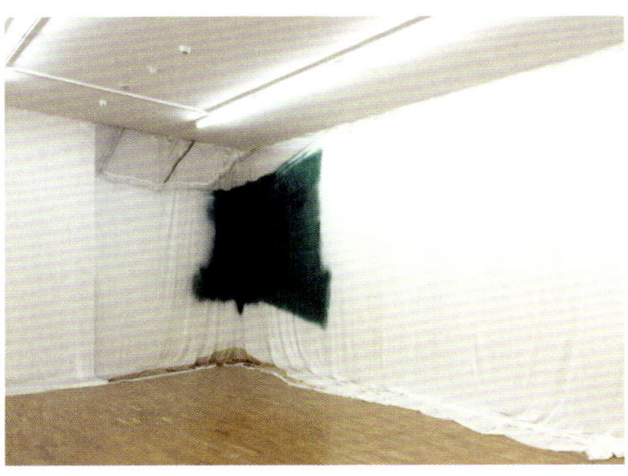

It's often not all that easy to pinpoint when an artist of talent becomes an artist of abundant, risk-taking vision; however, in Katharina Grosse's case we can do so, and this involves an especially cathartic work from 1998 in Bern, Switzerland: her first public wall painting made with a spray gun.

Grosse had accomplished several wall works before (1995, 1996 and 1997), and she had also been experimenting with spray-painting. Yet, using the spray gun and air compressor to paint directly onto a wall, ceiling and the adjoining walls allowed her to radically extend her whole approach as an artist. Increasingly, she moved off the canvas into architectural spaces, making intensely colorful paintings by spraying jets of atomized acrylic paint first on walls and ceilings, then later also on floors, doors, stairways, and windows.

She pared painting down to its most basic essence – the application of pure color to a surface – and then amped that up to space-altering, stop-you-in-your tracks proportions and intensity.

Grosse's work in Bern also had an unlikely, in part accidental, genesis. In 1992 she was 'invited' to Château de Servières in Marseilles, France to participate in an art residency in the tough outskirts of the city largely populated by Algerian immigrants. Actually, a friend of hers in Germany, Thomas Kohl, who was an admirer of her work and who would later suggest her to the Maria Wilkens Gallery in Cologne, knew about the residency and encouraged her to apply. Grosse wrote an inquiring letter, in French, and got back a letter, also in French, politely thanking her for her interest. She misread this letter, thinking she had been accepted, and promptly wrote back gladly accepting the 'invitation' and presenting her available dates. This basically forced the Château de Servières to accept her – Grosse somewhat sheepishly admitted to me – although no strategizing was involved; instead everything was a language mistake. That language mistake was fortuitous.

In Marseilles there were all sorts of artists engaged with graffiti and ribald comics, not at all the kind of things with which Grosse was occupied, and they were employing spray-painting. 'Traditional' painting, in Grosse's recollection, was largely considered old hat and pointless, except for the work of Gerhard Richter. While she was in Marseilles, working away in the residency, a friend of hers showed her a spray gun that he had acquired. Grosse was curious and tried it out. According to her, she saw paint – and the painted surface – in an entirely new way. She saw dense areas but also clouds and 'particles', as she put it, along with mists, drips and varying textures. She saw paint as a thing, in a way independent of her; not just as an art material but as a vital material altogether. When back home in Germany she got her own spray gun, loaded it with oil paint (not knowing any better) and promptly made a mess of things, covering everything with a film of oil. She remained curious and kept experimenting – spraying canvases, now with acrylic paint.

In 1998 Swiss curator Roman Kurzmeyer – who has since gone on to write insightfully about Grosse's work, and to collaborate with her on exhibitions – invited her to make a projects-room exhibition at Kunsthalle Bern in the Swiss capital. That was quite an opportunity. Kunsthalle Bern is one of the more renowned European kunsthalles; this is where its former director, the visionary Harald Szeemann, curated the legendary and controversial exhibition of Conceptual and Process Art *Live in Your Head: When Attitudes Becomes Form* in 1969, and it is also one of several museums that hosted Gerhard Richter's first retrospective in 1986. It would have made sense for Grosse to exhibit paintings per se – paintings evenly spaced, as is usual, on the walls – abstract paintings, I mean, in the vibrant yet reductive style she had developed over the past several years. She did no such thing, and here is when the real risk kicked in.

Grosse accomplished *Untitled* (1998) after first building a model of the room and deciding on the placement of her painting (fig.19). With green acrylic paint – Golden Artist Colors Phthalo Green (Blue Shade) to be precise – she spray-painted a section of one wall, the corner where two walls intersected, a small part of the adjacent wall, and a bit of the ceiling, including the molding. This was important. Grosse did not situate things on one flat wall, and centered on that wall, but instead encompassed two walls, the corner, the ceiling, and, in her terms, the 'sculptural' molding.

Even in the photographic documentation this work is enthralling; encountering it in person was surely much more so. Parts were dark green, almost black; others were much lighter ('bottle green', as Grosse put it) depending on the pressure and the distance of the spray gun from the surfaces. This work was fuzzy and atmospheric in parts, crisp in others. Some parts were dense and impacted, others were vaporous. It was static yet seemed in motion. It was concentrated yet ragged and free-form at its edges. It seemed to be clinging to the walls but also rising up them and spreading across them like green steam. It seemed alive, almost like an organism; it seemed organic, as if it possessed a life force. It invaded the space aggressively yet also seemed delicate, almost ethereal. It signaled agitation but also serenity, disturbance but also loveliness. Without attempting to represent anything, without being an image of something, it still connected loosely with things in the world: fog rolling in, a cumulus cloud, burgeoning foliage. You could be mesmerized by this painting even though you were looking solely at green acrylic paint on white walls and a ceiling, nothing more than that. Right here is when Grosse learned something crucial. A painting could generate its own spatial logic. It could disturb and transform a room rather than fit neatly within it. It could use the room, not be used by it. It could make its own circumstances, its own reason for being. And as it did so, it could be exquisite – but also unruly and rough.

Right here is the absolute genesis of Katharina Grosse's radical work, which has often been mischaracterized as site-specific. It is not – certainly not in the sense that the site determines the work. Instead it is site-responsive, or perhaps site-transformative, and oftentimes site-disruptive. Right here is also the genesis of Grosse's 'carnivalistic' art, in Bakhtin's sense of the word. The space as it normally is and the part of it that Grosse transformed through painting both clashed and combined. In Grosse's terms, 'the collision of the built space with the painting space was the key to this work'. What that entailed was a willingness to trespass across borders – in this case, between ceiling and walls. In Grosse's carnivalistic art borders, and all the categories and hierarchies they imply and enforce, are not fixed but instead are fluid and dynamic, subject to fresh interpretation and insights. This is fundamental for her art, but also for the implicit politics in her art, and really for her world view. As she has explained,

> I feel border districts to be zones of extremely dramatic theatricality, because that is where highly diverse interests overlap, intertwine and are compelled within a narrow space to engage in competition, to exist in simultaneity. In border areas, we experience mutually exclusive things in an instant, as a paradox. Borders are negotiation-spaces that have to be created again and again. My prototypes provide models for thinking through border-spaces, as it were. How would it be if the borders of objects were not so binding for us? If it were possible for objects to be redefined, to be newly materialized by a constant change of perspective? Would we then not encounter our loved ones differently, our neighbors, strangers or the community?[9]

Kurzmeyer, in an article he wrote about Grosse in *Parkett*, alludes briefly, and rather diplomatically, to 'some consternation amongst the Kunsthalle's staff' and a 'cool reception' when Grosse finished her work and presented it.[10] My conversations with Grosse suggest that this is quite an understatement: in fact, much worse happened. The director, Bernhard Fibicher, was adamant in his opposition, even pressing for the work to be removed – and we can forget about some predictable clash between a female avant-garde artist and a male old-school director. Back then, and now, Fibicher was and is a major and accomplished director and curator, attuned to the nuances and visons of really adept and idiosyncratic artists, including many female artists. Essentially, his argument was that Grosse's work was not radical or space-altering enough as a *sculpture* could be and that the criteria did not exist to discuss it as a *painting*, especially one that was not congruent with the architectural space.

For Fibicher, Grosse's work didn't fit with the room, it didn't behave like a painting should, it was too flippant and easy, it was illogical, it was an eyesore and maybe even a laughing stock – and there were numerous others at the museum who shared his opinion. Grosse remained steadfast, believing in and advocating for her work, which must have required considerable courage. She had, after all, done something really risky and fresh, and this often entails anxiety and vulnerability for an artist. Fibicher was well-established and famous; she was neither. Her wall painting survived and was exhibited. It has since been critically acclaimed many times, not only as an important work in Grosse's early career but as the single most important work. This, incidentally, is not the only time that Grosse's unorthodox (to say the least) paintings have met with strident opposition – often, but not exclusively, from men.

Katharina Grosse was born in 1961 in Freiburg/Breisgau, Germany, the second of three siblings (she has two brothers). Her mother, Barbara Grosse, is an artist, focusing on printmaking – albeit one who downplayed her career given the demands of raising three children (Grosse told me that she doesn't believe that her mother felt compromised or sorely restricted by this). Her father, Siegfried Grosse, was a linguist, specializing in medieval German. As a young child, she moved with her family to Bochum, long a center for coal and steel production in the Ruhr, which is the industrial heartland of Germany, when her father became a professor at Ruhr University, the first new university established in then West Germany after the Second World War. He was also founding professor of the German Institute at the university.

A few words are necessary here about Bochum – which as a municipality dates back to the ninth century and Charlemagne, and which in the nineteenth and twentieth centuries was a major industrial center. In 1943 and 1944 a large part of the city, then home to some 191,000 inhabitants, was leveled during Allied bombing. Thousands were killed and many further thousands displaced, as they fled the city seeking relative safety. Much of the industrial infrastructure was destroyed. During the whole Nazi period, of course, the Jews of Bochum were harassed, rounded up, deported, and killed.

This was the Bochum to which Grosse and her family moved, a city still emerging from mayhem and trauma – although she, of course, as a young child, would have known nothing of this. Bochum was also a focal point in a revitalizing West Germany. Education was key as things shifted from heavy industry to a new service economy, and as the country sought to move from a recent barbaric past to a humanistic present and future.

Grosse emphasizes how important the new university was, and not just for the city but for the whole region. It attracted an influx of new residents and it also fostered a democratic educational environment. As Grosse puts it, the children of workers, intellectuals and those attracted by the city's developing new economy all studied together and intermingled. This impact extended to the primary and secondary schools, which were excellent, and Grosse counts her primary- and secondary-school education as among her most formative influences. She also underscores how thoroughly the post-Nazi context conditioned her education. Some of her teachers were older and had served either in the war or in National Socialist government

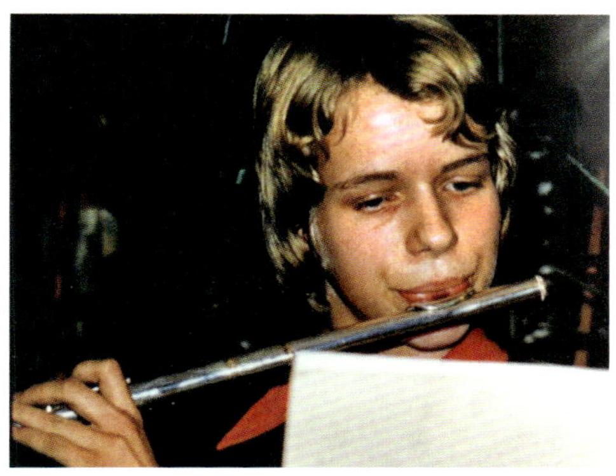

21. Katharina Grosse, *c.*1973

structures. In pedagogy, and also in public discussions, memory of the Nazi era, and the ways that adults dealt with their own conflicted experiences and choices during that period, suffused her time in school.

Grosse's was a classical education that included nine years of Latin; she would also study English, French and Spanish. In addition to languages, literature was a favorite – especially Shakespeare. Music was a constant. Grosse benefited from a government program that guaranteed a musical instrument and lessons for every child. She played and studied the flute for many years and was part of a symphony orchestra – although she admits that, while avid, she was 'not great' yet was 'adventurous'. She especially recalls performing US composer Charles Ives's *The Unanswered Question* (1908, revived 1930–5) with its unusual combination of solo trumpet, four flutes and a string ensemble; the trumpet player was at the back of the audience, not on the stage, and the flutists were interspersed through the audience, thus eliminating the distance between performers and spectators and, by extension, between artwork and viewer – something Grosse would later do in her own work many times. Ives's combination of different tempos for the instruments (steady strings; thoughtful, solemn trumpet; flighty, and at times frantic, flutes) along with his mix of melody and dissonance also fits with Grosse's combinatory, eventful and sometimes jarring aesthetic. Still, while visual art was a constant for Grosse at this stage by no means did she think of herself as an artist – nor did she have any aspirations to become one. That would come later.

Also essential was the education Katharina Grosse received from her family, including the familiarity with visual art that she absorbed from her mother and the education that she generated on her own. When I asked Grosse about her early artistic influences, I fully expected her to cite her mother, which she did, but she also underscored the importance of her father who, according to her, was 'theater crazy'. He used to enact performances in a miniature paper theater and present puppet shows for the three children, and he would also recite 'little bits' of stories over time, instilling imagination in the children and leaving them hungry for more: Tristan and Isolde, Percival, the Brothers Grimm fairy tales (which Grosse's mother also read to the children).

Grosse's family went frequently to the theater, and Bochum, despite being a mid-sized German city, had a world-class theater – Schauspielhaus Bochum – and a world-class theater director in the German-Jewish Peter Zadek, who had been born in Berlin in 1926 and basically survived because his family had managed to emigrate to London in 1934.

Zadek was theater director in Bochum from 1972 to 1979, and Grosse recalls being entranced by his production of Shakespeare's *The Merchant of Venice* – by the stage set, the make-believe wonder of it all, the lighting, the acting, all the visual drama. Grosse thought she saw Zadek's *Merchant of Venice* when she was a bit younger, but research shows that the production was in 1972, when she was 11 years old.

I was somewhat incredulous that a child so young could have been so enamored of this complex play. 'You see things differently as a kid', Grosse explained. 'You find it fascinating that Shylock is offering to cut one pound of flesh out of his breast. And you wonder, hey, how does he know it's going to be a pound?' She also recalls how Zadek built a stage out of slate into the audience; that stage was very noisy. The performers wore high wooden shoes ('from the Japanese theater', Grosse said) and the sound they made when they walked on the slate evoked what you might have heard way back when on the stone streets of sixteenth-century Venice. Years later Grosse would make many painting installations that extend into the audience and that break down the distance between artwork and viewer. Her room-filling *Inside the Speaker* (2014) at Kunstpalast Düsseldorf – with acrylic on soil, fabric, and glass-fiber-reinforced plastic objects – was part colorful wonderland, part invented indoor landscape and part heaped-up debris (fig.22). Viewers could navigate through it on walkways – not just looking at, but wholly immersed in, this engrossing installation.

As a teenager and young adult Katharina Grosse steeped herself in culture – especially visual art, theater and music – even though none of her friends were doing the same, and even though she had zero awareness that she would one day become an artist.

She went with her family, but more often on her own, to museum after museum, exhibition after exhibition, and she points out that in the Ruhr there were lots of excellent museums, including the Museum Folkwang in Essen with paintings by Romantic painters Caspar David Friedrich and Carl Gustav Carus, and Expressionist Ernst Ludwig Kirchner.

Grosse also went to performance after performance, and she sometimes traveled far to do so, including waiting for three hours to get a ticket to a Peter Brook piece at his Théâtre des Bouffes du Nord in Paris and going to the Avignon Festival in France for an Ariane Mnouchkine production.

When she was 19 or 20 years old, and still before she conceived of herself as an artist, Grosse used to take the night train (as this was the most inexpensive way of traveling) throughout Europe to visit museums, in Lisbon, London, Paris, Madrid, Florence and many other cities. I asked her if she was focusing on a particular area – painting, for example – or on specific artists. 'I saw everything', she declared, although contemporary art hardly registered. She took the night train to Paris to see the Louvre. She would go to museums during the day and then theaters at night. She amassed a trove of postcards, an archive of artworks that she had seen or wanted to see, which became a lexicon of sorts. She learned by looking, not reading; from direct experience rather than catalog images. When she finally entered art school, Grosse was astonished to discover that most of her fellow students had never been to the Louvre.

Katharina Grosse graduated from high school and entered Ruhr University intending to study English and Art History, after also considering Psychology. Because of her excellent grades, she received a coveted stipend to support her English studies, which allowed her to travel to England and Wales for tutoring and to gain more familiarity with the language and culture. But during this first year things began to shift, and not because of any plan. Grosse began to make paintings

right and following spread

22. Inside the Speaker   2014
Kunstpalast Düsseldorf

Acrylic on fabric, soil, and glass-fiber-reinforced plastic
450 × 4170 × 1870 cm (177 × 1642 × 736 in)

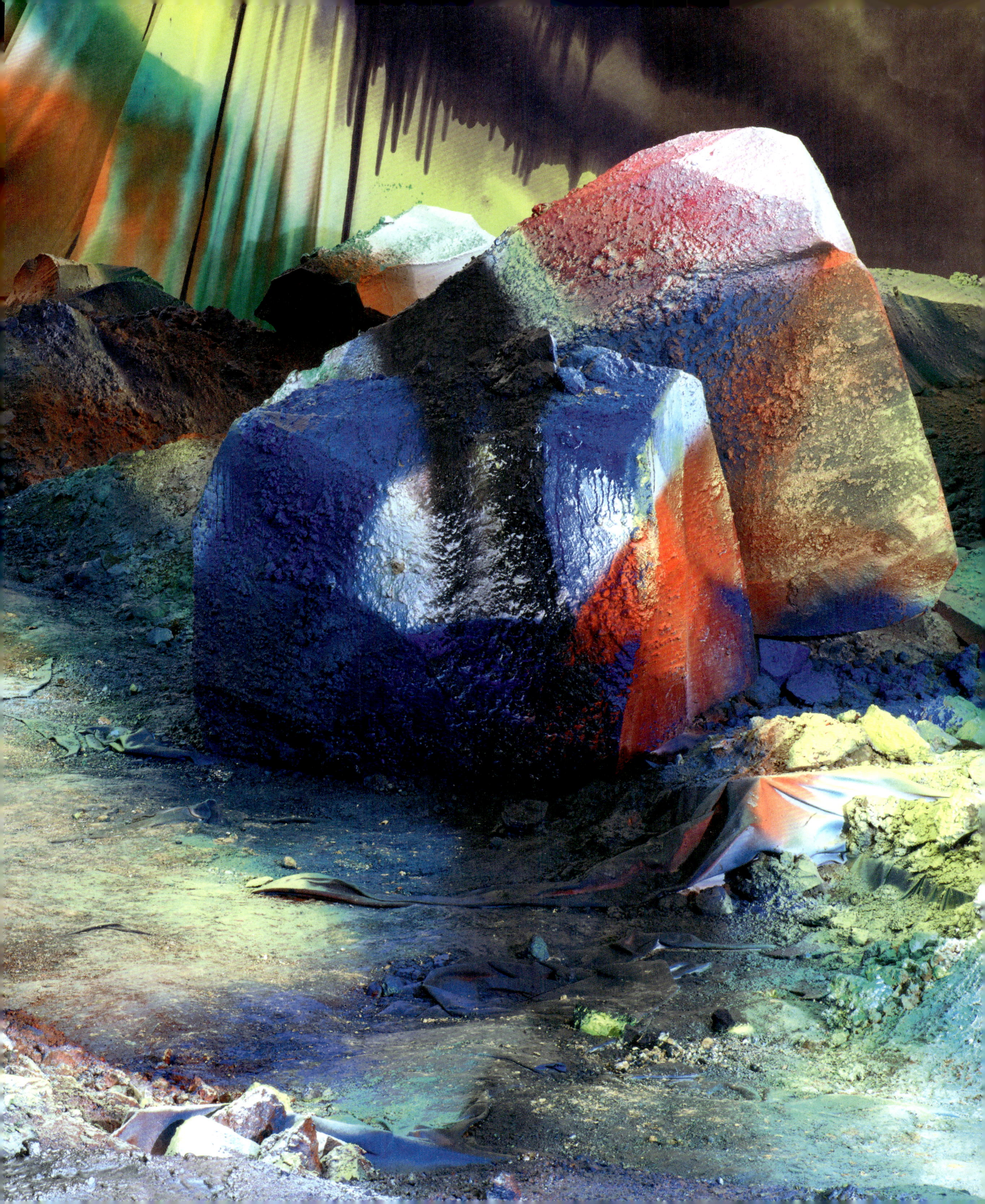

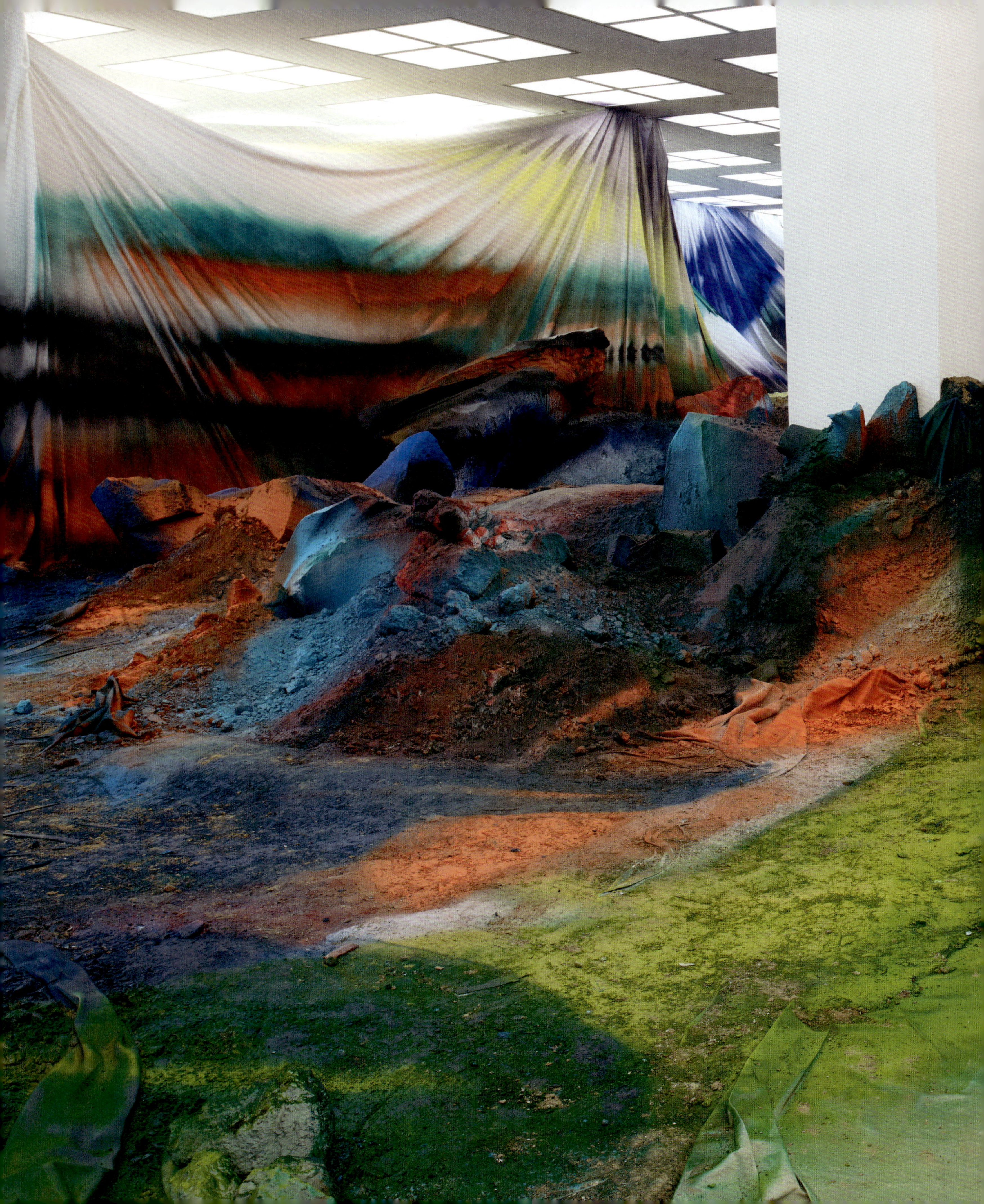

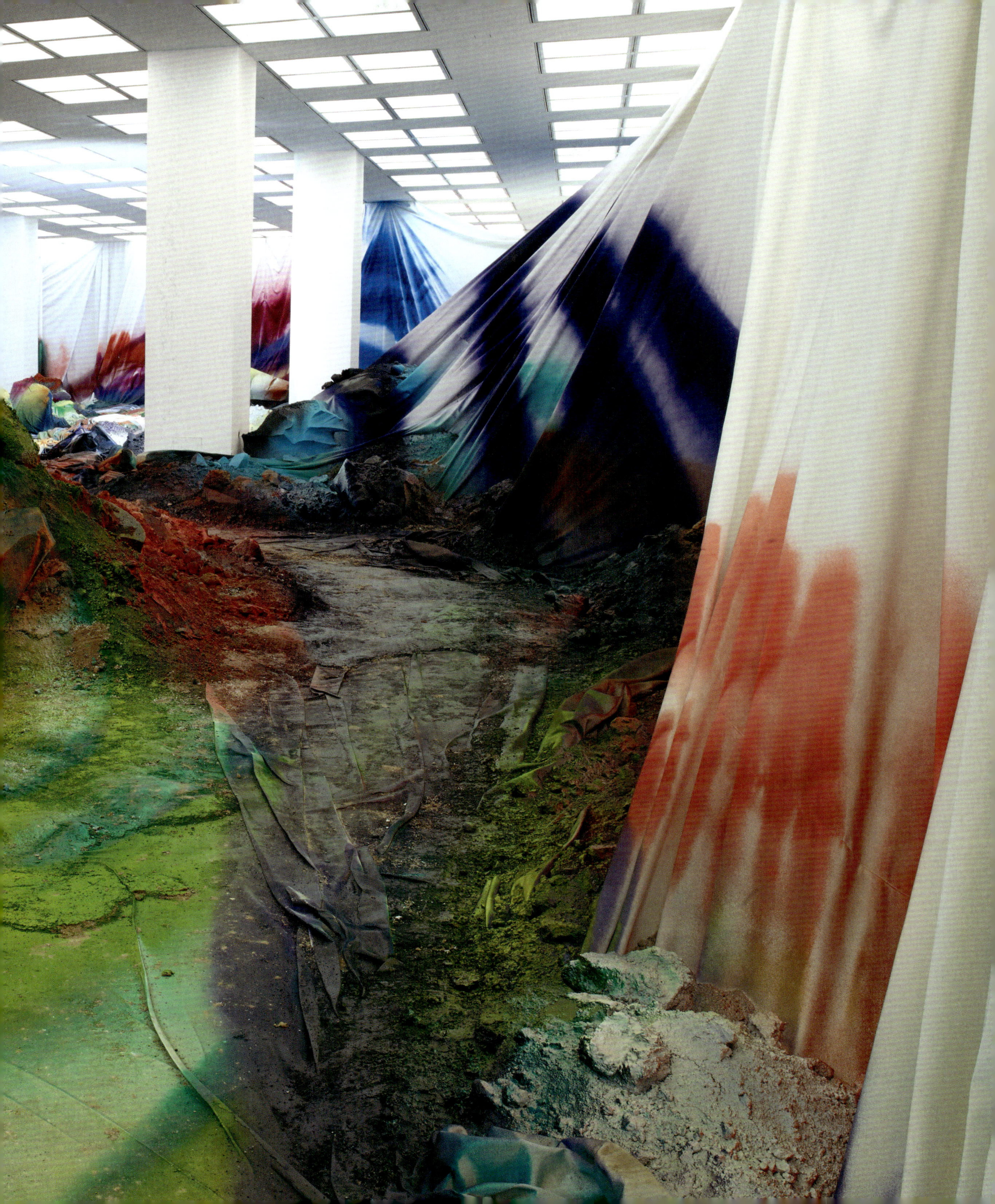

and drawings in earnest. She just did so, on her own. At the university she attended lectures by eminent art historian Max Imdahl, took a whole seminar on Renaissance sculptor Gian Lorenzo Bernini, and learned from painter Hans-Jürgen 'Hänner' Schlieker. She took a special course on 'eccentric and marginalized twentieth century composers', sitting in a listening booth ten hours a day over three weeks absorbing Karlheinz Stockhausen, Ives, John Cage and others. There was also an art center at the university spanning visual art, music and theater, which anyone affiliated with the university could attend – students and faculty, but also secretaries and workers. Grosse would attend classes and study during the day and go to the art center in the evenings and on Saturdays to work in the studios.

Also during this first year of studies Grosse's mother chanced upon some small paintings that Katharina had made, and she thought them very good. With her mother's encouragement, Grosse signed up, through the university's art center, for a week-long *plein air* painting excursion in the north of Germany. In Grosse's archive I happened on a treasure, an image of one of the paintings she made during this excursion (*Untitled*, 1982). It's a remarkable, and remarkably prescient, work. Instead of painting the landscape she focused on grass, in fluctuating green shades. There is a yellow triangle on the left. I asked Grosse about this. 'It's my tent,' she explained, 'I painted the tip of my yellow tent.' Here is an origin painting with its interplay of colors, all equal, with a natural material (grass) and a cultural one (the tent) linked via paint. Another painting was of 'a little gate with hinges', which Grosse sold to a friend of her mother for 100 DM (her first sale) allowing her to buy her own paintbrushes and oil paints. I found it hilarious that she went far out in splendid nature and painted a humble gate. The teacher encouraged her to apply to art school. This is precisely what Grosse did, initially not knowing a thing about art schools – even their names – while realizing that if accepted she would have to relinquish her coveted stipend, which could only be used for English studies rather than art.

Grosse applied to exactly one school, the quite small and relatively unheralded Kunstakademie Münster, and was surprised when she was accepted. Traveling to Münster she took the first cheap room she could find – a laughably small one that, in her view, had probably been used in former times by a maid. It had no heat, hot water or stove but she had two hot plates and the room had a skylight letting in 'diffuse light', which is why she took it. From what I gather, Grosse began working intensely from day one, composing painting after painting. She was usually the last person in the studios (which closed at 9 pm) and she befriended the janitor, who could also procure art materials like canvases at a reduced price since there was no bona fide art store in Münster.

In Germany's unique art-school system, after the first year of studies students choose which professor to work with, and if the professor accepts they'll be in that class for the duration. At summer's end Grosse was uncertain how to proceed, but then she made the first of two momentous, against-the-grain art-school decisions. At a time when many of her fellow students were in full flight from painting – and especially figurative painting, believing it creaky, old, and restrictive – she entered the 'classic painting class' of Norbert Tadeusz, *the* figurative painting professor at the school.

He had 'great skills' and was 'a really good draftsman' but what drew Grosse to him most were his colors. 'He had all the raw colors in his work, that's why I went to him', she told me. 'I liked his color scheme. And I liked him.' Tadeusz was on sabbatical at the time, and was an artist-in-residence at Villa Romana in Florence. Grosse went to visit him there, to 'meet that guy that could be my teacher, and to see what he says'. An alcoholic, he had stopped drinking but had a bottle of wine and asked Grosse if she would like something to drink. 'We were sitting in the sun,' she told me, 'and it was really hot and I drank the whole bottle of wine. It was all very blurred, that meeting.' Blurred or not, things totally clicked.

Tadeusz, from a working-class background in the Ruhr, who always wore 'super expensive clothes', even while painting, 'Italian shirts and stuff'; who was also always 'a little run down'; and who drove 'a Jaguar that would only run on three cylinders or something and wobble along' had studied with Joseph Beuys ('He knew everything about Beuys', Grosse said), was friends with Blinky Palermo (together the two of them visited the US), was a lover of jazz and was part of the Cologne art scene. He died in 2011. 'Nobody knows him now', Grosse told me, and she's mostly right about that. I sure didn't. But now I do, and I also think his paintings very much merit renewed attention – for instance, *Untitled* (1982), in which bright blue and orange inflatable mattresses in a swimming pool float upon water streaked with blue, green and yellow. He proved to be an engaged and exemplary teacher, encouraging Grosse as she experimented in different genres – including life drawings, still lifes, landscapes, portraits, and large self-portraits – and as she also experimented with materials, including painting with tar and encaustic (she boiled candles to make her own encaustic). At one point Tadeusz didn't just suggest that Grosse make a really large painting, he told her to do so – adding that if she wouldn't do it, he would. He also instructed Grosse to take good photographs of her paintings, as if he either knew or sensed what the future might bring.

After studying in Münster Grosse began hearing of the larger and more famous Kunstakademie Düsseldorf, with its roster of big-name professors including Gerhard Richter, Nam June Paik, Bernd and Hilla Becher, Tony Cragg, Michael Buthe, Dieter Krieg and Markus Lüpertz. A friend of hers left Münster to enter the Richter class. Grosse, too, realized that she was outgrowing Münster. 'I couldn't develop any further', she said. 'Using color, I had the feeling I was coming to a dead end. I understood I used it to draw things I saw, rather than to think with color.' She had moved out of her studio to squat in a decrepit industrial space where she made 'huge amounts of paint' and composed large self-portraits. Tadeusz visited her there, and recognized as well that she was outgrowing Münster. He also said that she would be great for Düsseldorf. Grosse decided to apply.

This was Grosse's next momentous decision. She considered Gerhard Richter but settled on Gotthard Graubner ('the color guy', she calls him, adding that 'he could whistle an entire symphony from memory'). Again, her friends – especially her female friends – were astonished that she would consider entering the class of the 'macho' and 'authoritarian' abstract painter Graubner, who seemed straight out of a vanishing era when most artists were painters and most painters were men. To apply, Grosse strapped her paintings to the roof of a borrowed orange BMW ('it needed a push to go'), drove to Düsseldorf, and the first professor she went to see was Graubner – who immediately accepted her.

In hindsight entering Graubner's class in 1985 was exactly what Grosse needed, as she transitioned from figurative painting to abstract paintings based on color. Yes, Graubner was authoritarian, conservative, impossible, and he almost never included female students in shows that he arranged. Still, for Grosse he was inspirational and supportive. Among his more renowned works are his *Farbraumkörper* (Color-space bodies), slightly swelling or bulging paintings that look from a distance like bright monochromes but that are filled with layers of colors and gradations of tones, and that also resemble concentrated mist. Graubner helped to inspire a significant change for Grosse. 'He shifted my attention from looking outside the painting field into it', she told me, adding that 'it wasn't like he said I shouldn't paint things'. Rather than focusing on what she saw outside the canvas or had in her mind, Grosse began to focus on what was right in front of her: 'I started to move my observations more and more towards the canvas while I was painting on it.' She also learned from Graubner, who instructed his students to not 'give up on a work, just go on, on the canvas. That's your building site.' According to Grosse, 'This idea that it [a painting] is a building site was an interesting image for me, because it made me think of street building, or house building, or digging a hole.'

Among Grosse's fellow students in Düsseldorf were quite a number who, like her, have gone on to considerable acclaim – including Andreas Gursky, Thomas Ruff, Monika Baer, Katharina Fritsch, Thomas Demand, Reinhard Mucha, Dirk Skreber, Andreas Siekmann, Corinne Wasmuht, and Ull Hohn. This was a fertile time at that renowned, highly competitive art school, and Grosse was part of a rising generation of German artists who worked hard and adventurously in their studios, met frequently in the evenings at the punk bar Ratinger Hof to carry on and talk shop, and who would rather quickly become central figures in contemporary art of the 1990s and 2000s, not only in Germany. She also cites as influences Nam June Paik's videos (especially their colors); Kasper König, who taught a class in art in public space, where 'whoever was connected with him was dragged to Düsseldorf and that little classroom' including the young Jenny Holzer and Jannis Kounellis; the 'energy' of the Neue Wilde, or New Savages, Neo-Expressionist painters, including Cologne-based Walter Dahn, Jiří Dokoupil, Jörg Immendorff, and Peter Bömmels; Jan Hoet's famous exhibition *Chambres d'Amis* (Guest Rooms) occurring in 1986 in 58 private

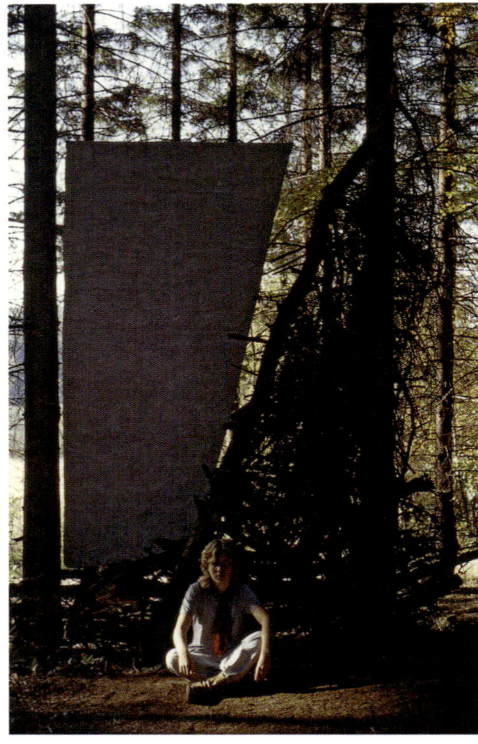

23. Katharina Grosse in front of an outdoor work of hers at Möhnesee, 1982

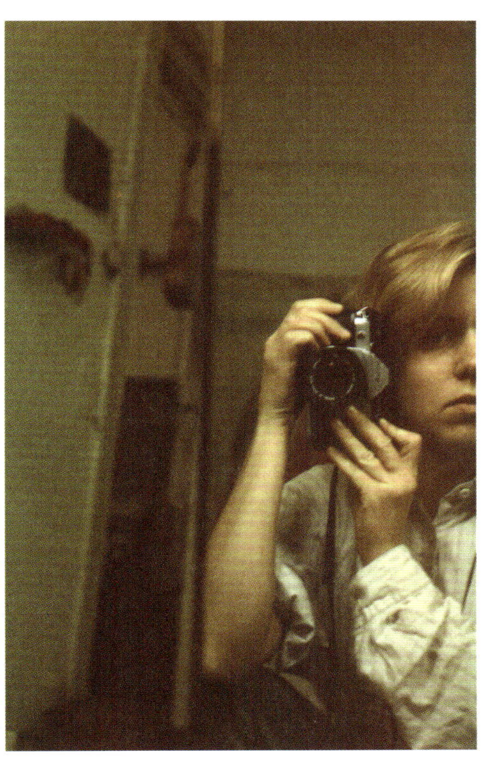

24. Katharina Grosse, self-portrait, mid-1980s

houses in Ghent, Belgium; and the also famous retrospective exhibition *Bilderstreit – Widerspruch, Einheit und Fragment in der Kunst seit 1960* (Iconoclasm – Contradiction, Unity and Fragment in Art since 1960) in 1989 in Cologne.

Working primarily in oil on canvas Grosse developed serious painterly chops and continued to explore different styles and subject matter – from Color Field-influenced abstractions, still lifes, landscapes, and various forms of pared-down geometric abstraction to large, Neo-Expressionist self-portraits, *plein air* painting in a cemetery, and a series of paintings based on stills from Nam June Paik videos. She increasingly gravitated to color, saying she was realizing that 'color has to be right in front of your face, to spring into your face, as a loving but very aggressive punch. I wanted it to get to you like the voice in a song, that it approaches you without you realizing that it does.'

All through this early period Grosse continued to question and explore what constitutes a painting, including grinding her own pigments, mixing her own paints, and experimenting with different ways of making paintings. For *Untitled* (1989) (fig.25) – with its multiple brown tones so different from the brilliant ones with which she is identified – Grosse affixed clumps of paraffin to the canvas and also applied raw pigment. For another painting, also called *Untitled* (1989), she embedded dry brown leaves on a dark teal ground with thin white streaks (fig.26). This painting prefigures by many years Grosse's numerous painting installations, in which she combined acrylic spray-painting with trees, rocks and soil.

Grosse also experimented with other mediums – including video, film, sculpture, and photography – at one point cutting up a Super 8 film and gluing its parts back together, not because she was skeptical of or exasperated with painting – and certainly not because she was influenced by any 'painting is dead' nonsense – but because, as she put it in an interview, 'I really wanted to see whether painting would matter enough in the end for me to dedicate my life to it.'[11] It did, and she has – to remarkable effect.

After Grosse finished her studies in 1990 she enjoyed some modest success (later, this would escalate). In 1992 she was a prizewinner and months-long resident at Villa Romana in Florence, a major honor for an emerging German artist. The next year she won the Schmidt-Rottluff Stipendium, another top award that provided her with much-needed funding and also an important exhibition. She had a one-person show the same year in the small and short-lived Maria Wilkens Gallery in Cologne ('my first exhibition with an invitation card!', Grosse enthuses). She had solo exhibitions at Kunstverein Hochrhein in Bad Säckingen, Germany (1993), the Altes Kunstmuseum in Bonn (1994), and the Mark Müller Gallery (1995) in Zürich, among others. Grosse's paintings were garnering interest. A viable professional career was assembling.

Color is essential in Grosse's paintings from this early period: color as a thing, a material, and not a descriptor of something else. The emotional resonance of colors is important, as is the complex interplay between them – what happens when a particular crimson touches a specific yellow-gold, or when an orange tone partially covers a dark-green one.

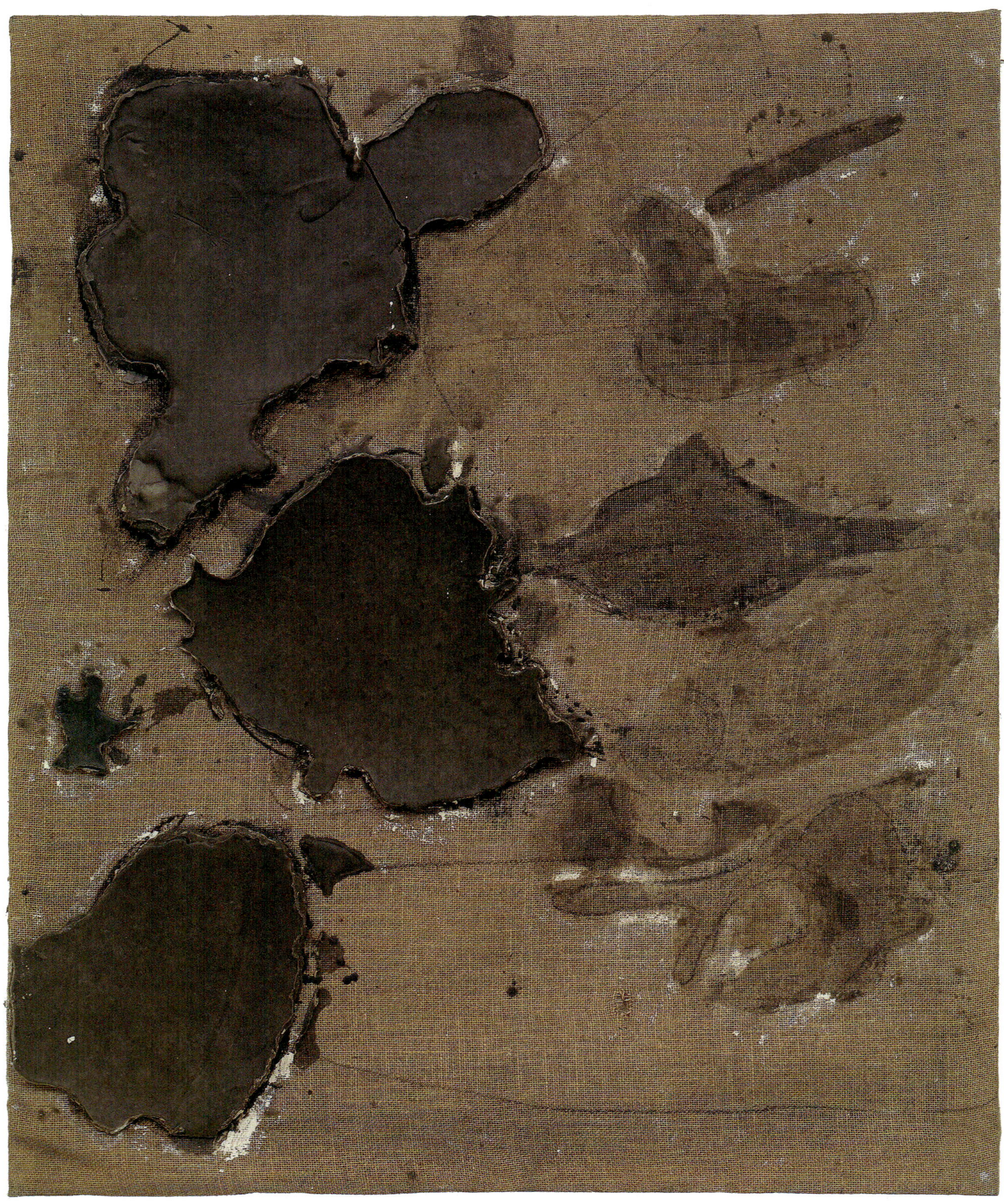

25. Untitled   1989

Paraffin, pigment on canvas
106 × 88 cm (42 × 35 in)
Kunstmuseum Stuttgart

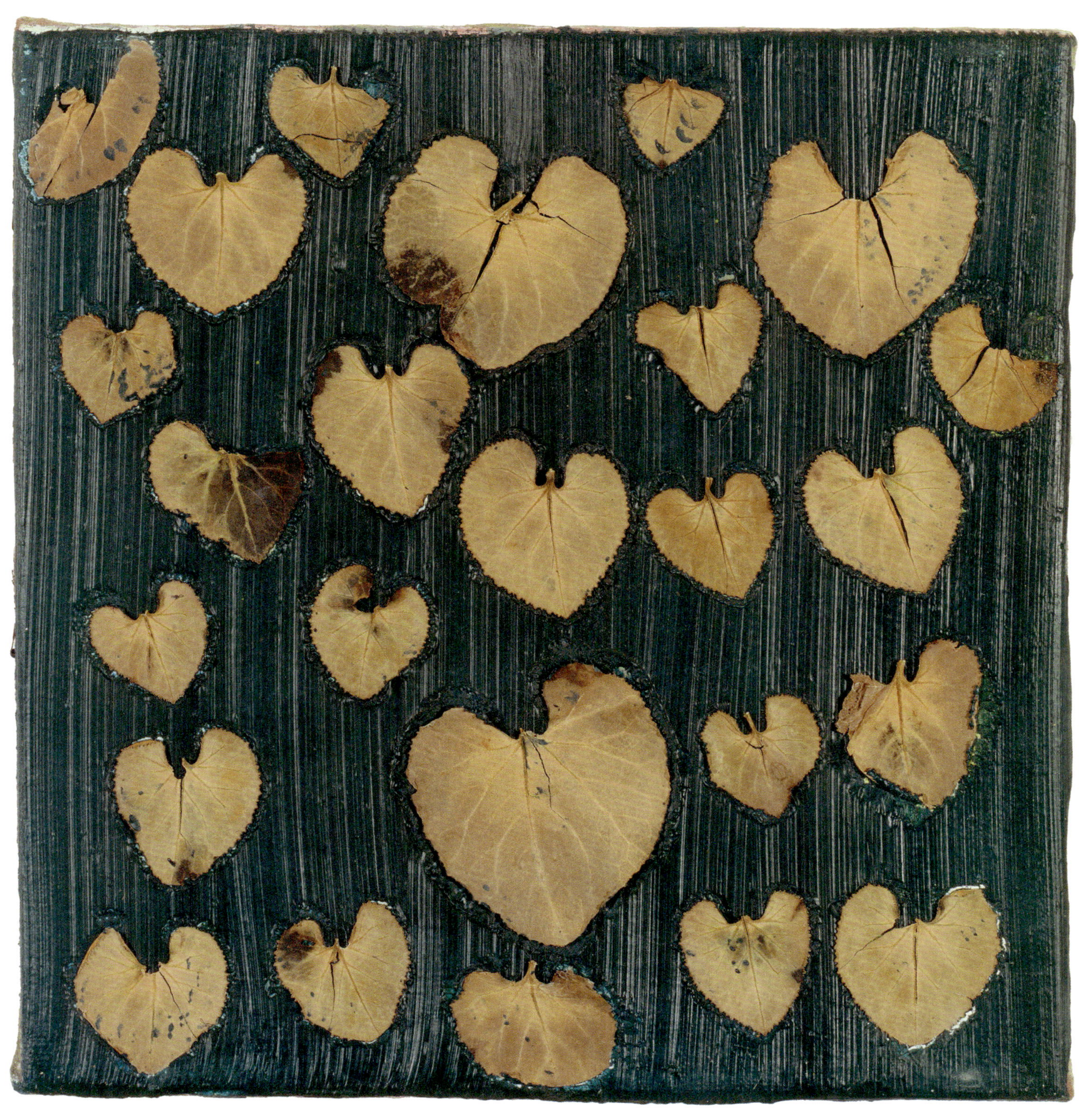

26. Untitled   1989

Oil and leaves on canvas
30 × 30 cm (12 × 12 in)

In *Untitled* (1991) multiple colors – including red, pink, light blue, purple, and muddy green – cover the canvas in curving, vertical bands and streaks (fig.28). You sense how inquisitive Grosse was, investigating the relationships between these several colors and these irregular, abstract shapes; you sense how vital and 'alive' colors were for her. In *Untitled* (1994) three different orange tones abut, and also partially cover sections of a green ground (fig.29).

This was also the period in which Grosse began making large two-color oil-on-paper paintings, portable works that she could roll up, transport, attach to the wall with pushpins, and that would cover much of the wall (which they did for her 1995 exhibition at Mark Müller Gallery). They were about as close to the wall as could be without being directly on it, and they are the immediate precursors to her breakthrough spray-painted works. From a distance some look like monochromes, like the tawny red *Untitled* (1995) (fig.30). Look closer and you see all sorts of subtle tones in the vertical, slightly bending brushstrokes. Others involve multiple colors – for instance, the really large *Untitled* (1995) with yellow, green, white, blue, and black adjacent rectangles in varying widths, all rendered with vertical brushstrokes on several sheets of paper (fig.31). Grosse's paintings from this period especially connect with so-called Radical Painting from the 1980s and 1990s in Europe and the US, with its focus on monochromes or near-monochromes and color, and including the work of painters Marcia Hafif, Joseph Marioni, Günter Umberg and Olivier Mosset.

1995 was also the year that I first met Grosse – not in Germany but in Williamsburg, Brooklyn, during her second visit to New York.

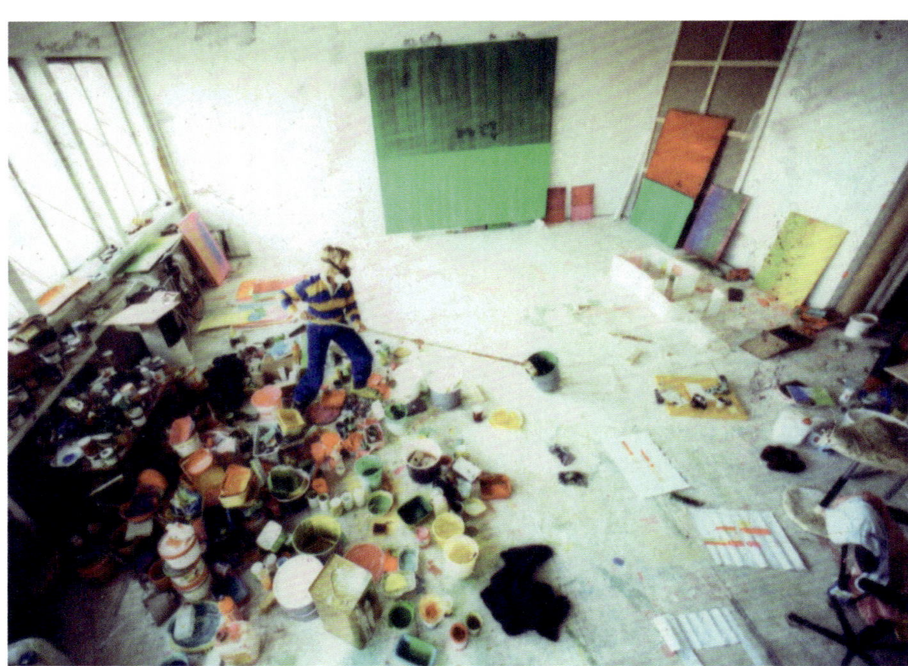

27. Studio view, Düsseldorf, 1995

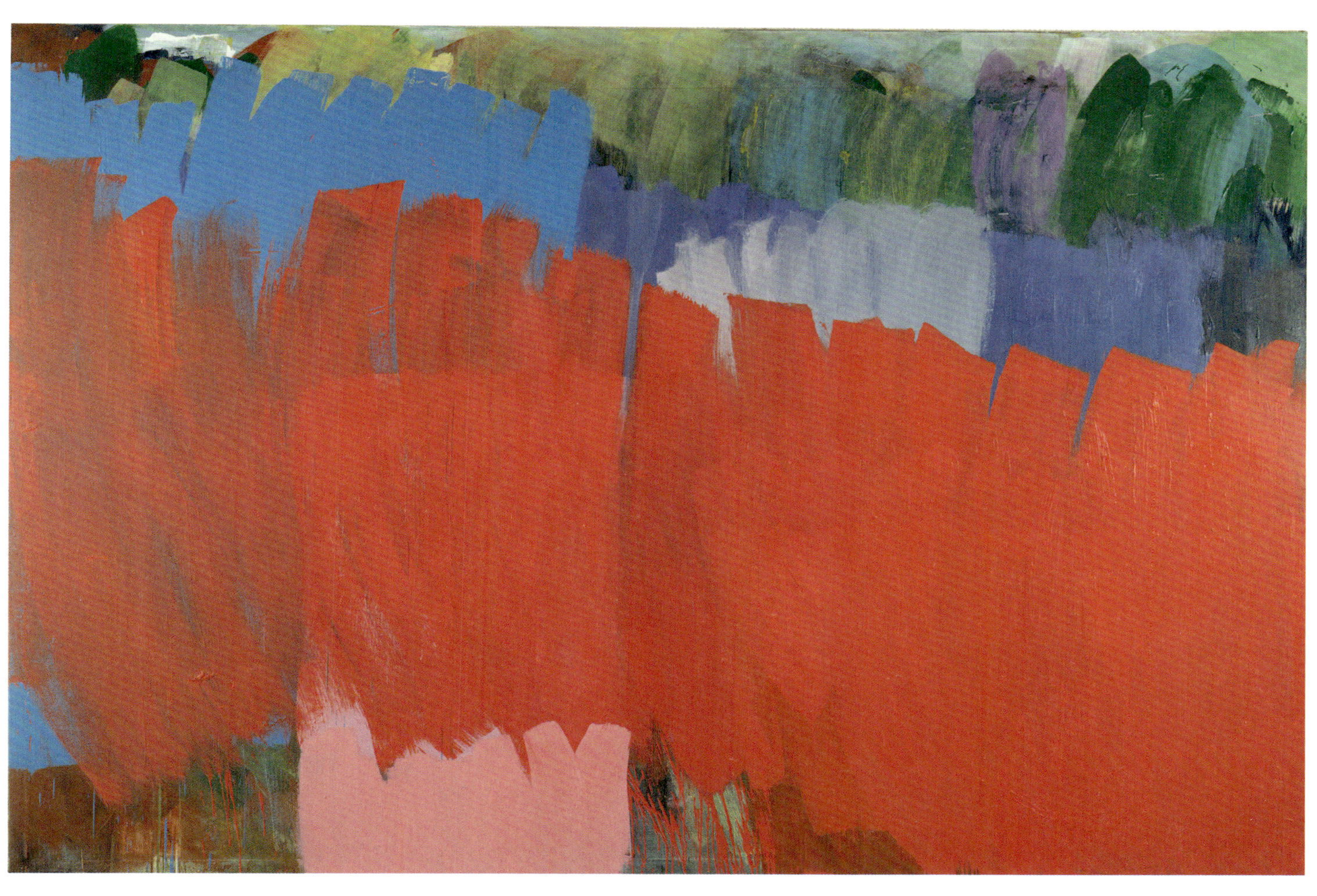

28. Untitled   1991

Oil on canvas
200 × 300 cm (79 × 118 in)

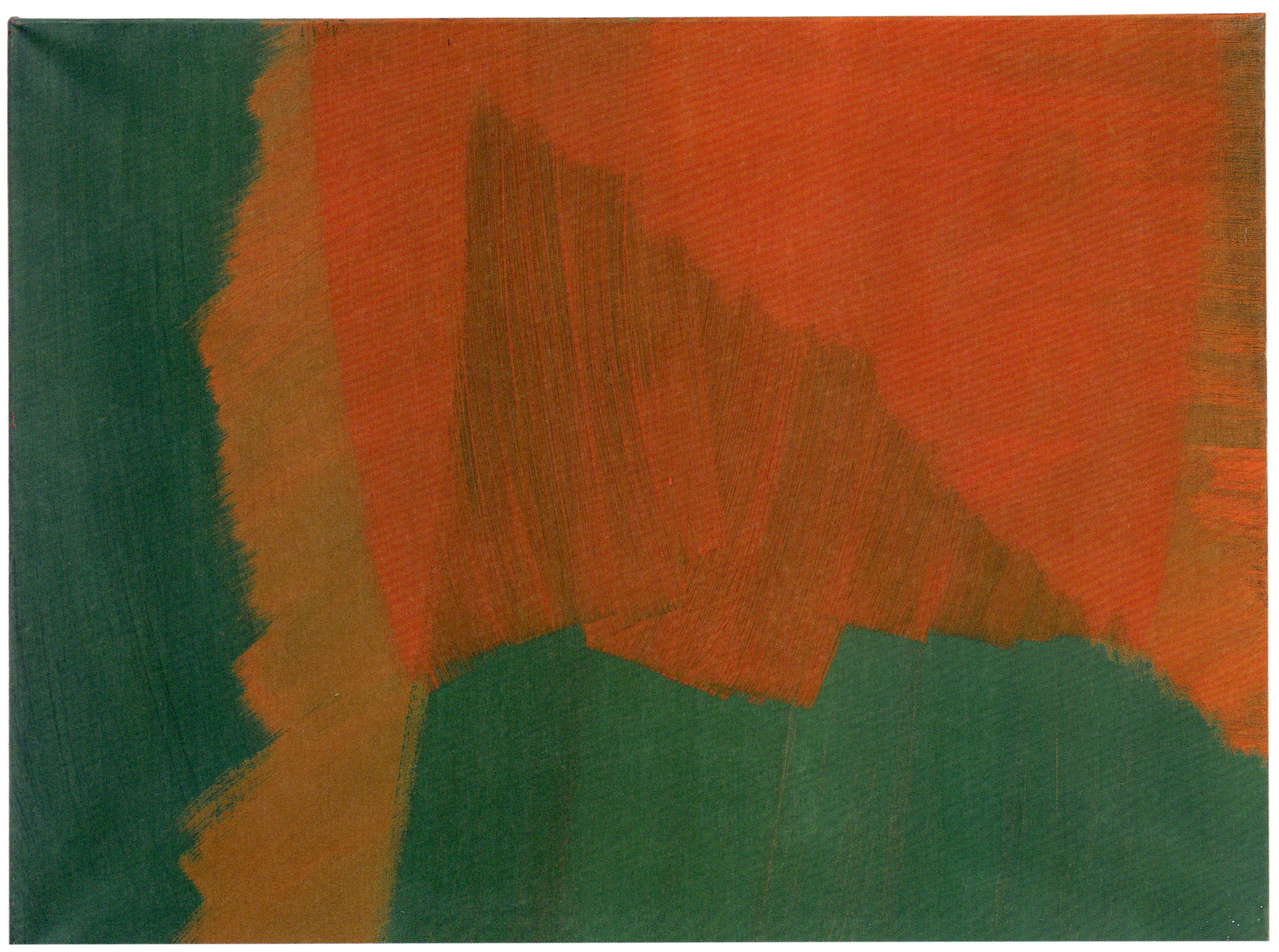

29. Untitled   1994

Oil on canvas
70 × 93 cm (28 × 37 in)

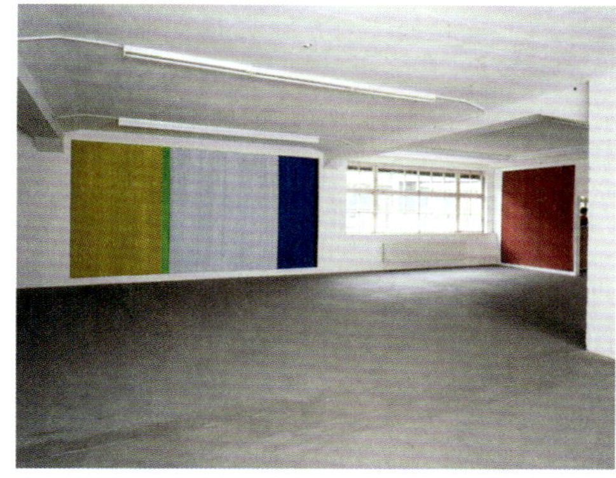

30. Malerei scannen   1995
Gallery Mark Müller, Zurich, Switzerland

When I met Grosse only a handful, or maybe less than a handful, of New Yorkers knew anything about her. She showed me the paintings that she was working on, and also photographs of others. I was impressed. Many were quite reductive, but also very vibrant. In the oil on canvas *Untitled* (1995) slightly curving bright-green vertical brushstrokes partially cover an underlying dark ground (fig.32). This painting, as Grosse correctly notes, is 'extremely delicate because the pigment is open and exposed nearly like dust' and the paint appears to have been 'combed' onto the canvas, not applied with a paintbrush. The oil on canvas *Untitled* (1994) features abstract vertical bands in blue, crimson, several oranges, teal, and light green, rendered with prominent vertical, horizontal, and diagonal brushstrokes – and it is completely captivating (fig.33). I have no doubt that had Grosse continued to work primarily in this vein she would have gone on to a distinguished career as an Abstract Colorist. But that is not at all what she would do.

Instead, while maintaining a practice that also includes copious paintings and drawings per se, what she did was develop and propel her new-found spray-painting aesthetic. And as her works grew larger and more complex, she also increasingly introduced distinctly carnivalesque elements.

Grosse's breakthrough wall painting in Bern in 1998 led to numerous others over the next several years (roughly 1998–2004), including ones in New York, Switzerland, and Marfa, Texas. With all of them, Grosse established a principle that would guide her work from then on. Nothing would be repeated. Everything would change, and keep changing. One work would lead to the next – opening up fresh possibilities, new means of both execution and perception, fresh research, new consciousness.

In New York, for a group exhibition at The Drawing Center (an exhibition of drawings and also one that continues to perplex her, since her work wasn't a drawing) Grosse presented a variation on her piece in Bern but with a significant twist (*Untitled*, 1999). It was again largely green, wrapping around parts of two walls and encompassing the corner of the space, but now she added in yellow – prominent at the top, but glowing around the edges of and through the green (fig.34). This was the first time that many people in New York had seen a work by Grosse, and that work was something of a sensation; people still talk about it 20 years later. There were at the time (and, in some cases, still are) many expert Colorists in New York, including Helen Frankenthaler, Mary Heilmann, Stanley Whitney, Amy Sillman, the late Marcia Hafif (a friend of Grosse's), and many others. In the background were long-deceased pioneers like Mark Rothko, Hans Hofmann, Morris Louis, et al. Grosse's painting just didn't look or behave like anything else at the time, or before that time. It was physical and optical yet seemed atmospheric and ethereal – and it was made with a spray gun, not with a paintbrush. It also had so much life.

That same year Grosse was artist-in-residence at the Chinati Foundation in Marfa, Texas, the amazing, way-off-the-beaten-track art institution that sculptor Donald

following spread

31. Untitled   1995

Oil on paper
265 × 485 cm (104 × 191 in)

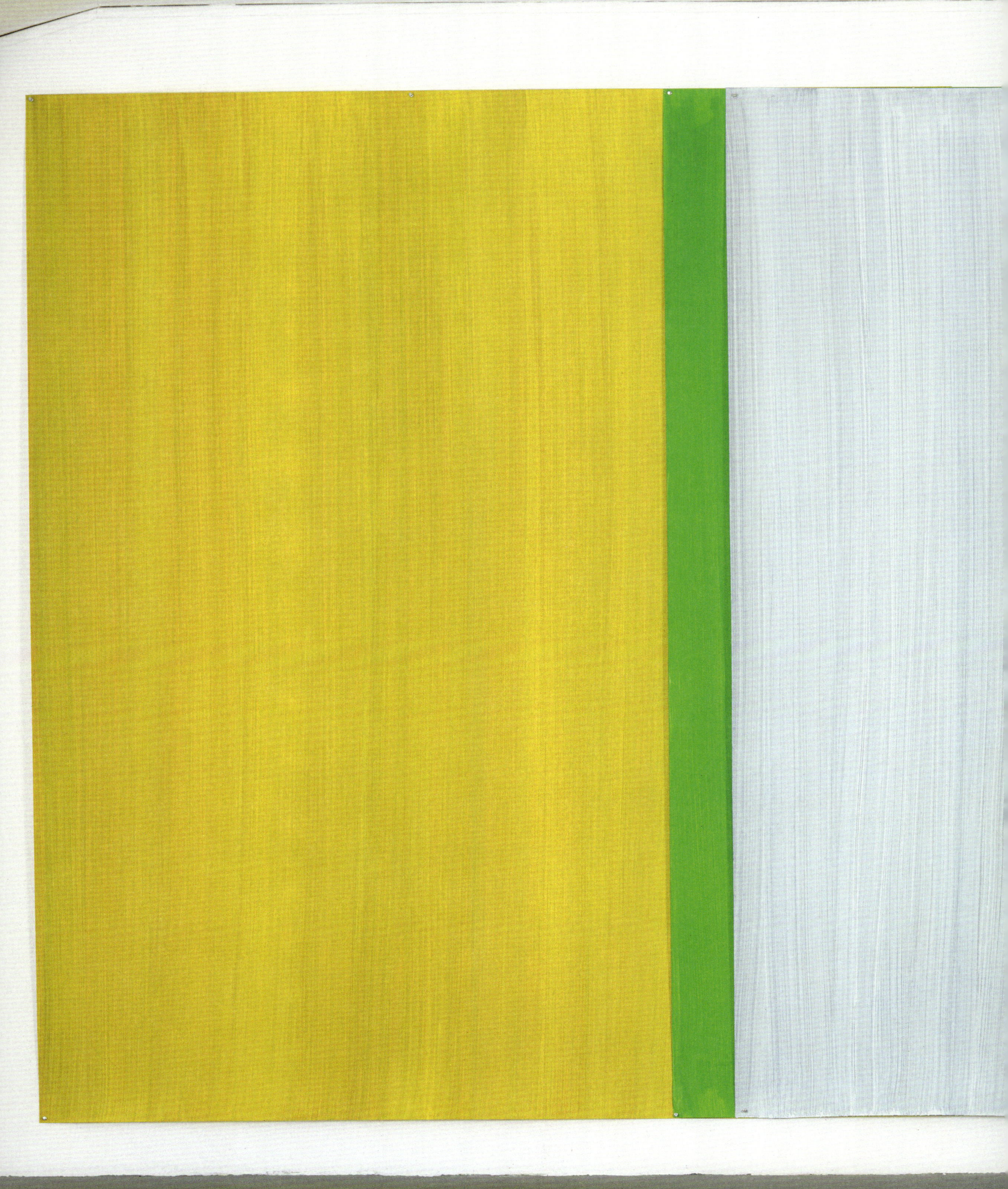

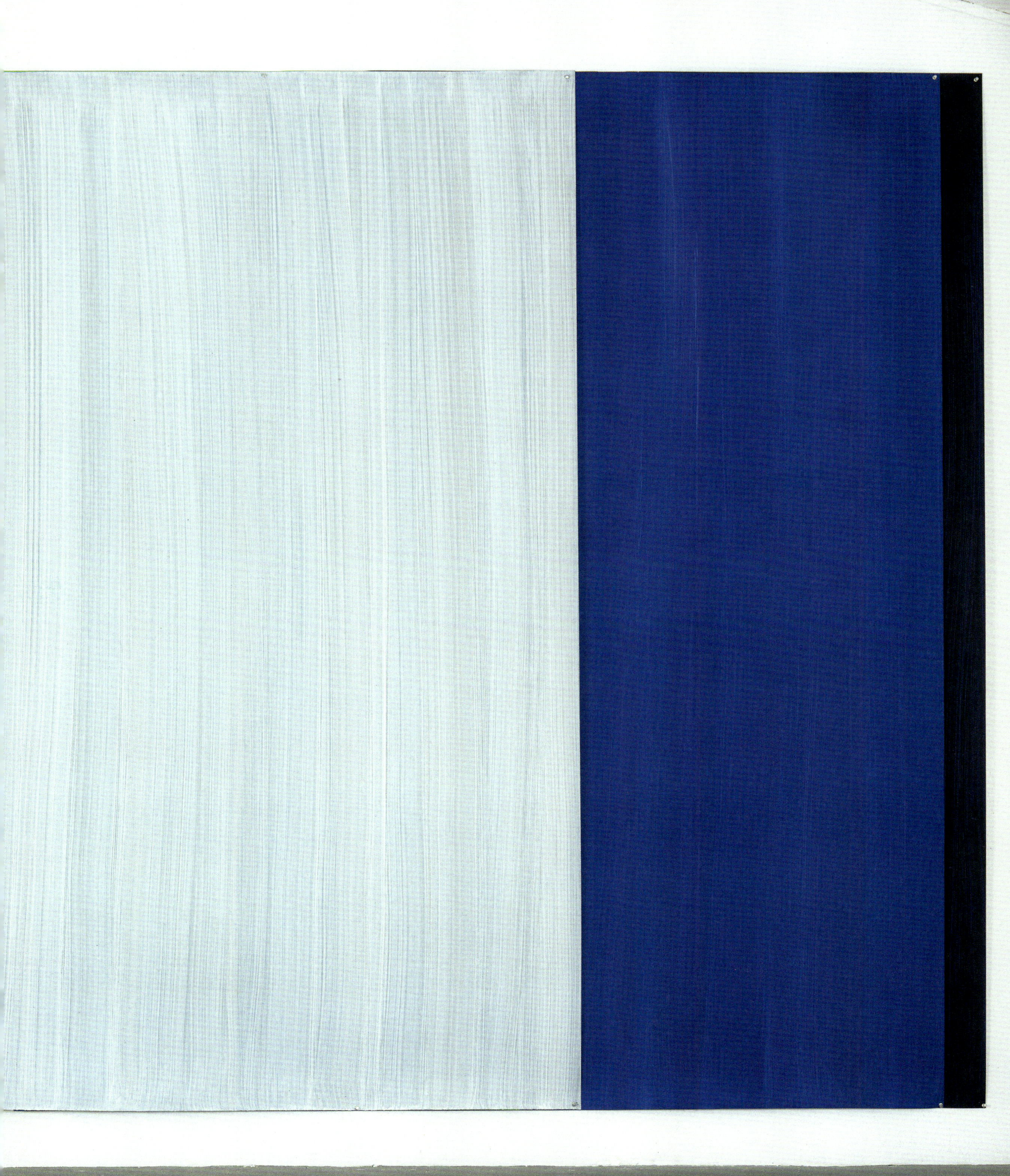

32. Untitled   1995

Oil on paper
240 × 240 cm (95 × 95 in)

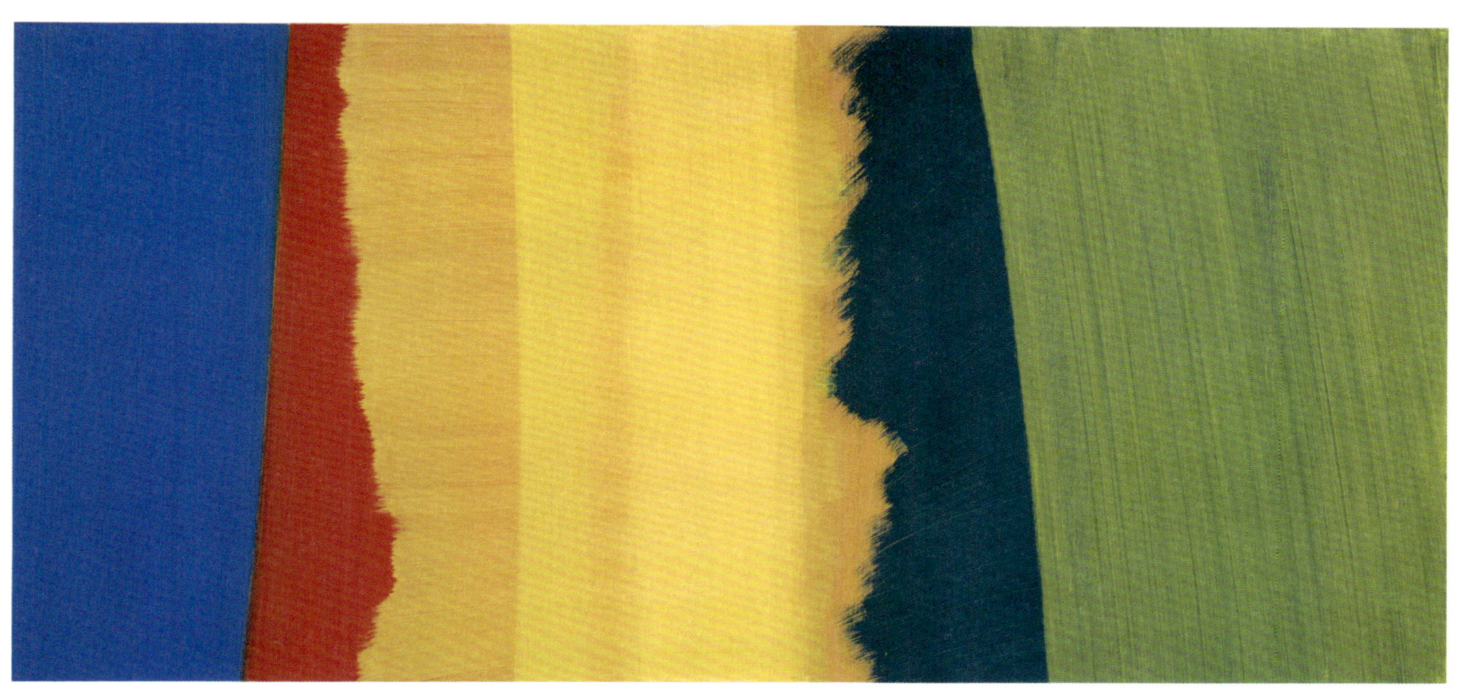

33. Untitled   1994

Oil on canvas
163 × 343 cm (64 × 135 in)

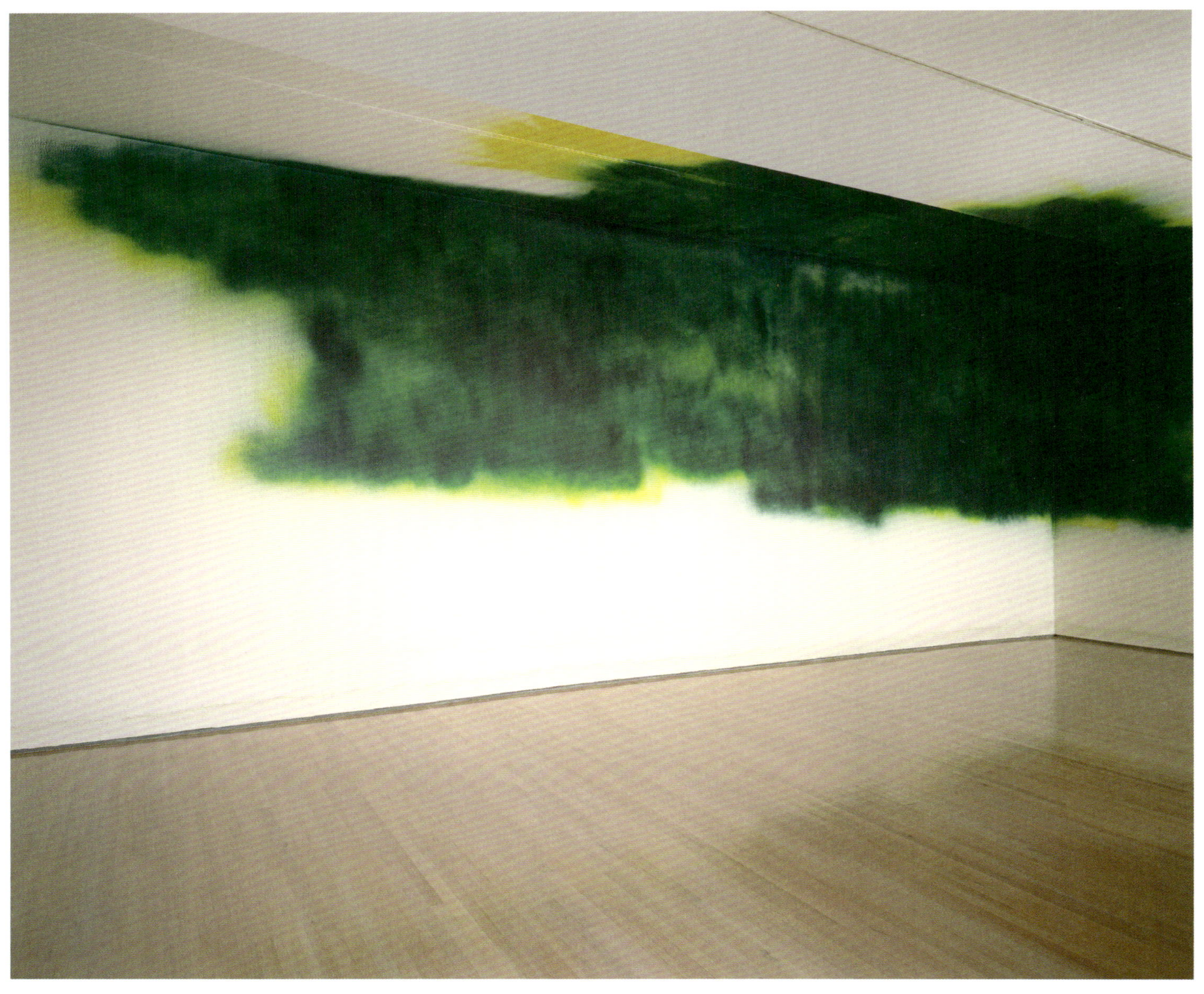

34. Untitled   1999
The Drawing Center, New York

Acrylic on wall
405 × 1481 × 233 cm (159 × 583 × 92 in)

Judd built from scratch (with help, of course, from many others) by buying property
and renovating weathered and abandoned buildings in a remote West Texas town
in the high desert, a three-hour drive from El Paso. (Some of the structures housed
German prisoners of war during the Second World War, which is why you can still
see inscriptions in German on some walls.) Grosse's residency included an exhibition
in one of the foundation's properties, the Locker Plant, a former butcher's shop in
downtown Marfa. In the back of this space was a walk-in cooler (for the meat), with
one light bulb; this was Grosse's studio, where she made paintings and drawings. She
could also work on the patio. It would have made ever so much sense for her to work
in the studio and on the patio, and then display the fruits of that work in the large
front room in an exhibition of paintings for the Chinati Foundation's Open House.
This is not at all what she did.

Instead, in the front room Grosse went all out with her spray gun, now using
multiple colors – yellow, pink, and green – for her work with the comical title *Cheese
Gone Bad* (1999) (fig.36). Because of how the colors combined, some parts seemed
quite dark – almost charred – while others were considerably lighter. Mixing short,
aggressive marks with softer and gentler ones, this work seemed to be billowing and
smoldering, drifting and glowing. The walls, door, and part of the ceiling didn't just
display a painting, they were alive with a living painting – and Grosse emphasizes how
important it was for her to include the door, a functional structure in the room. The
whole space wasn't a static container; instead, it became an active, vital force. This
is when Grosse learned that a painting on the walls, door, and ceiling didn't involve
only those elements but instead the entire building, the whole context – including the
air and all sight lines, including the outside, which would prove crucial for her going
forward. This is also when she really began to explore the chromatic and at times
jarring interplay between, and layering of, multiple colors in architectural spaces.
You could see, and be amazed by, this painting from up close, from outside through
the windows, from across the street, and from quite some distance away. It had a
plugged in, cinematic look. It seethed and glowed, hinting at a vibrant, West Texas
sunset. It also seemed fiery and molten, like an abstract version of a volcanic eruption.

Cheese Gone Bad has subsequently been written about many times, and images of
it have been reproduced endlessly. But what has rarely – maybe never – been noted
is the fact that Grosse made two wall works in Marfa – the one public; the other in
the office of Steffen Böddeker, whose position was Public Affairs Administrator. In
the latter case Grosse painted parts of two walls, the door, and the ceiling fluorescent
yellow, and she loved that she did this in a normal office space, not an exhibition
space (*Office, Marfa*, 1999) (fig.35). As we looked at the image, with the yellow almost
swarming into the office, Grosse explained, 'The color does something different.
It kind of invades the space. It's coming through the building. It's not really on top
of a surface . . . it goes through the wall and goes on behind the wall.' She also likes
'how naturally' Böddeker had her work 'as his companion'.

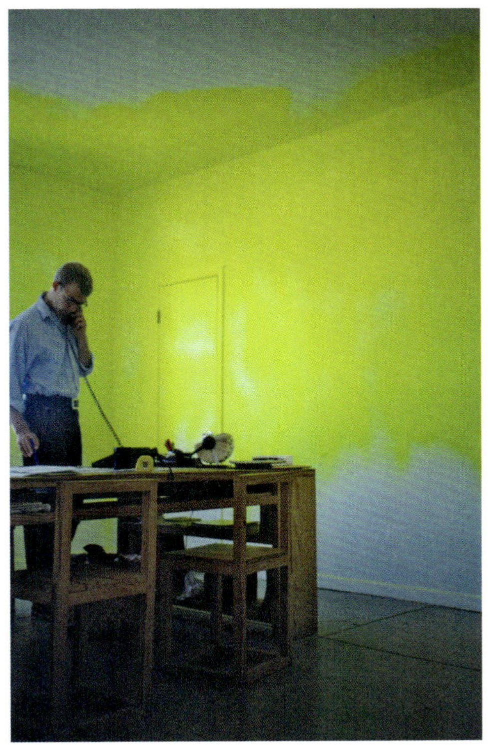

35. Office, Marfa 1999
Chinati Foundation, Marfa, Texas

Acrylic on wall

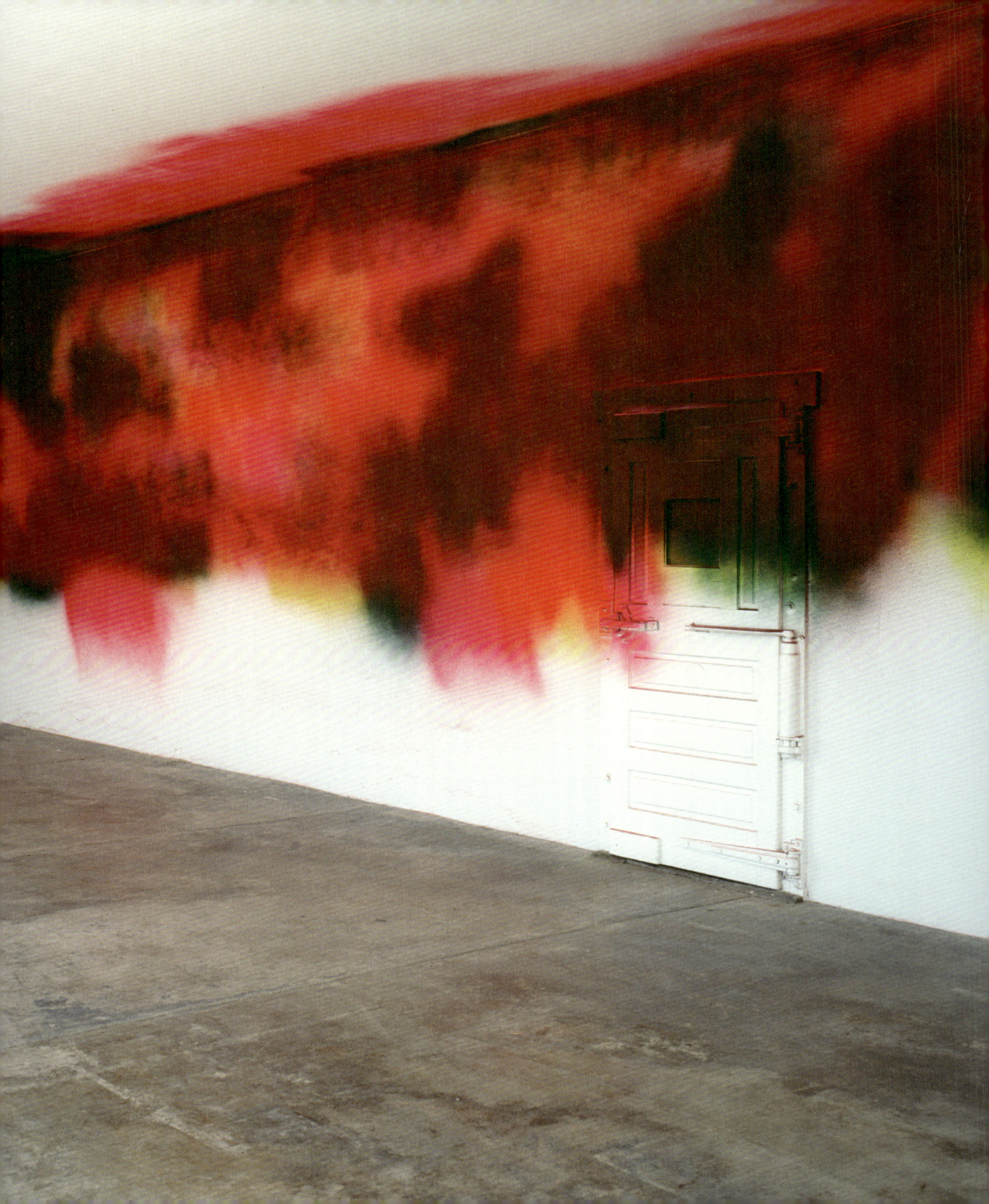

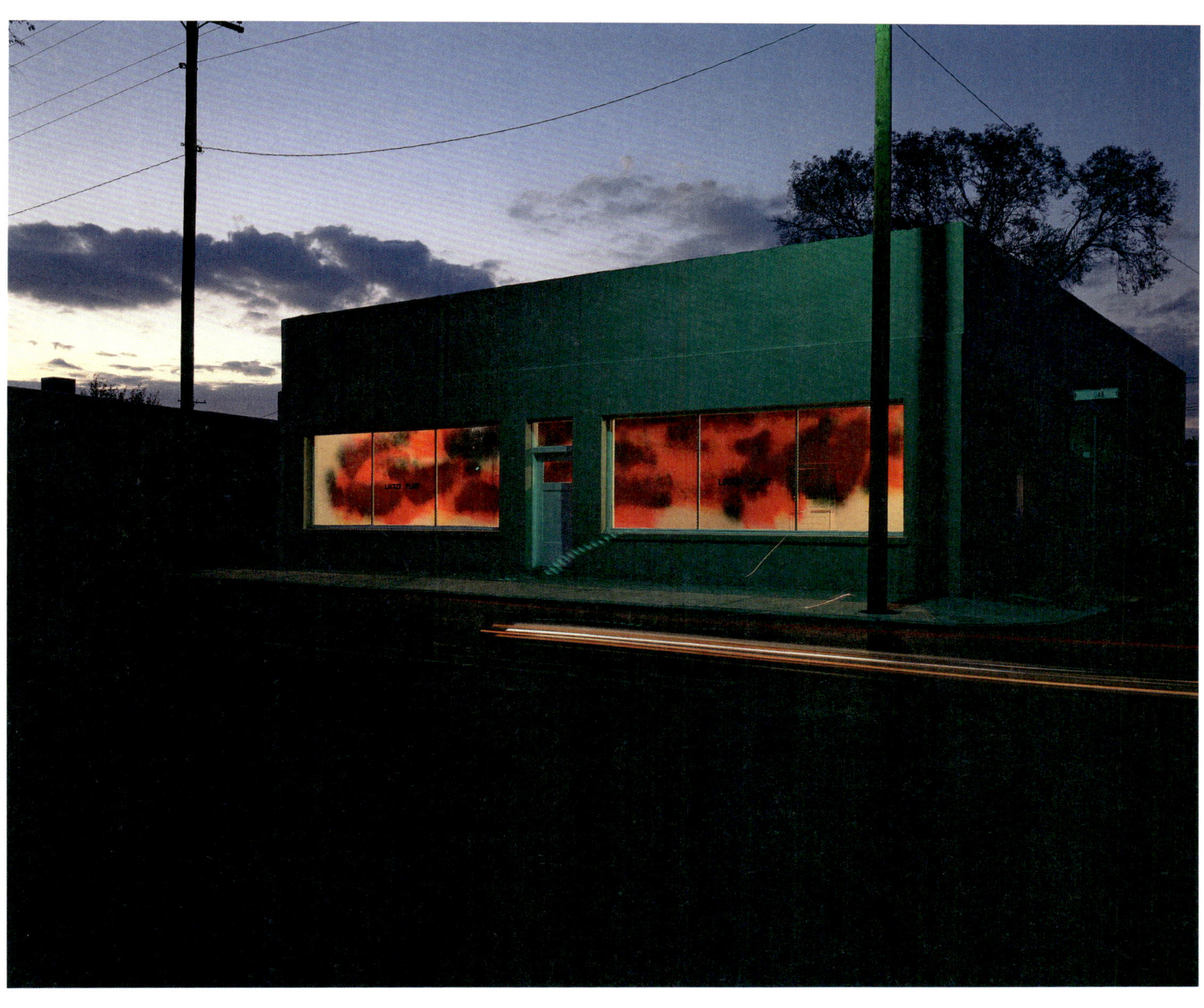

above and left

36. Cheese Gone Bad   1999
Chinati Foundation, Marfa, Texas

Acrylic on wall
357 × 1464 × 671 cm (141 × 576 × 264 in)

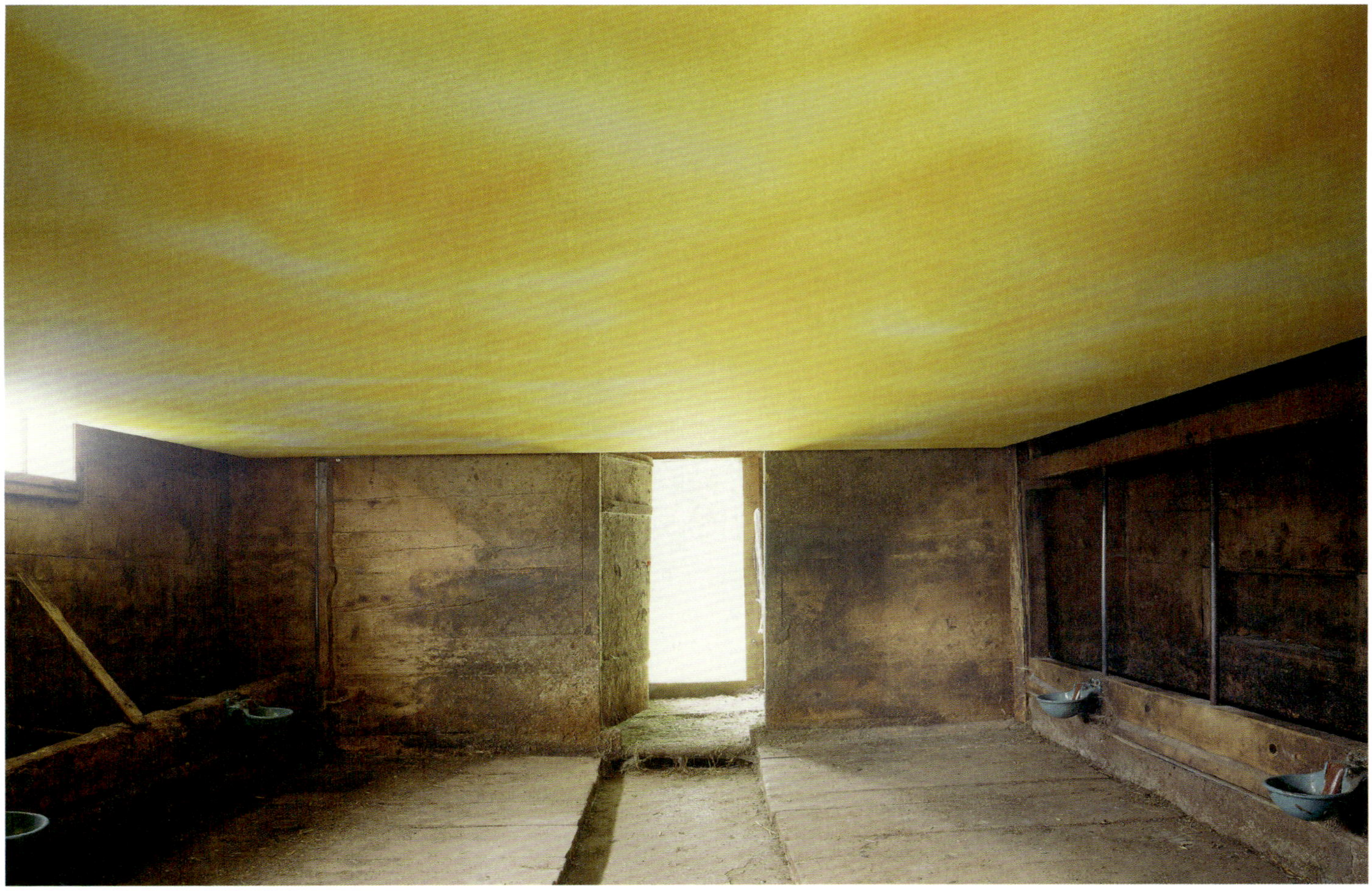

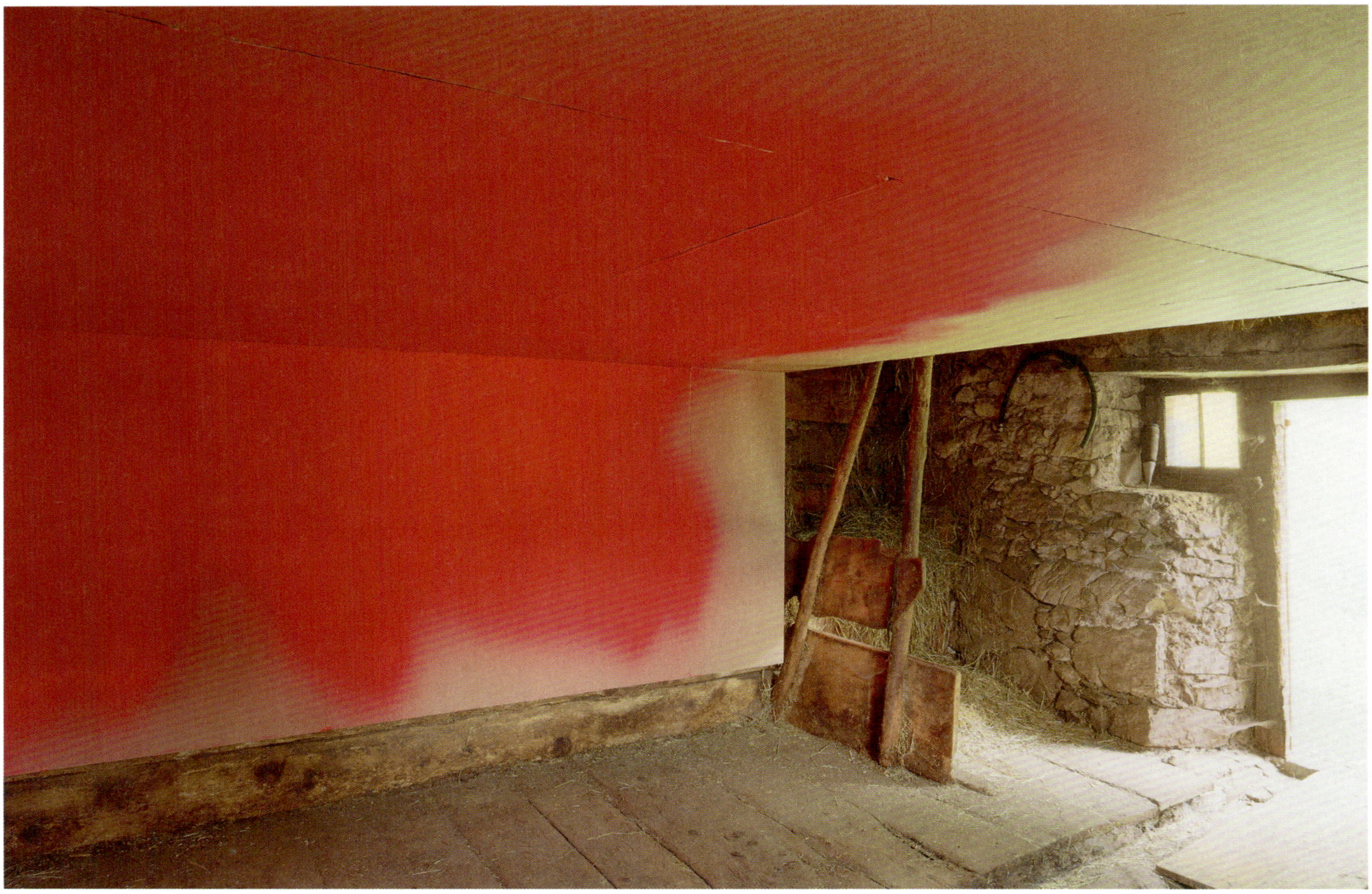

37. Untitled   1999
Atelier Amden, Switzerland

Acrylic on cardboard
125 × 343 × 289 cm and 496 × 432 cm
(49 × 135 × 114 in and 195 × 170 in)

Also in 1999, Roman Kurzmeyer invited Grosse to participate in the inaugural exhibition of his extremely unorthodox Amden Atelier, located on a small farm in Amden, Switzerland high up in the mountains above the elongated lake Walensee. Grosse describes Amden as a 'spiritual' place, once attuned to the esoteric teachings of theosophist Madame Blavatsky, pointing to its past as an artists' colony and the adopted home of Swiss painter Otto Meyer-Amden. Her works were to be in two functioning stables, which sheltered cows in the winter. She couldn't paint on the rough walls or ceiling, and she also wanted to make overhead paintings, so she had to build two constructions out of durable cardboard. She recalls hiking up with Kurzmeyer to the stables through 'deep snow' in the 'bitter cold winter' to take measurements for her constructions, scrambling among the cows to do so, passing the tape measure underneath them and through their legs. Later, she built two structures in the stables in relation to the windows and the dramatic outdoors; these allowed her to make overhead paintings – one red, and one yellow (*Untitled*, 1999) (fig.37). 'I wanted to introduce something very light,' Grosse said, 'something that is not like a painting per se' but instead is as if 'a puff of wind' had come in. 'That's when I realized that the setting is so important', Grosse continued, meaning not just the stables but the whole environment, adding that the buildings in which she worked were 'a little like the stable of Mary, Joseph, and Jesus in a Christmas play, a cliché stable in which religious rituals and the meat industry meet'.

Untitled (2001) on parts of the ceiling and walls of the Y8 International Sivinanda Yoga Vedanta Center in Hamburg, Germany was made three years after Grosse's big move from canvas to architecture (figs 38 and 39). It was a dynamic confection of green and orange streaks, yellow stains, ragged magenta marks, and billowing purples, among others, fixed in one position but seemingly drifting and shifting like Technicolor

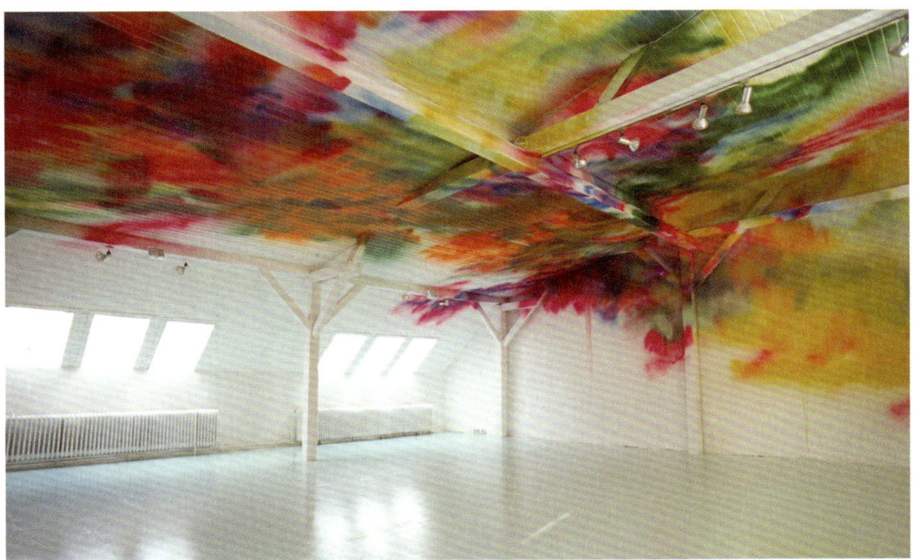

38. Untitled   2001
Y8 / International Sivananda Yoga Vedanta Center, Hamburg

Acrylic on wall
440 × 1000 × 1000 cm
(173 × 394 × 394 in)

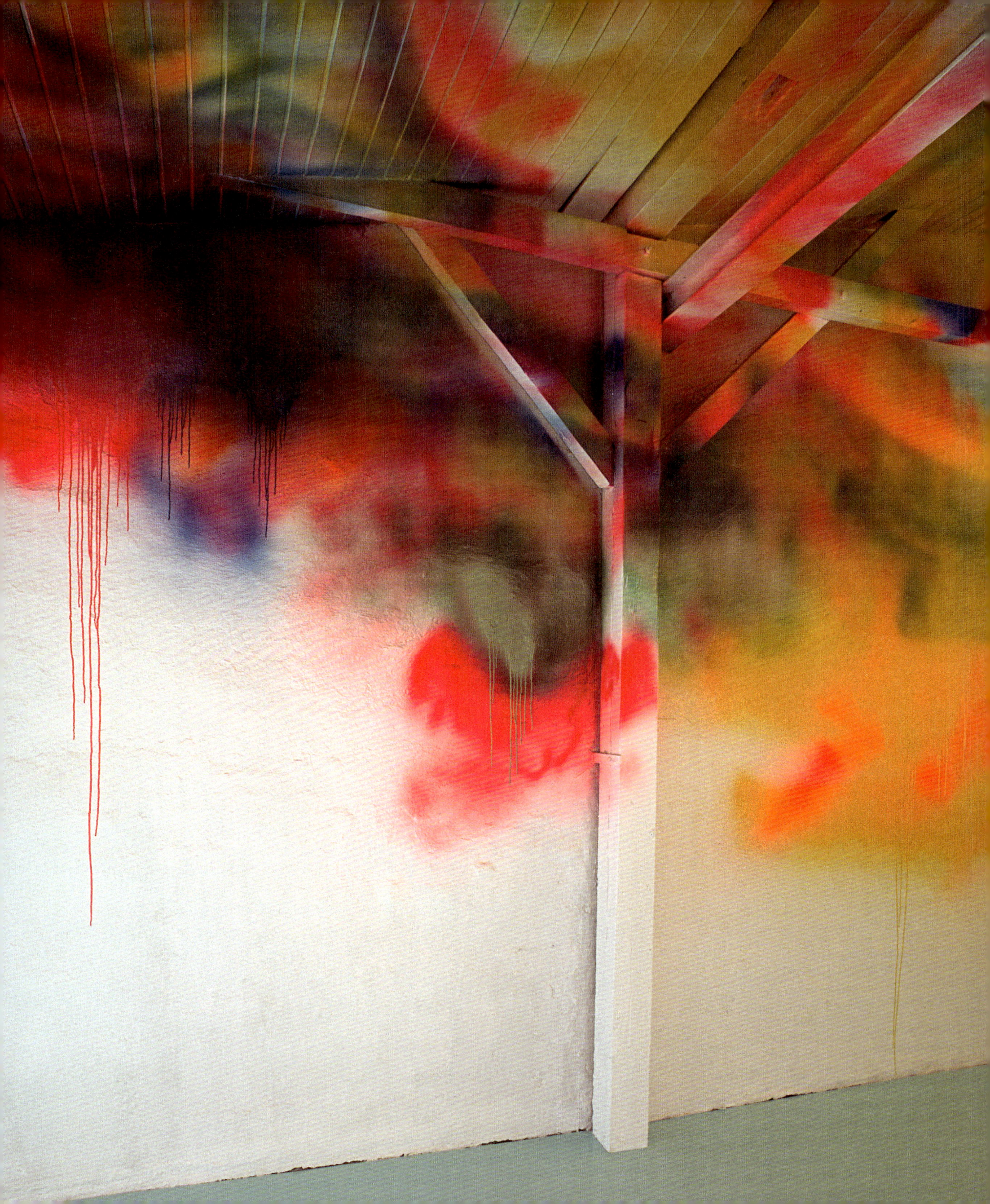

clouds. This work was commissioned by the artist duo Benita and Immanuel Grosser, who found Y8 and who had also brought yoga as art into other art spaces, including New York's Pat Hearn Gallery and Dia Center for the Arts (now, Dia Art Foundation).

Two years later in Helsinki, at the impressive (and impressively curving) Steven Holl-designed Kiasma Museum of Contemporary Art, Grosse composed another dynamic painting – here, on the walls and ceiling of the museum's top-floor exhibition space. This work featured pinkish-white and yellow streaks in multiple directions layered atop a purple-blue smear; a tangle of sizzling reds that abutted a jutting, loosely triangular light blue; yellow-golds that seemed to be dripping down the wall; and combinations of light and dark green that seemed to be flying overhead (*Untitled*, 2003) (fig.40).

I imagine that for some viewers Grosse's work resembled graffiti or, even worse, vandalism – and what on earth was that doing in Finland's top museum for contemporary art? I imagine that it was, for some, an unmannered travesty of a painting – brash, disruptive, busting out of a frame to sprawl all over the place. I also imagine that many others were startled and delighted; they had likely never before encountered a painting like this, perhaps never even imagined that there could be such a risky and exuberant painting – especially in a major museum. Grosse's painting also had an unusual role in the museum. By day it was accessible. In the evenings, when the building was closed, it remained illuminated and visible from outside through large windows. It beamed wild color and energy out into the city, out into the Finnish night.

There is a streak of gleeful rebellion in Grosse's work from this period, a raid on paintings as constrained devices and on the rigid, rectilinear architectural spaces in which her paintings were usually located. Made from broad swathes, streaks, curves, squiggles, drips, stains, bands, granular particles, and diaphanous mists, Grosse's motion-filled paintings flooded spaces with vivid colors and layers of colors, rose up walls like brilliant vapors, swept across ceilings, and jutted across floors at willfully askew angles.

Even when modestly scaled, Grosse's assertive, colorful works can ignite a space. At the fantastic (and now no longer extant) house museum SAFN in Reykjavik – which displayed the collection of Pétur Arason, a businessman and top art collector in Iceland, and artist Ragna Róbertsdóttir – Grosse's multicolored ensemble featured prominent yellows, dripping greens, blues, magenta, and bursting orange on parts of three walls, a large painting leaning against a wall, and the ceiling (*Untitled*, 2004). It looked intensely vibrant next to a Richard Long sculpture on the floor with dark rocks arranged in a curving strand (*Atlantic Lava Line*, 1995) and a wonderful Lawrence Weiner text piece (*The Light of Day*, 1996) on the wall that evokes colors in Iceland generated by 'the light of day' and 'Iceland spar': THE LIGHT OF DAY (SUCH AS IT IS) & ICELAND SPAR (AS CLOSE AS PURE) TO FORM COLORS (ON THE SURFACE OF THE EARTH)

39. Untitled   2001
Y8/International Sivananda Yoga Vedanta Center, Hamburg

Acrylic on wall
440 × 1000 × 1000 cm (173 × 394 × 394 in)

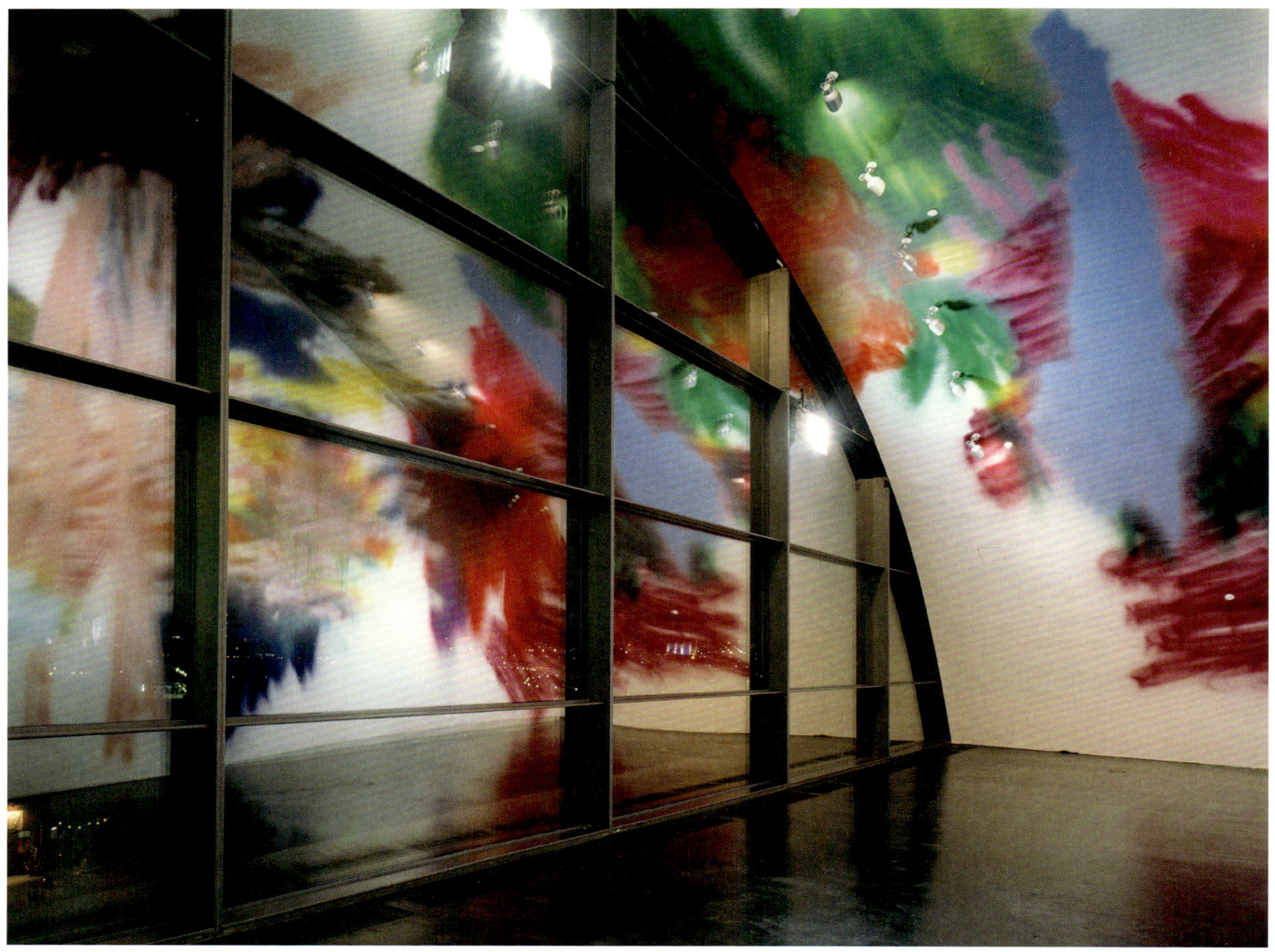

above and right

40. Untitled   2003
Kiasma Museum of Contemporary Art, Helsinki

Acrylic on wall
790 × 2140 × 670 cm (311 × 843 × 264 in)

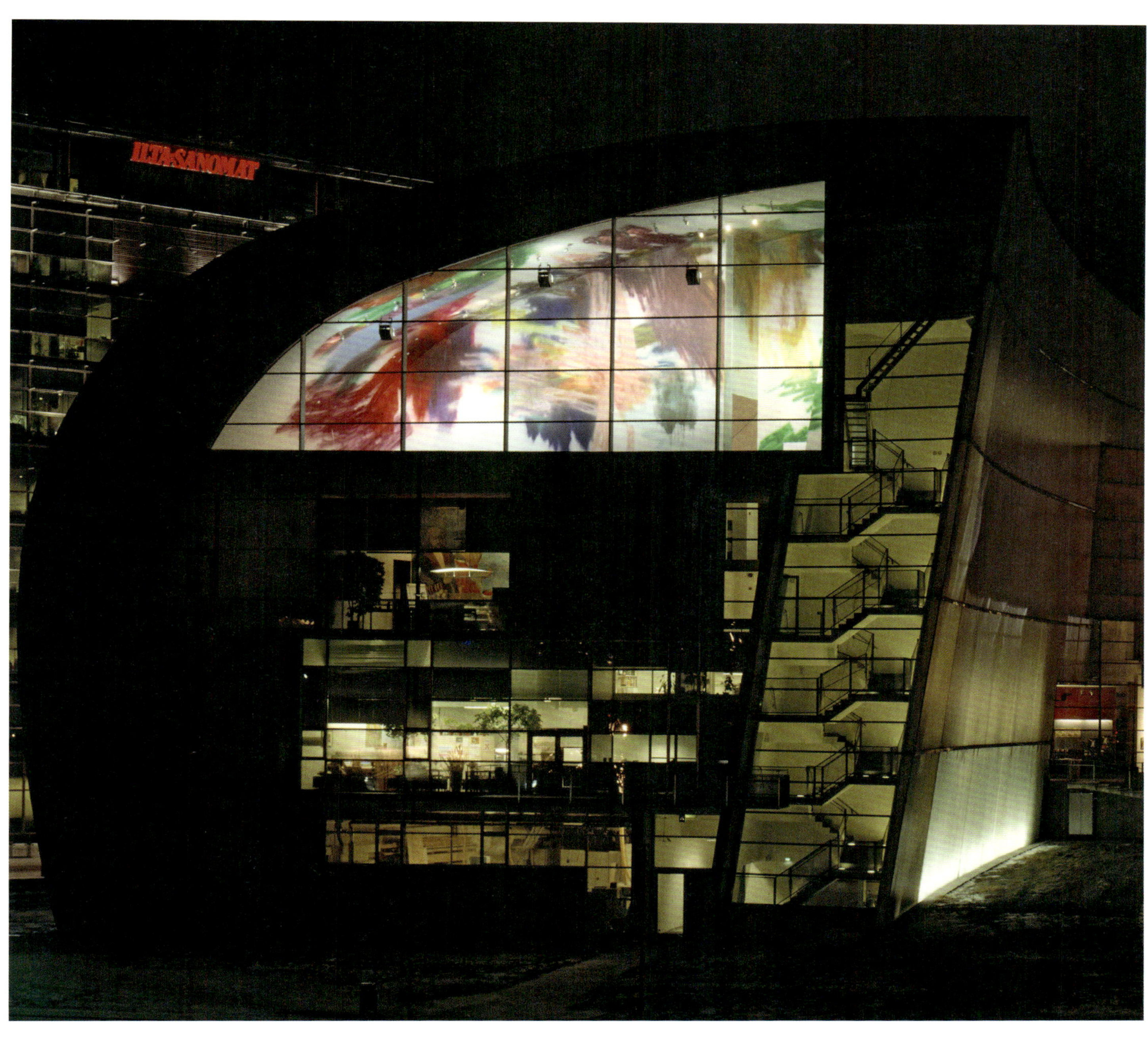
ILTA-SANOMAT

These works were distinctly non-hierarchical; no part was more or less important than any other, and you often couldn't see the whole work from a single vantage point because of its size or because of how it was dispersed through a space (this non-hierarchical approach would continue). *Cool Dolls* (2002) spanned several rooms at the Ikon Gallery in Birmingham, UK (fig.41). Viewers encountered a dense, spreading mesh of red, orange, green, blue, and purple marks in one room. Elsewhere a large burst of yellows, greens, and oranges merged with fuzzy, russet streaks that seemed half-disappearing, while another room featured forceful, almost frantic dark greens (mixed with lighter green tones) on two walls and rising up the roof trusses. This was a work not just to be seen but to be experienced, from different positions and while static; while made in that way and no other, it also seemed in constant flux – a quality that many other works by Grosse possess as well. Throughout Grosse's work there is always more to discover, always a fresh perspective, and the same painting or painting installation can look markedly different not just on a second visit a week or so later, but in the next minute. The same painting or painting installation can also have very different effects. Some parts can be 'loud' and jarring, while other parts, much softer and suppler, can be frankly entrancing.

While Grosse's painting installations are far closer to abstract painting than any other contemporary genre, she declines the label of abstract painter. Instead, her works are the visual manifestations of her nuanced thought and emotions as she moves through, responds to, and thoroughly transforms particular sites over particular durations. How her consciousness (made visible through paint) affects matter and space, and how both affect her, is at the core of these works, and Grosse has said that the 'field' in which she works as a painter is 'the area where we think without words'.[12]

Even though Grosse's aesthetic is distinctly idiosyncratic, she has also absorbed and redirects (sometimes in a single work) a vast range of twentieth-century abstraction – from monochromes to Abstract Expressionism, Color Field to Pop, hard-edge to gestural, lyrical to minimal – while her work also hints at much older antecedents: Renaissance frescoes, for instance, which Grosse once studied intently in Florence; and Romantic paintings (think of Caspar David Friedrich's eventful clouds, J.M.W. Turner's and John Constable's sublime, color-streaked skies). While Grosse is hardly a latter-day Romantic her works often induce wonderment and sublimity, and while she never paints objects or scenes, clouds, sunlight, and shadows – endlessly variable – are potent influences. Grosse's intensely visual works seem suffused with elemental and sometimes invisible forces, with flowing powers and vibrational energy – and as much as they arise from analytical decisions, they equally involve total openness, instinct, and intuitive insights.

Despite Grosse's spray-painting technique, graffiti was never an influence. Unlike much of contemporary graffiti, Grosse's work is devoid of language and representational images. She doesn't tag anything; her name or initials never appear. She doesn't repeat a signature form in multiple places and she also doesn't

right and following spread

41. Cool Puppen (Cool Dolls) 2002
Ikon Gallery, Birmingham

Acrylic on wall
370 × 1200 × 700 cm (146 × 473 × 276 in)

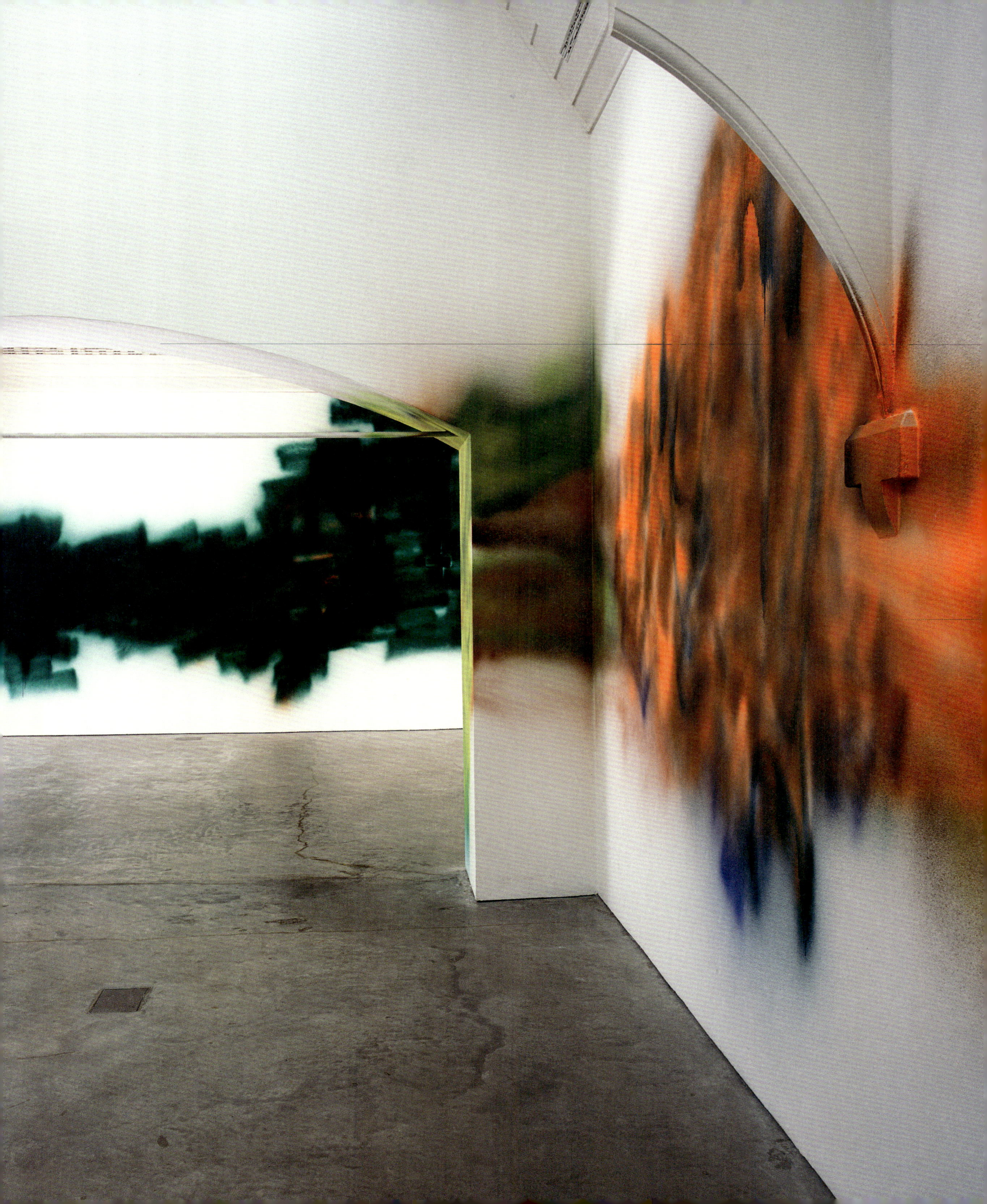

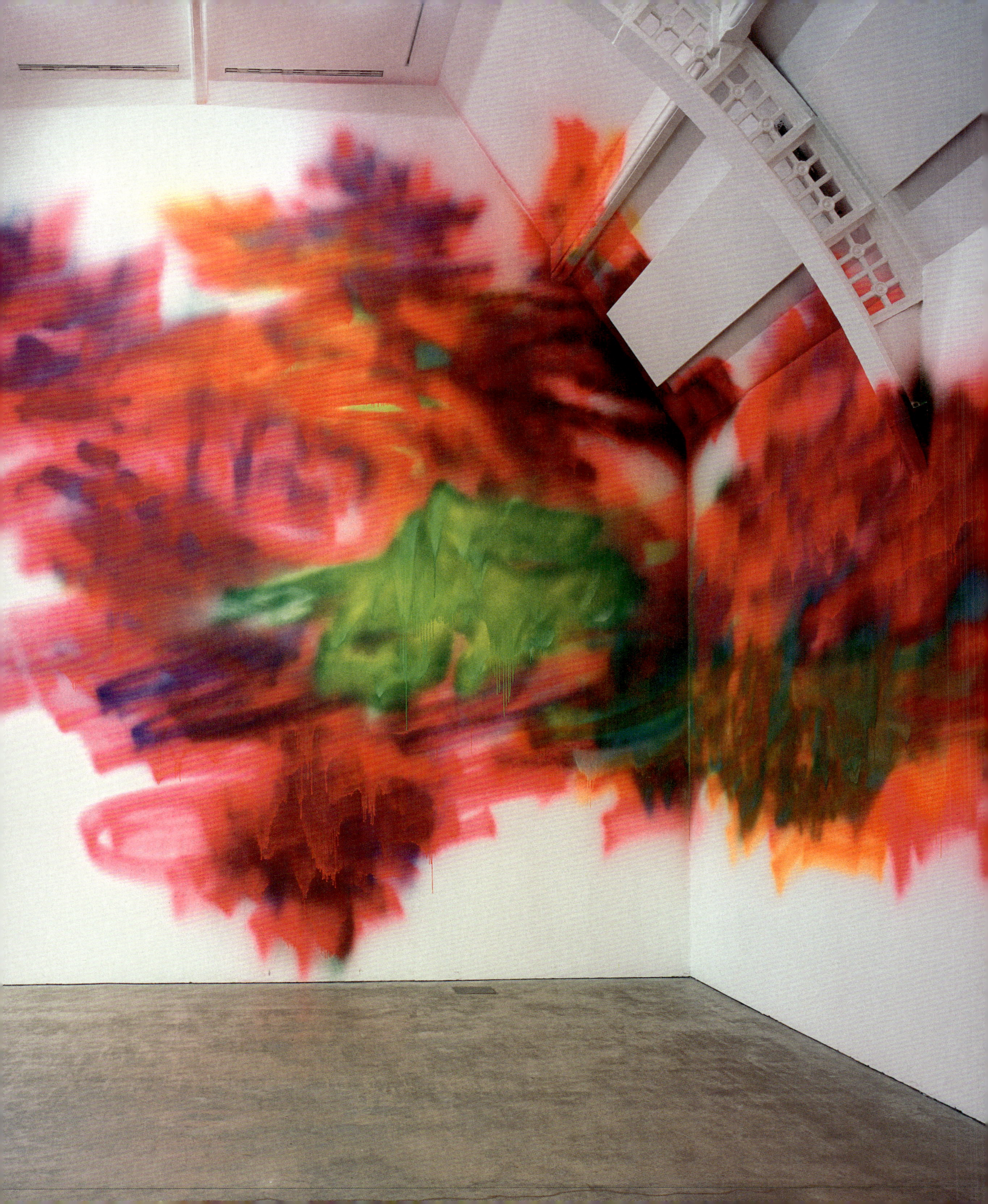

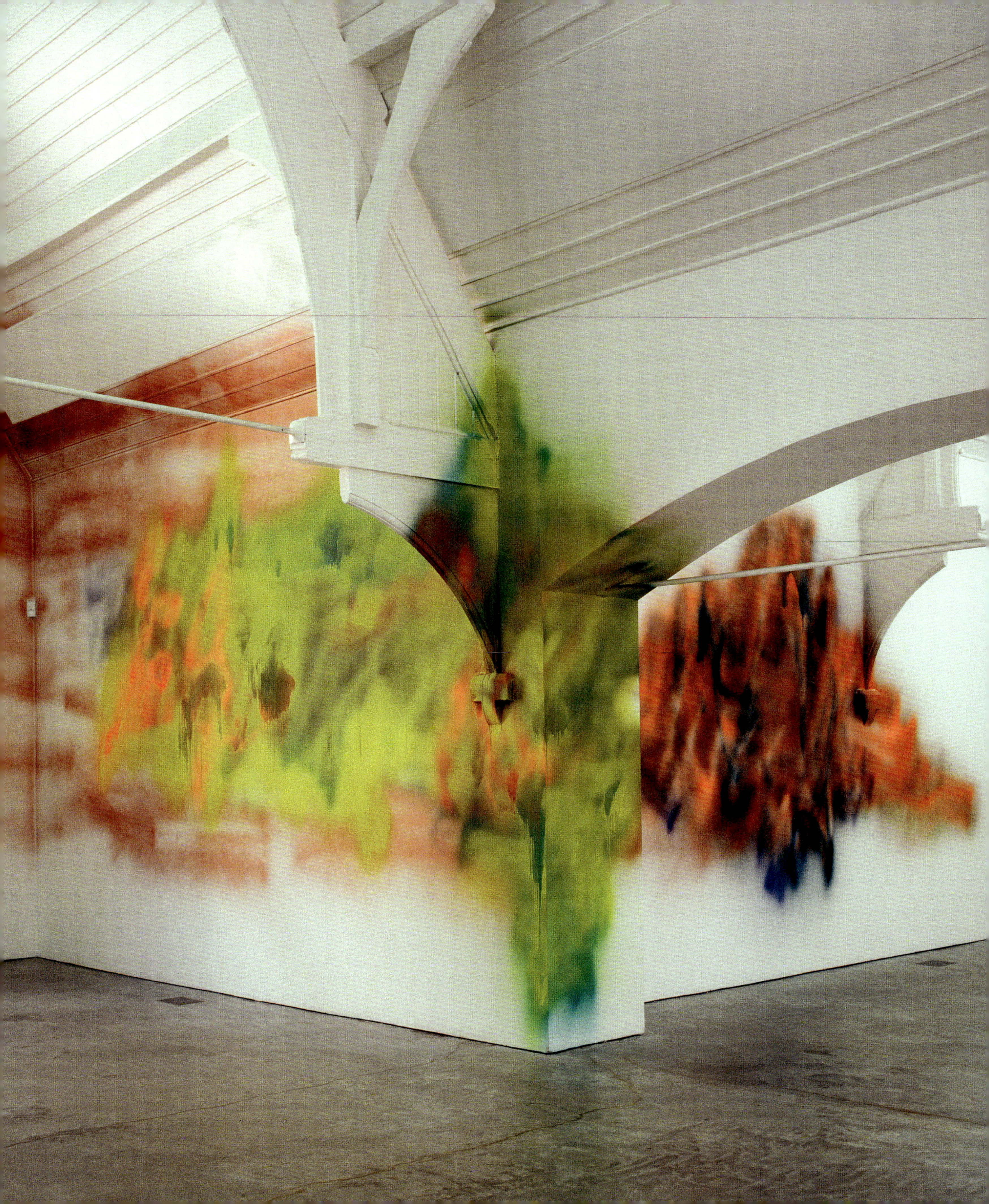

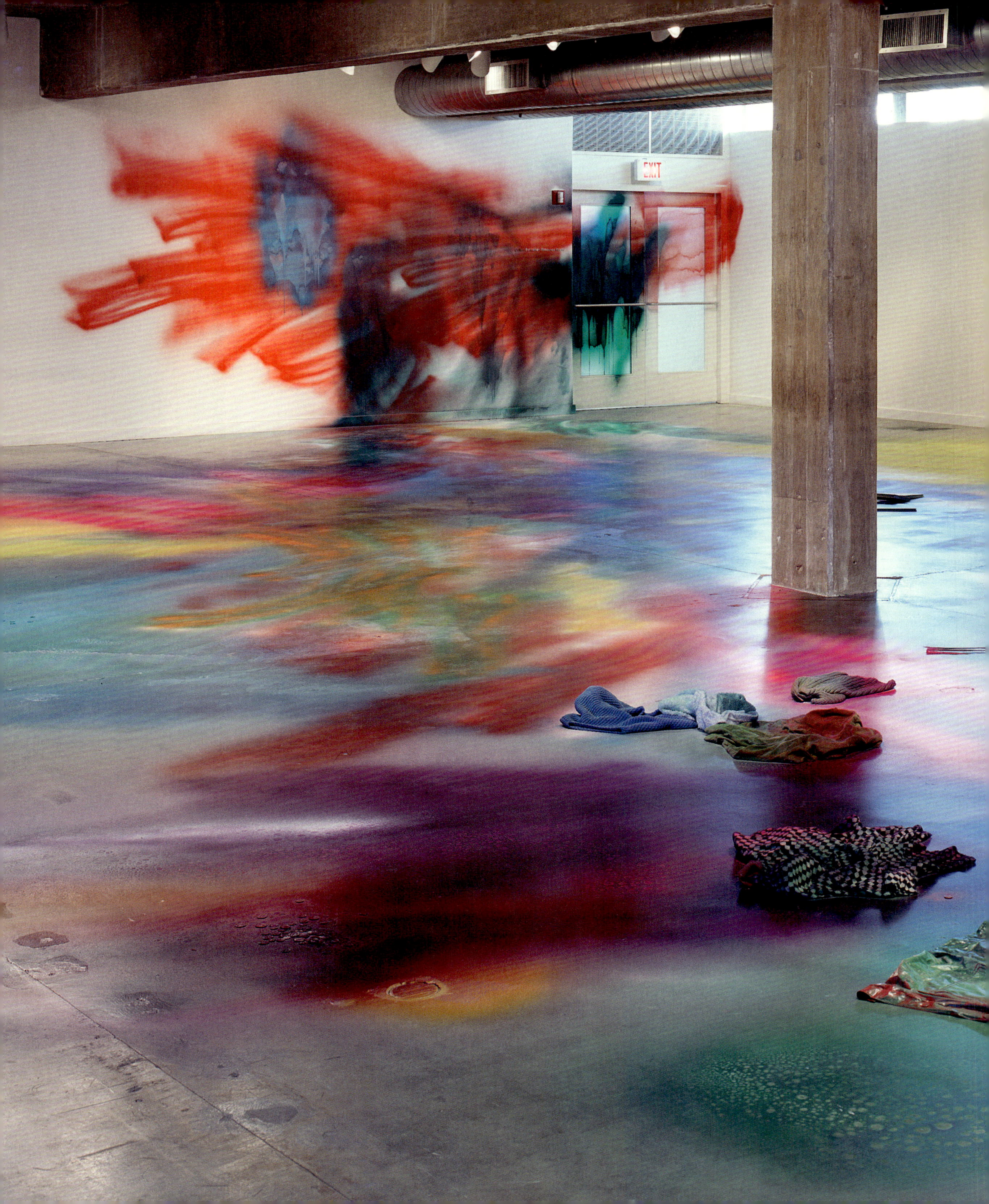

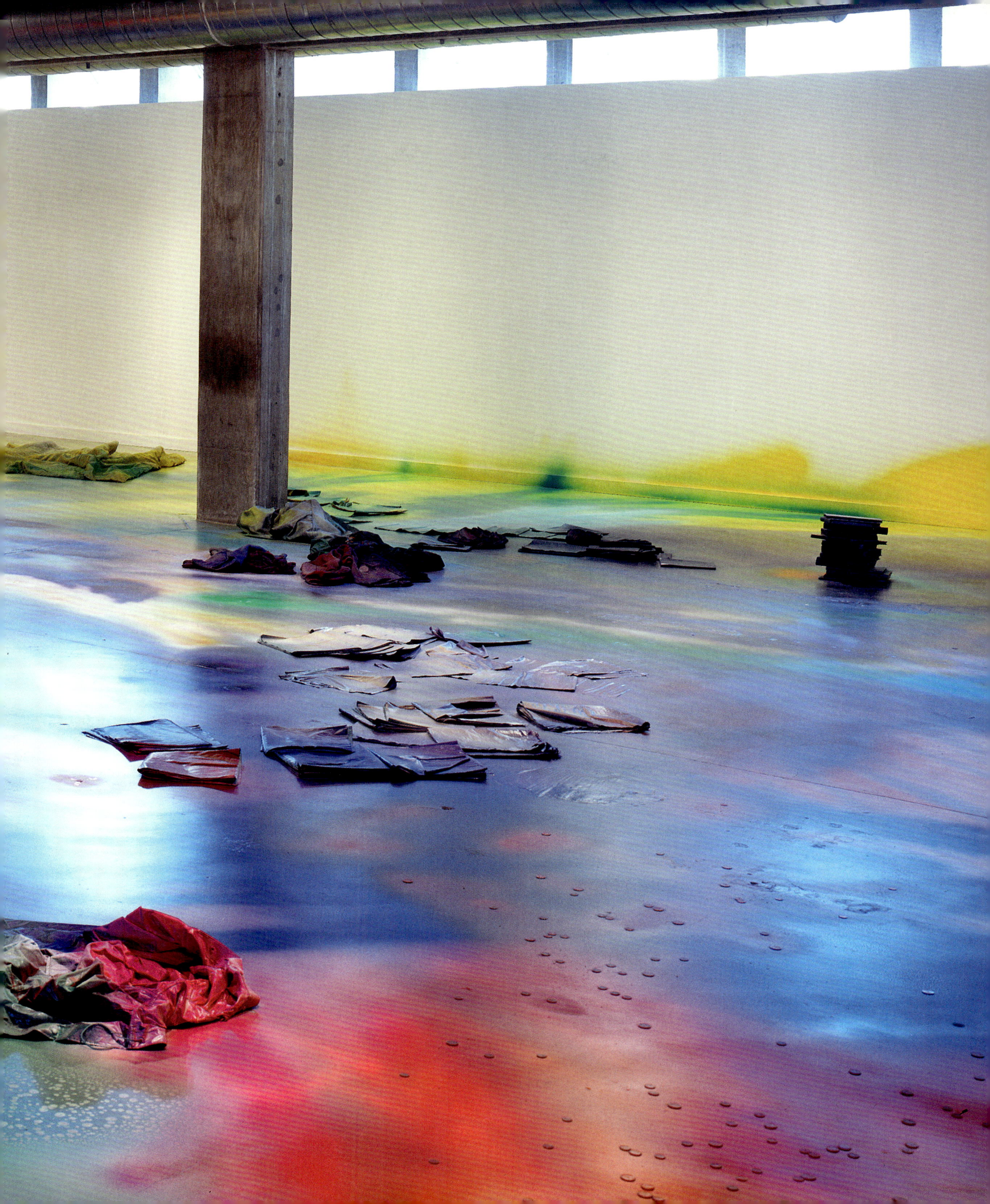

engage in guerilla-art activities. She is not interested in marking a space in order to claim it and assert her identity, or to deliver messages to others. She is interested in how her excessive, multicolored paintings simultaneously respond to and clash with the sites where they are located – really, in how they function as transformative forces.

Cy Twombly is an influence that Grosse has acknowledged, noting how his 'paintings are voyages in time that divert a linear understanding of time' by conflating the ancient past, present, and future. This non-linear time is especially pertinent for Grosse because in her paintings past marks (and thoughts, and feelings) are coequal with current ones; it's just not possible to determine what was made when. Grosse is also clearly attuned to Twombly's forceful scribbles and scrawls, and to the overall urgency of his work. According to her, with Twombly 'everything is urgent. He never leaves room for the slightest hesitation in finding the right tool or noting down a fleeting thought, but he puts precisely in play what arises in the moment', an analysis that also describes her own process.[13]

One thing is clear: in unprecedented ways Grosse has liberated robust, colorful painting – abstract or otherwise – from the canvas and studio, and oftentimes from the gallery and museum as well, allowing it to be a vital and surprising (and sometimes confrontational and controversial) force in the world at large.

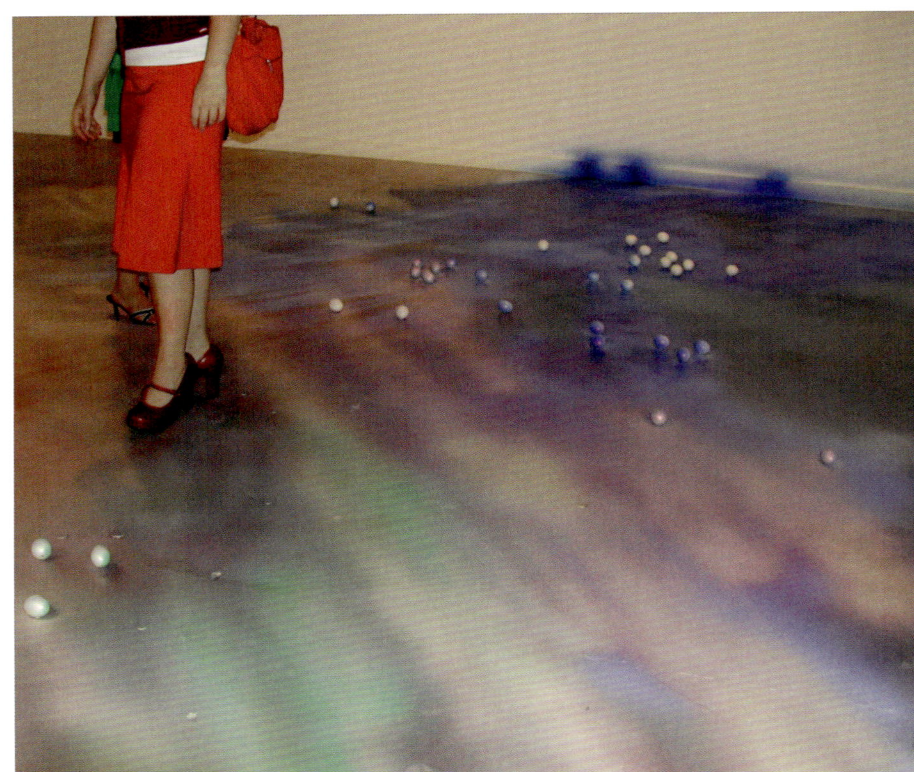

previous spread and left

42. Untitled   2004
Contemporary Arts Museum Houston

Acrylic on wall, floor, clothes, books and eggs
304 × 1798 × 2133 cm (120 × 708 × 840 in)

In a sentiment dating back to her university days, Grosse also began to feel restless about the sedentary, indoor nature of painting even as she was beginning to recognize that she was developing, in her terms, a 'visual intelligence' that is 'a crossover of methodical and analytical thinking and emotional abilities'. Grosse had also begun to yearn for an art capable of reflecting her particular experience: one in which she could employ her body more fully, an art revelatory of who she really is, and one able to embody her understanding of, for want of a better term, reality – not as something given or fixed but instead as fluid, performative, endlessly reconstituting itself. 'I realized that how I saw the world was not in terms of singular things', Grosse told me. 'I saw the world as a mesh, something cloudlike and quite unstable.'

The question was how to bring that sensibility into her art, and to do so she needed a new kind of painting – her spray-painting technique – which involved her mind, sight, emotions, and her whole body. Bending, crouching, standing up and extending her arms and hands, extending them even further via the reach of the spray gun (Grosse has said that painting in this way makes her 'bigger and much faster'), moving close to the wall or much further away, striding around, stepping back to take things in but then moving quickly back to the painting – all of these physical, bodily actions are fundamental, constituting a kind of painting performance (albeit one not intended for an audience). Still, the heart of the matter is the unfettered relationship between seeing and painting. Spray-painting allows Grosse to be, simultaneously, a viewer and a painter, as she has explained:

> My immediate physical relationship to the space is considerably reduced, which allows my visual perception of the special situation to develop its full potential. In this process, I am both the viewer and the cause of the painting action . . . Spraying permits actions that come directly from seeing, whereas the movement of the body influences painting lines with the brush heavily. The movement of the eye is much more closely connected to the movement of the spray gun. You move away from the system of measurements based on the body.[14]

In some videos documenting her process you see Grosse dressed in a head-to-toe white protective suit – replete with goggles, respirator, and ear mufflers – as she wields her spray gun while composing a work. She reminds us not of a painter in her studio but rather of a scientist in some top-secret laboratory; a member of a clean-up crew after a toxic disaster; an astronaut exploring an alien planet; or, perhaps, a costumed actor in a play. Nothing, you think, could be further from the concentration, intimacy, and control normally associated with the act of painting than Grosse, in that garb, as she copiously sprays her chosen surfaces.

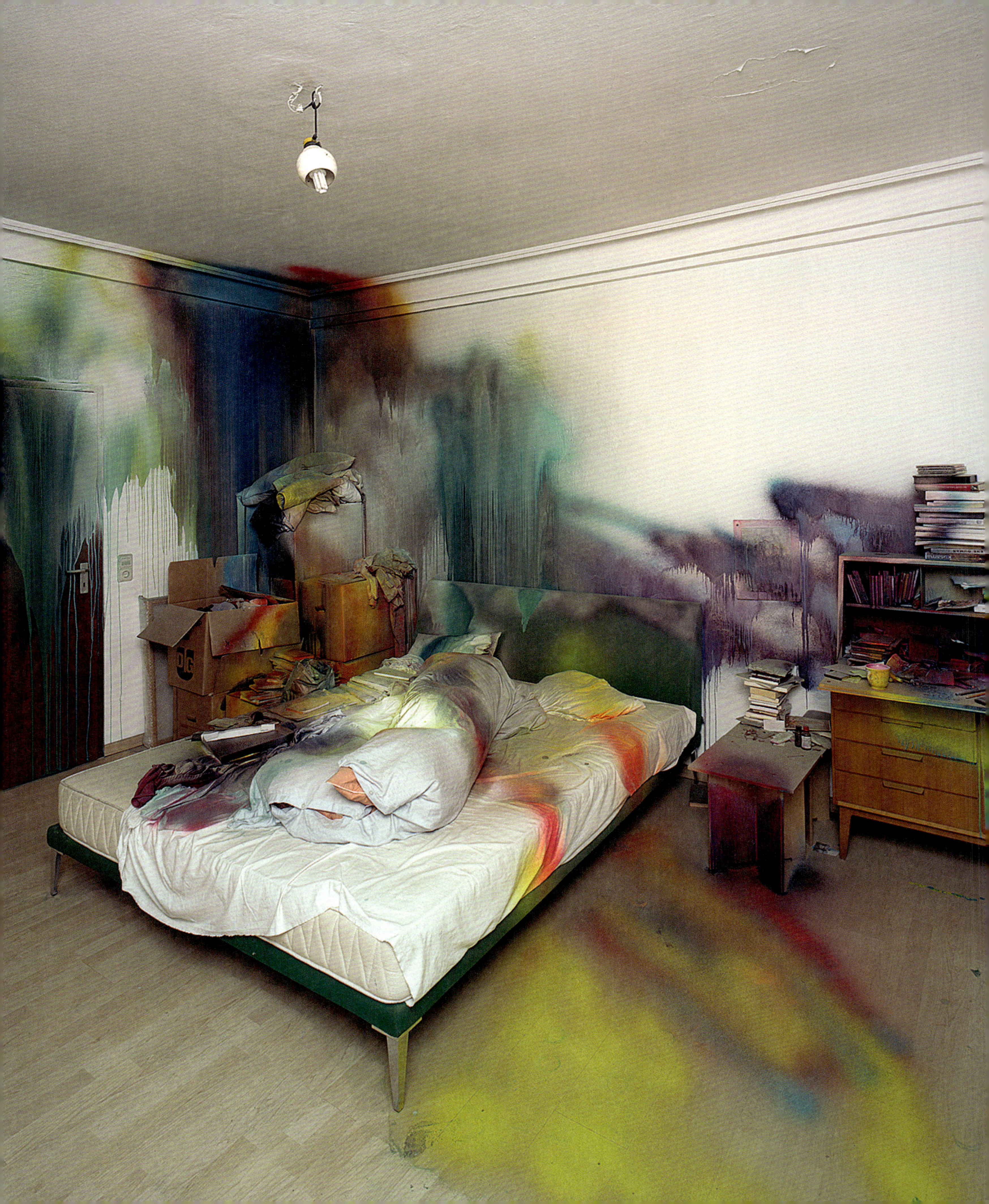

3   The Carnival Expands

As consequential as Katharina Grosse's move from paintings on canvases to in situ paintings on architectural surfaces was, so too was how she extended things even further by incorporating objects – domestic ones like a bed, clothes, books, and furniture and nature-based ones like soil, rocks, and trees – all spray-painted or, rather, partially painted.

By 2004 Grosse's career was flourishing and she was already renowned for her many architectural paintings exhibited in far-flung locations, at numerous sites in Germany but also in Switzerland, the US, Australia, Austria, South Korea, Brazil, and Italy. She was represented by important galleries: Galerie nächst St. Stephan Rosemarie Schwarzwälder in Vienna, Barbara Gross in Munich, Christopher Grimes in Los Angeles, and Mark Müller in Zürich (Helga de Alvear in Madrid, Gagosian, and the König Galerie in Berlin would come later). She had become a professor at Weissensee Kunsthochschule in Berlin and was dividing her time between Düsseldorf and Berlin, maintaining two apartments. Her life had grown more complex and, in a way, cluttered. In part to see what she could do without, and in part to work in a much more direct way from her daily experience and with the stuff of her immediate life, Grosse decided to spray-paint her Jasper Morrison bed – the only high-end piece of furniture she had ever bought – exactly as she had left it when she got up that morning, along with books, the walls, clothes, furniture, and the floor in her Düsseldorf apartment (*The Bed*, 2004) (fig.43).

There was yellow-gold on the floor, mixing with hazy crimsons, turquoises, and oranges. There were red and yellow streaks on the bed along with purple and yellow stains; a spreading green blob on the headboard; and dripping greens, purples, and blues on the walls. Cardboard boxes full of books and other possessions, a night table, piles of books, and a small commode were all partially painted. Grosse's painting conjoined walls, floor, bed, and objects, which otherwise could have easily seemed separate and distinct. This bed-altering, clothes- and books-transforming, apartment-spraying action – not part of any exhibition, accomplished solely for reasons all Grosse's own, and shown to exactly three people – was a pivotal work in her early career: the first time she moved off the wall, into the space, and began to incorporate objects in her art.

This work would lead in the same year to Grosse's *Infinite Logic Conference* (2004) at Magasin III in Stockholm, which featured a bed protruding from the base of the wall and next to it a pile of books (fig.44). The bed and books were partially painted, and the rest of the installation involved wildly painted walls, ceiling, and floor along

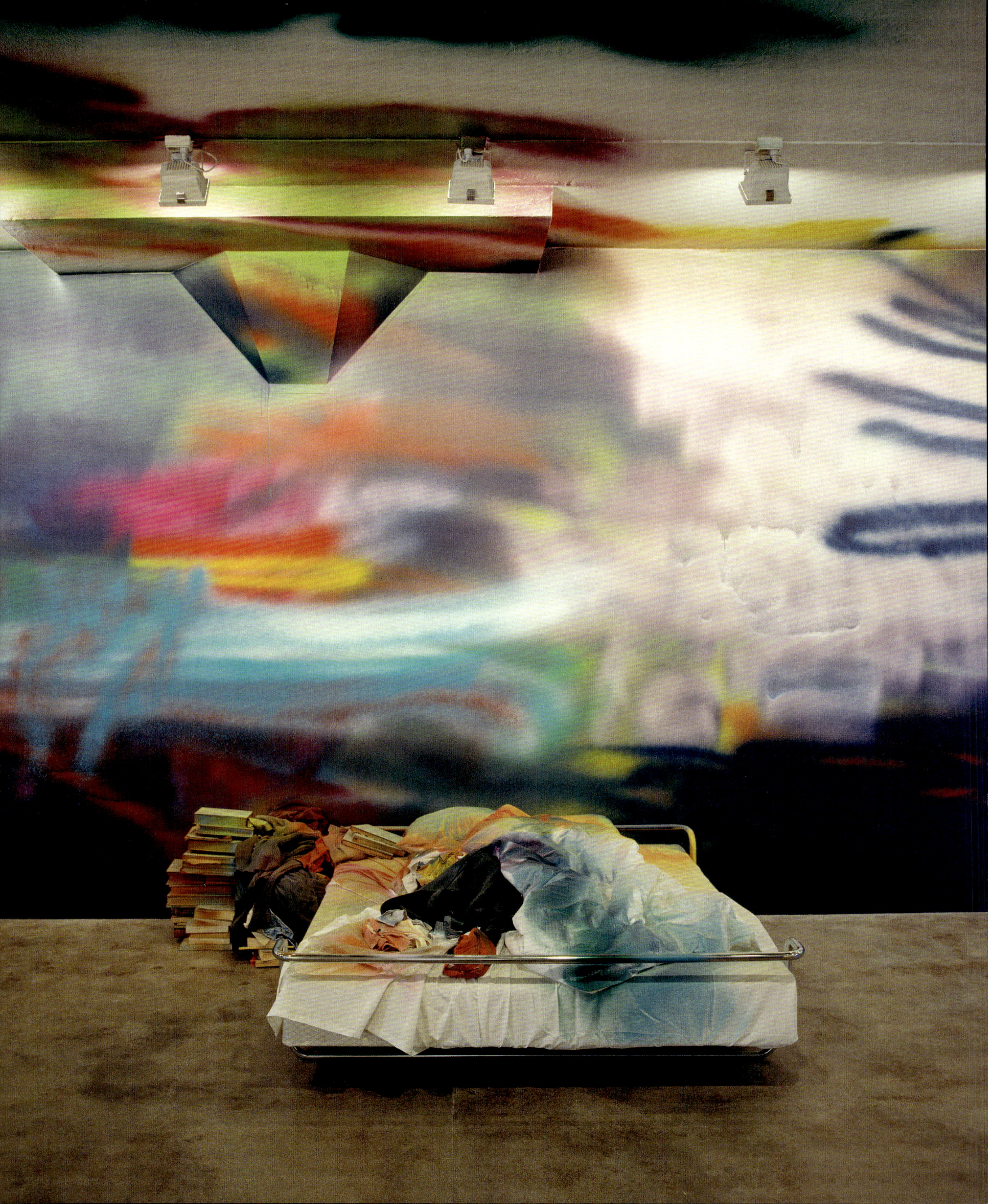

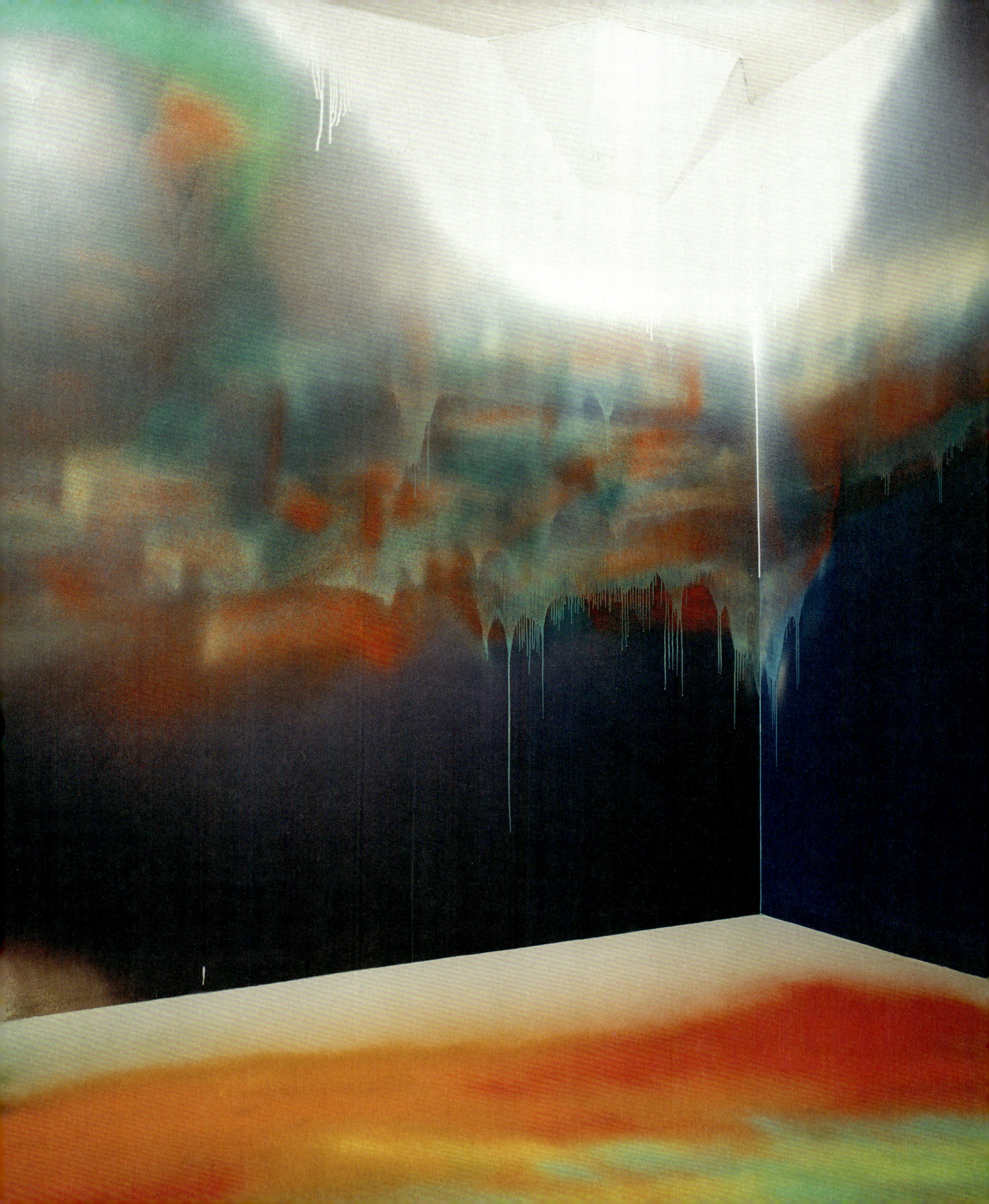

with three large abstract paintings on canvas. A vibrant environment full of colorful, dreamlike phantasms seemed to emanate from the bed and the books. According to Grosse, this was 'an enlargement of . . . a dream experience' in which 'the museum space seemed transformed into a version of a domestic space, where imagination and functions overlapped'.

Also in 2004 came *Double Floor Painting* (2004) at Kunsthallen Brandts Klædefabrik in Odense, Denmark (fig.46). The floor and the walls were a riot of colors and various shapes, with a yellow burst on the wall linked to a broad yellow band angling across the floor, with recurring bright magentas, repeating greens, and traveling purples. Grosse also installed large, unframed painted canvases on the walls, which seemed to be gathered by the wall paintings ('You did not know', Grosse said, 'if you were looking at a painting or the painted wall') and she thoroughly blasted a Montana bookcase – 'a quintessentially important piece of furniture for the Danes', which was packed with books – with her colors. Eliminating distinctions between canvases and walls, furniture and architecture, floor and walls, Grosse's work was an enlarged, hallucinatory, carnivalized version of, according to her, 'a living room'.

Grosse first worked with spray-painted soil for the group exhibition *Raumfürraum* at Kunsthalle Düsseldorf (*The Poise of the Head und die anderen folgen*, 2004) (fig.45). In the corner, a mound of soil (an 'island', Grosse called it), lightly spray-painted, was atop white paint, as if light was coming from underneath it. A large painting featuring several colored bands (among them yellow, blue, green, pink, and orange) leaned against one wall; its colors were repeated on the walls as seemingly oscillating streaks. Another painting featuring mysterious black semicircular forms ('magnified spray dots', according to Grosse) leaned against the adjacent wall. Right here was a condensed version of how Grosse uses paint to connect canvas, wall, objects, and floor.

This would lead to many more works with soil – which functions in Grosse's work as a malleable sculptural material and an outsize, rather comical, version of a painter's raw pigments but also as a primal material on its own. At the same time it sometimes suggests landscapes, abstract indoor versions of vast places outdoors, and also connects with, and provides an extremely updated take on, Robert Smithson's famous 'nonsites' – notably, his *Nonsite (Essen Soil and Mirrors)*, 1969, in which red soil and scattered rocks are displayed on and next to twelve mirrors.

Grosse's 2005 exhibition at Palais de Tokyo in Paris combined painting, floor painting, large paintings on canvases, and painted soil (*Constructions à cru*, 2005) (fig.47). Colors on the walls and floor – among them purple, turquoise, pink, yellow, and green – spread across parts of the soil mounds and swept down the stairs. Directly at the large glass wall in the Taipei Fine Arts Museum in Taiwan, soil and small rocks spilled across Styrofoam constructions and under two wooden benches – an indoor version of a geological slump (*Untitled*, 2006) (fig.48). Grosse painted everything (except for the benches) green, blue, purple, orange, greenish-yellow, and

right

45. The Poise of the Head und die anderen folgen (. . . and the others follow)   2004
Kunsthalle Düsseldorf

Acrylic on wall, floor, soil, and canvas
900 × 900 × 1000 cm (354 × 354 × 394 in)

following spread

46. Double Floor Painting   2004
Kunsthallen Brandts Klaedefabrik, Odense

Acrylic on wall, floor, canvas, and various objects
680 × 3800 × 1100 cm (268 × 1496 × 433 in)

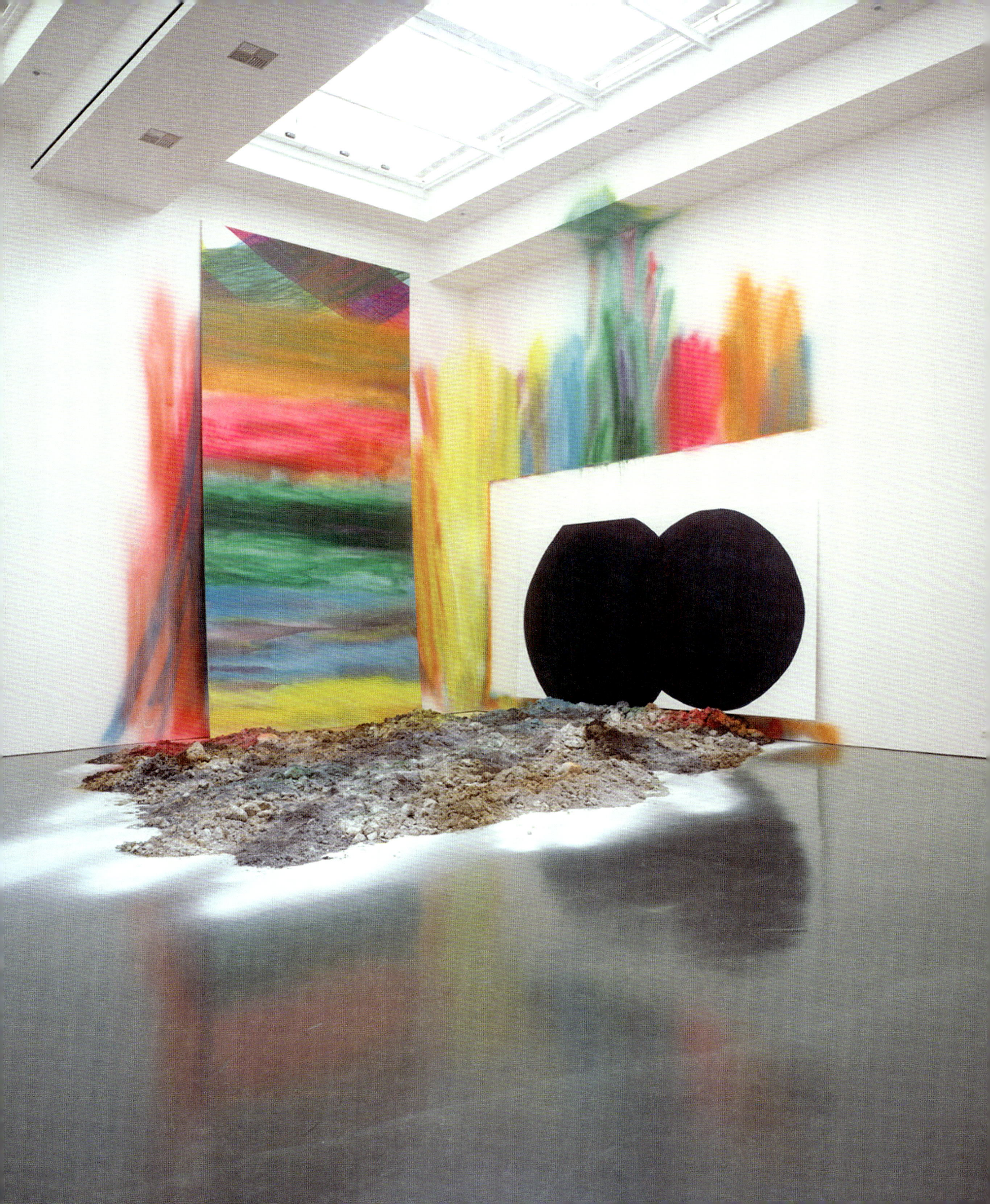

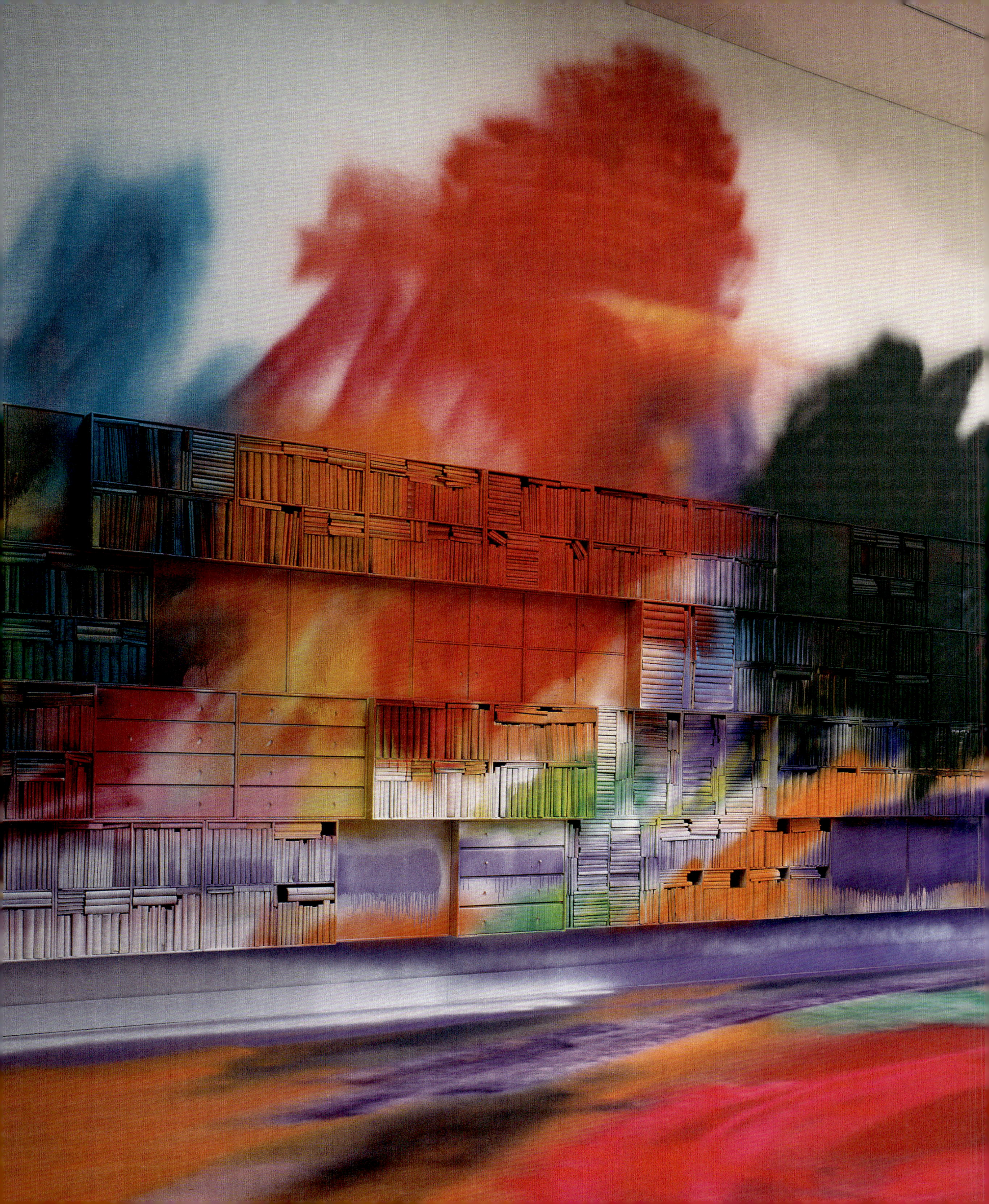

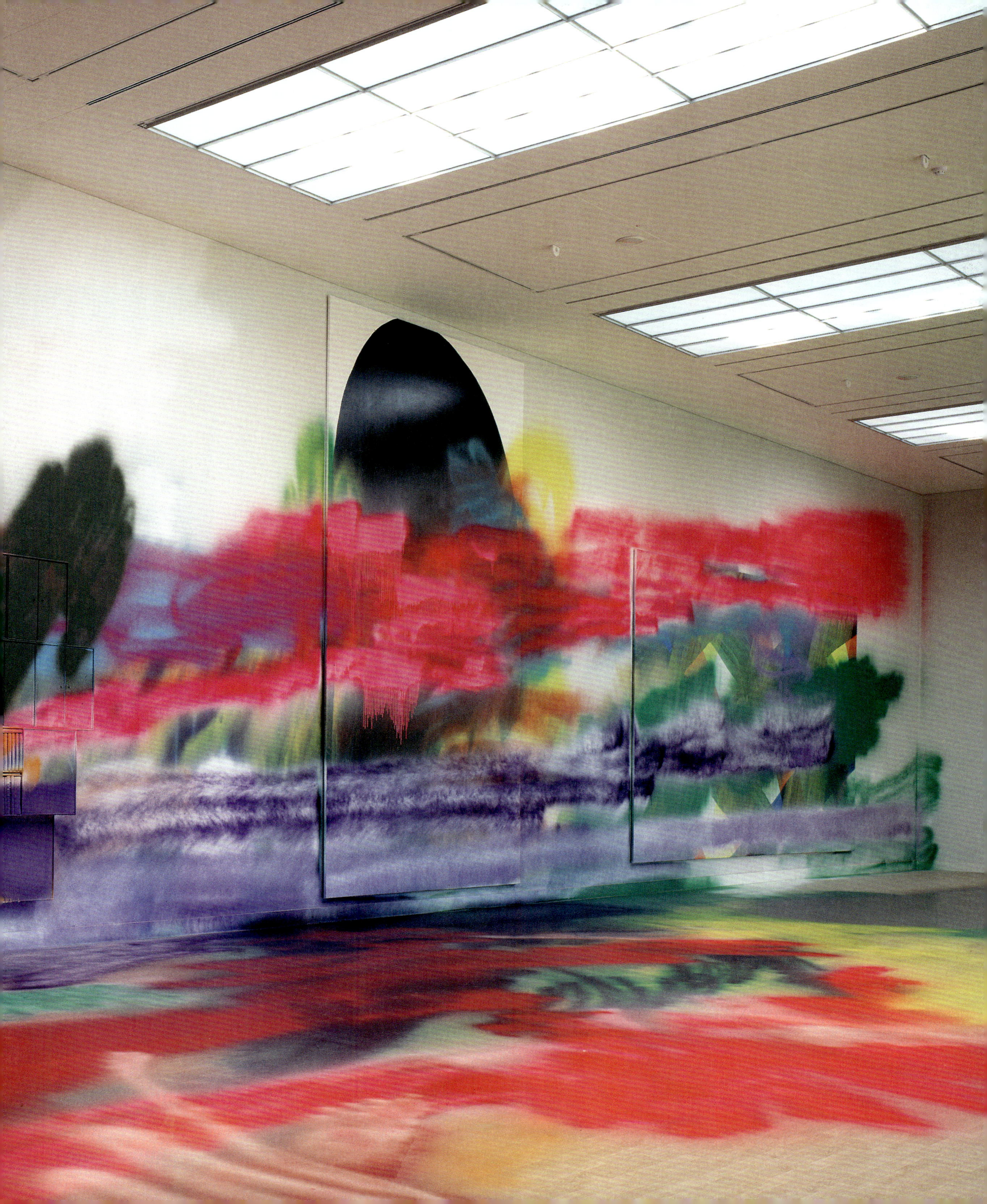

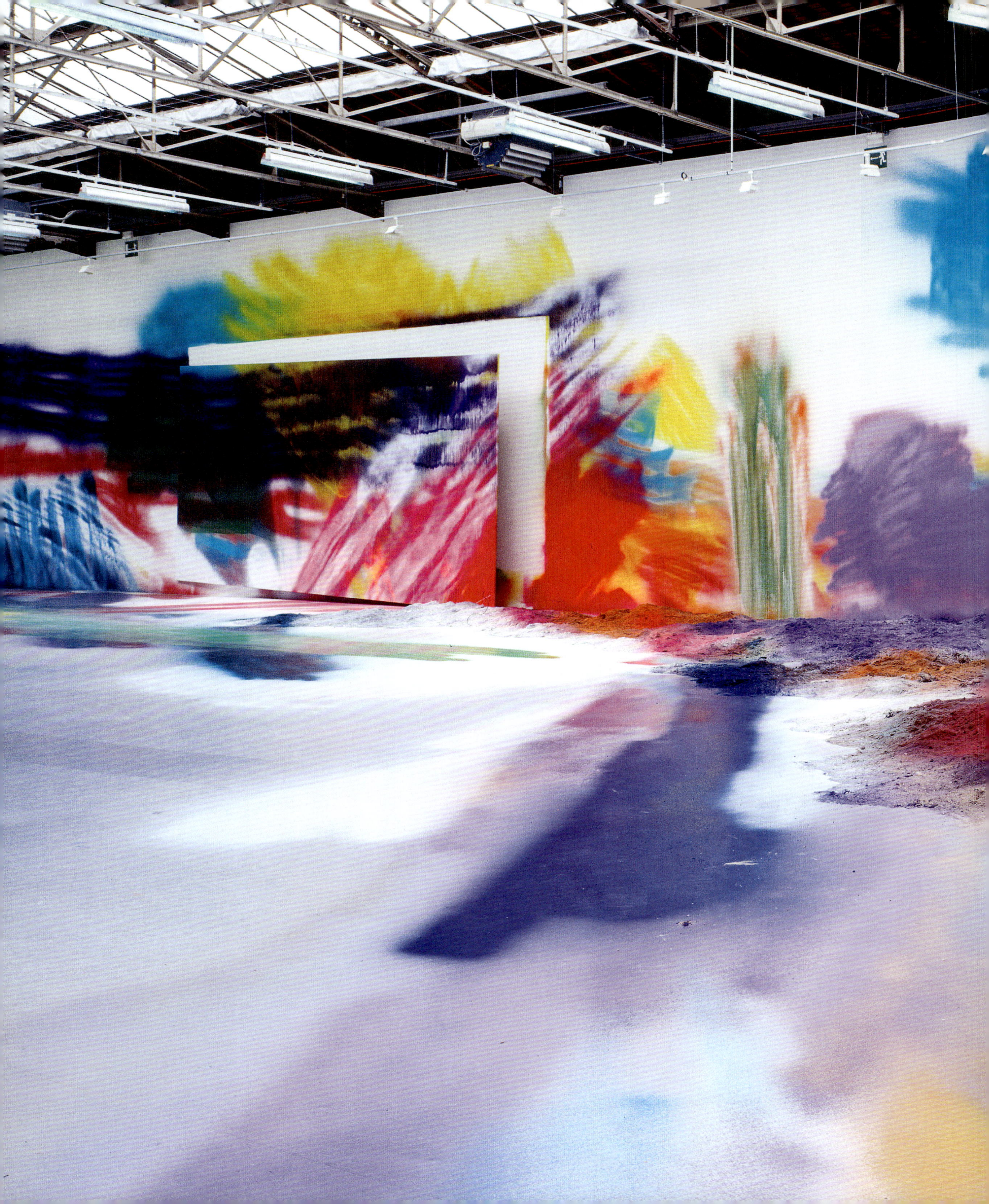

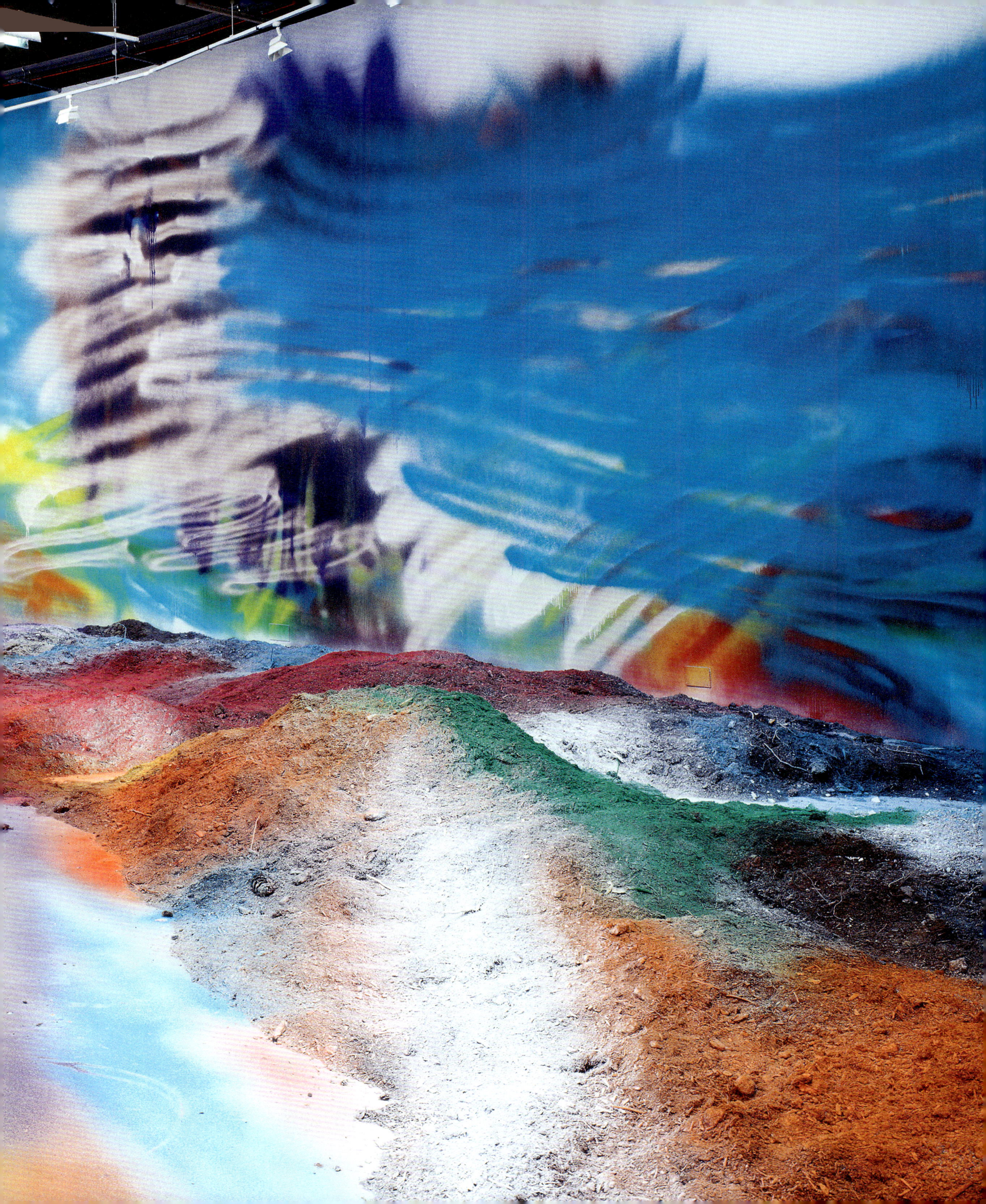

several more colors. She also painted parts of the glass wall with her bright colors. Depending on your perspective, and especially from a distance, it was as if Grosse's multicolored work was bisecting the museum's wall, simultaneously sliding in from outside and angling up toward the outdoors and the sky.

As part of her 2013 exhibition *Wunderblock* (another reference to Freud) at the Nasher Sculpture Center in Dallas, Texas, Grosse installed wall-to-wall mounds of soil painted green, rich blue, turquoise, bright red, orange, purple, and other colors too (fig.49). This earthy work was gorgeous, and it was also an updated take on another artwork made by a noted practitioner of Land Art, Walter De Maria, with his *New York Earth Room* (1977) featuring some 190 cubic meters (250 cubic yards) of rich, black earth covering the floor to a depth of 56 cm (22 inches). Previously, De Maria had made two other earth rooms, which no longer exist – one in Munich in 1968 and the other at the Hessisches Landesmuseum in Darmstadt, Germany in 1974. As opposed to De Maria's work, viewers could, quite literally, enter Grosse's work and walk on it, thus making a miracle of sorts. For centuries enraptured viewers had longed to enter a painting; now they could. So many did so that after the first weekend visitors had 'walked off' the vibrant colors, creating a tawny and brownish footpath, similar to a miniature hiking trail or a dirt-bike track, which surprised Grosse and the museum. She later repainted the work. Also in the exhibition was a huge and dramatic painting/sculpture hybrid made of acrylic on glass-fiber-reinforced plastic, which has become one of Grosse's signature materials (fig.51). Hinting at rocks, bones, and fossils, this work, with its electric colors, was both inside and outside, cutting through the glass wall of the Renzo Piano-designed museum to enter the garden.

In 2013 Grosse made her first work with a tree (there would soon be many), and it was almost accidental. A sizable tree was cut down by the city workers outside her

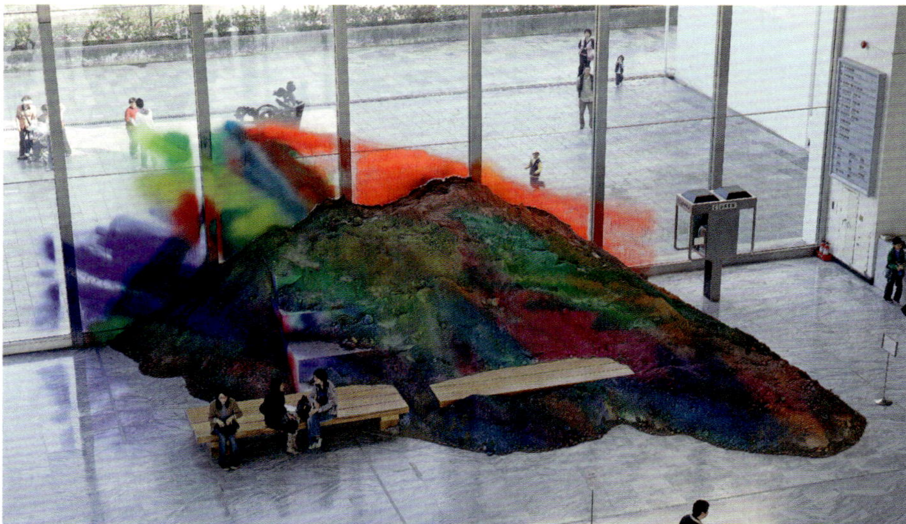

47. Constructions à cru   2005
Palais de Tokyo, Paris

Acrylic on wall, floor, soil, and canvas
670 × 800 × 1000 cm (264 × 315 × 394 in)

left

48. Untitled   2006
Taipei Biennial: 'Dirty Yoga', Taipei Fine Arts Museum

Acrylic on wall, floor, glass, Styrofoam, and soil
460 × 1050 × 800 cm (181 × 413 × 315 in)

right and following spread

49. Wunderblock   2013
Nasher Sculpture Center, Dallas, Texas

Acrylic on canvas, soil and wall
420 × 970 × 1400 cm (165 × 382 × 551 in)

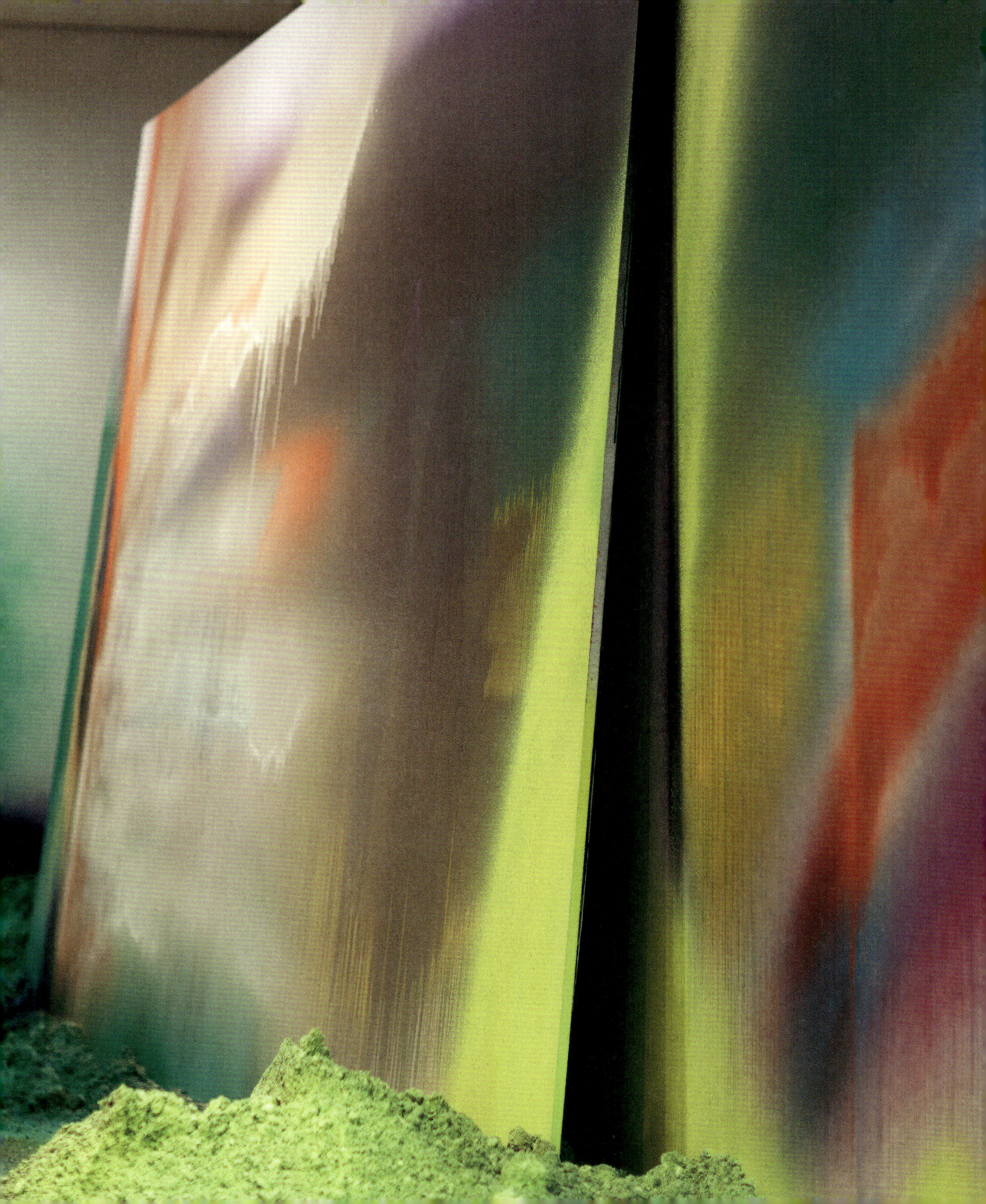

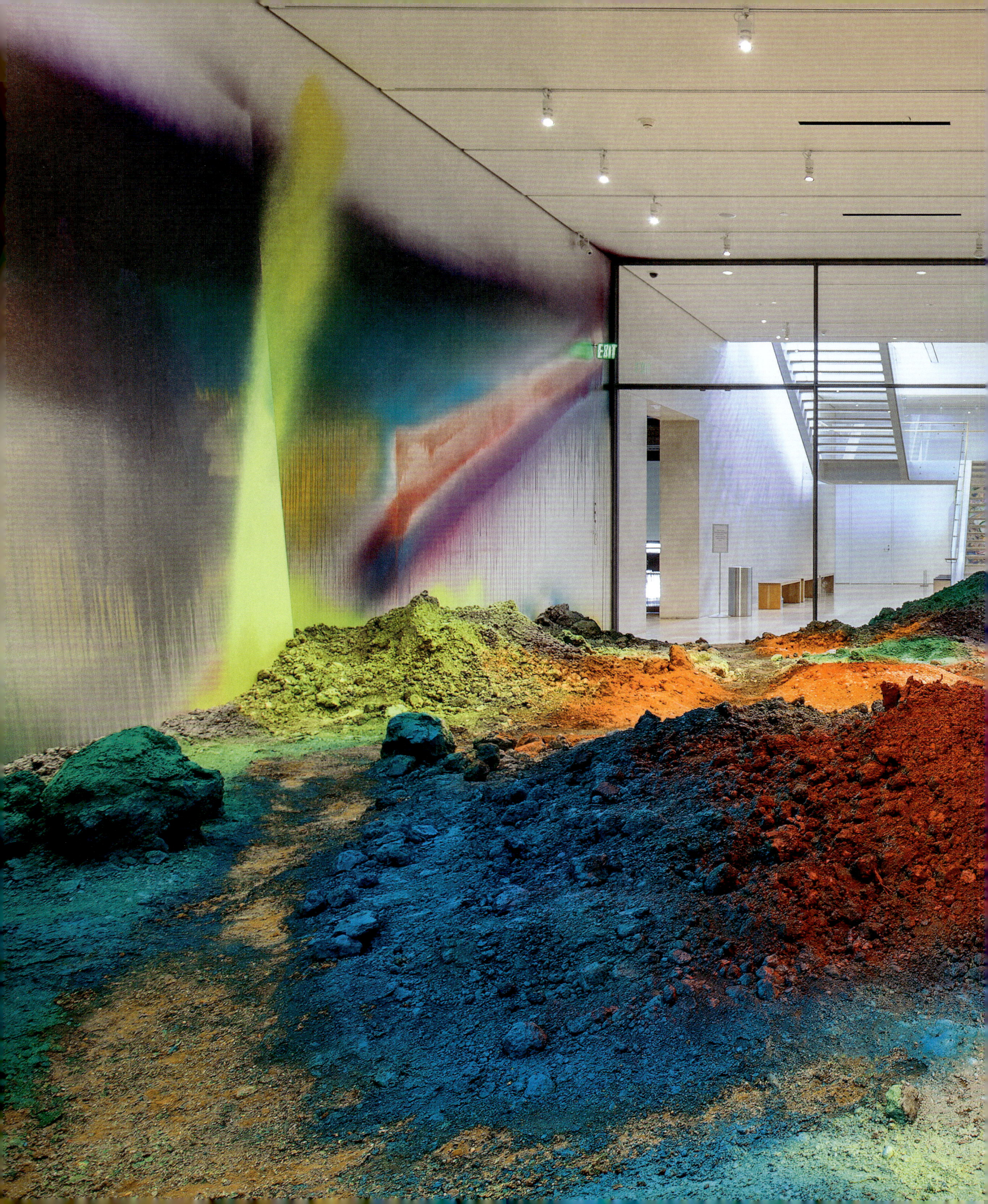

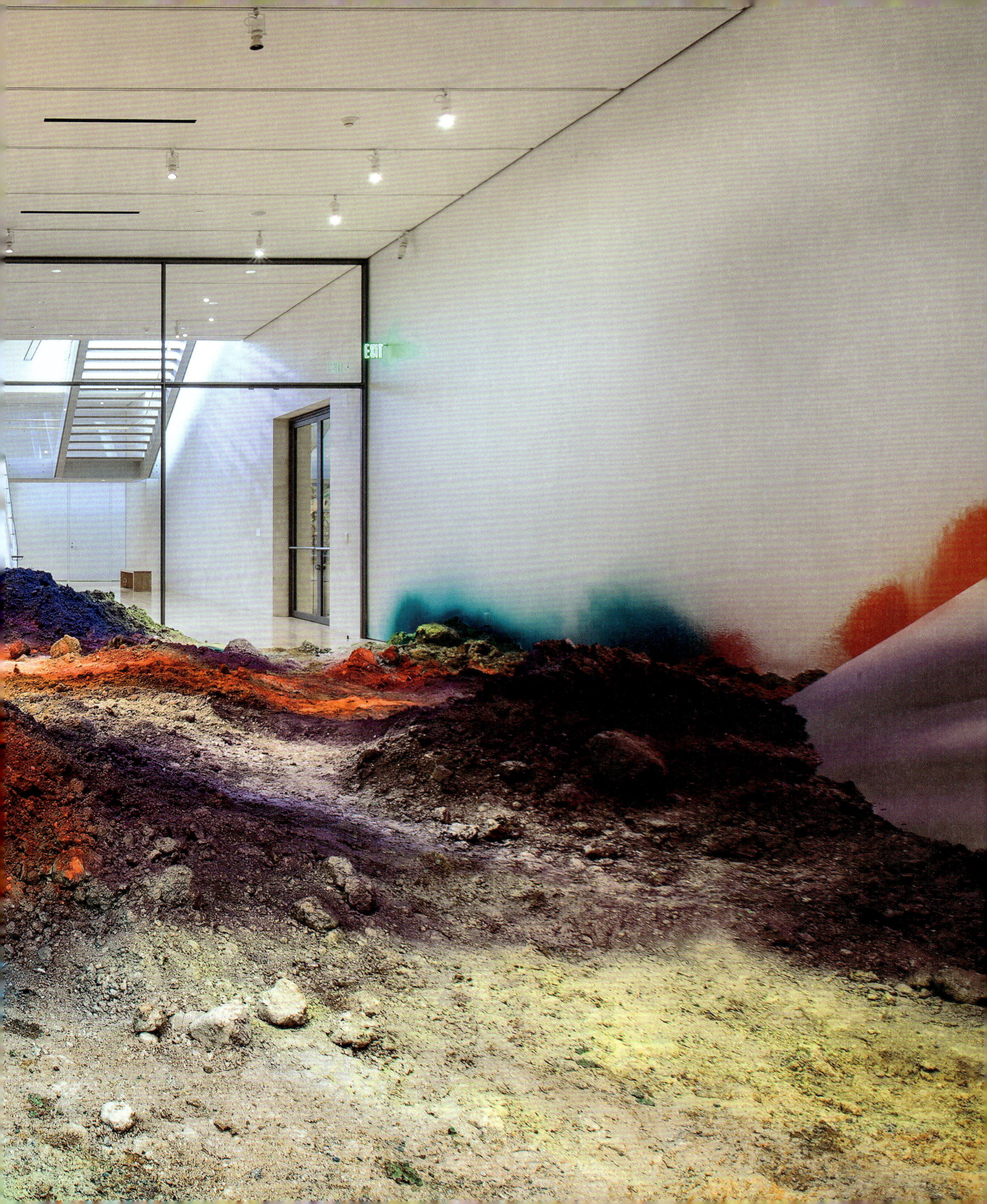

Berlin studio near the street, and before it was carried away Grosse and her assistants managed to whisk it into the nearby artist-run exhibition space Kurt-Kurt. There it was stacked it in a sculptural pile, and spray-painted purple, yellow, and light blue. This pile of painted wood served as the stage for Grosse's first sound and spoken-word performance with Stefan Schneider, with both thoughtful performers perched on the painting/sculpture a bit like animals or birds (*my writing desk, the snow field*, 2013) (figs 52 and 53). The gallery is located in the birth house of noted German-Jewish writer and journalist Kurt Tucholsky. Schneider interviewed some of the inhabitants of the house at the time, and excerpts of the interviews were incorporated into the performance. This engagement with, and transformation of, a dead tree in a gallery, making for a potent nature/culture amalgamation, has a precursor – albeit one that was little known for many years. For Robert Smithson's *Dead Tree* (1969) (fig.50) – a work destroyed at the end of the exhibition, but which has since been reconstructed three times – the artist installed a large tree on its side, along with mirrors, in Kunsthalle Düsseldorf. One of the more striking and unusual things about Katharina Grosse is how she introduces aspects of Land Art into her centrally painterly aesthetic – more on this topic a bit later.[15]

Very quickly, raw, rough, painted trees would become prominent components in Grosse's artworks. She 'threaded' three large trees among the rectangular columns at Museum Wiesbaden, a historic building dating back to 1915, displaying them with swooping, spray-painted fabric (*Seven Hours, Eight Voices, Three Trees*, 2015) (fig.54). The orange and yellow roots of one tree looked hallucinatory and ecstatic; the blue, purple, and yellow roots of another did too. At the Garage Museum in Moscow, white fabric, spray-painted with a dizzying array of colors, sloped from the sides of the room and covered the floor. Nestled at one end were three brilliantly painted trees (*yes no why later*,

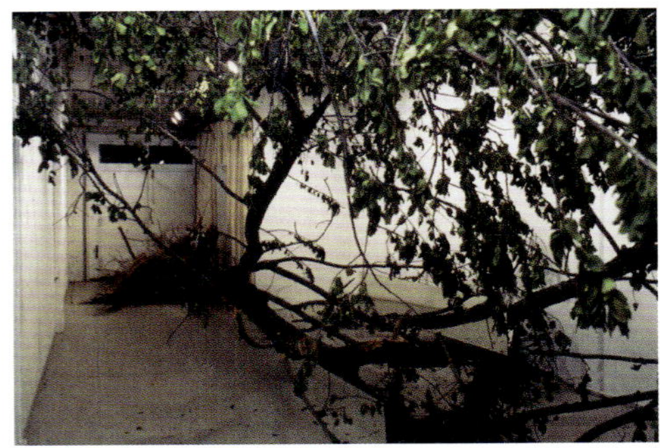

50. Robert Smithson
Dead Tree　1969

Tree, soil, mirrors
1219 cm (480 in)
Installation at Pierogi (a recreation of the work originally exhibited in *Prospect 69*, Städtische Kunsthalle, Dusseldorf, Germany, September 1969)

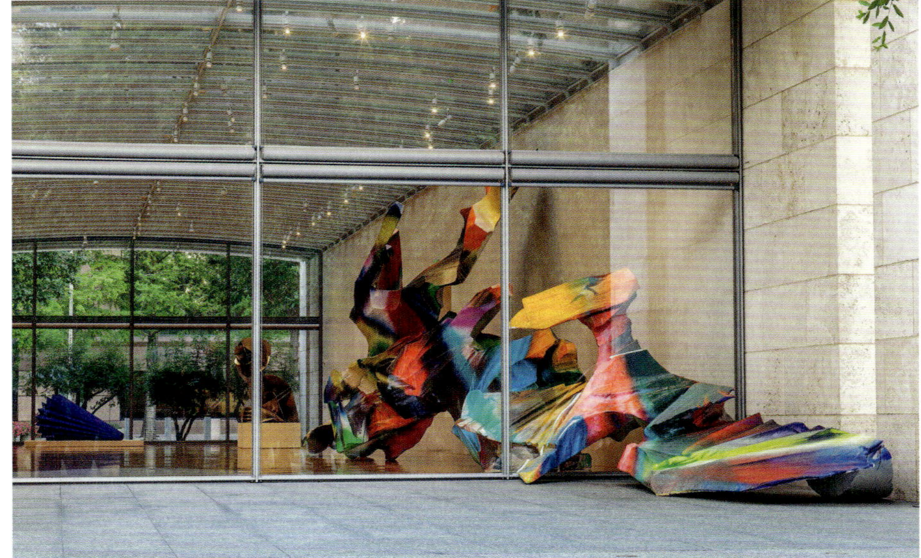

51. **Wunderblock**　2013
Nasher Sculpture Center, Dallas, Texas

Acrylic on glass fiber reinforced plastic
430 × 260 × 2,040 cm (169 × 102 × 803 in)

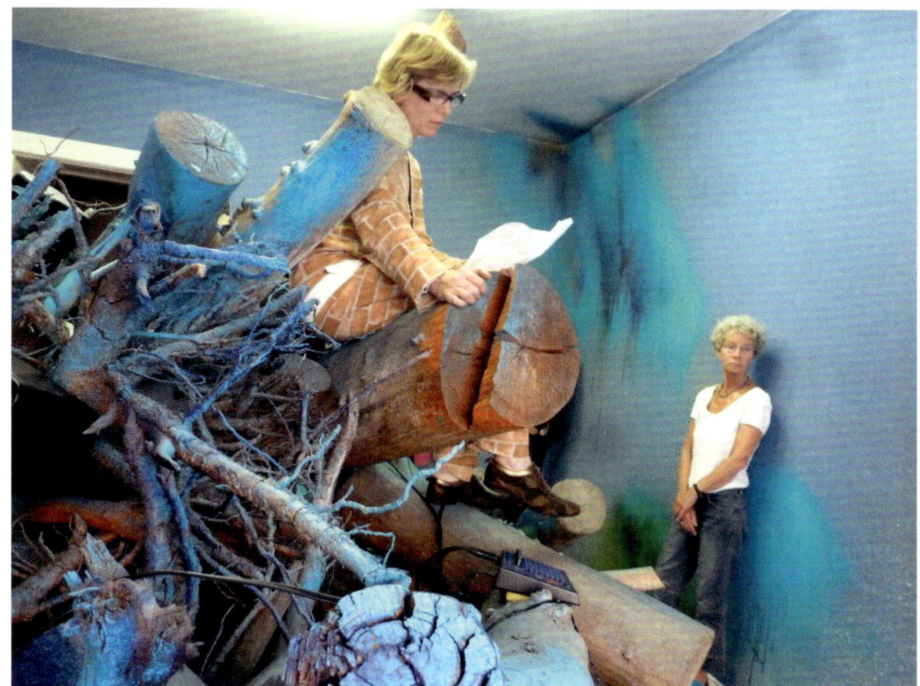

2015). Grosse's works can be quite humorous; in fact, they can sometimes be a total riot. This one was another of her absurdly exaggerated and enlarged versions of, well, painting – with the trees as paintbrushes, and the fabric as a really massive canvas.

Things (my emphasis), like the trees in these two works, never appear in Grosse's works as mere props, nor are they really found objects in the sense of commonplace objects given a new context and assigned a new meaning as art, such as have often been presented ever since the work of Marcel Duchamp. Here is how Grosse describes her use of objects: 'I am using the tree like I use the bed, or the soil, or the house as these primordial conditions which we all know and need to live.'

Implicit in 'these primordial conditions' is a distinctly non-anthropocentric understanding that we, as humans, are part of the non-human world and partners with inanimate things, not their lords and masters. Very evident in Grosse's work is the fact that these things – whether a bed, crumpled clothes, rocks, soil, or a tree with tangled roots – maintain their own vitality and agency, even as she ushers them into artworks. While Grosse spray-paints these things, she almost always leaves parts untouched; logs and trees with all their textures and colors, the textures of soil, shapes of trees and rocks, shadows cast by objects and sunlight slanting in, and sections of bare walls are as much components of her artworks as anything else.

In her excellent book *Vibrant Matter: A Political Ecology of Things* (2010), the American political theorist, philosopher, and author Jane Bennett has written of 'vibrant matter and lively things', of 'thing-power' and of 'the vital materialities

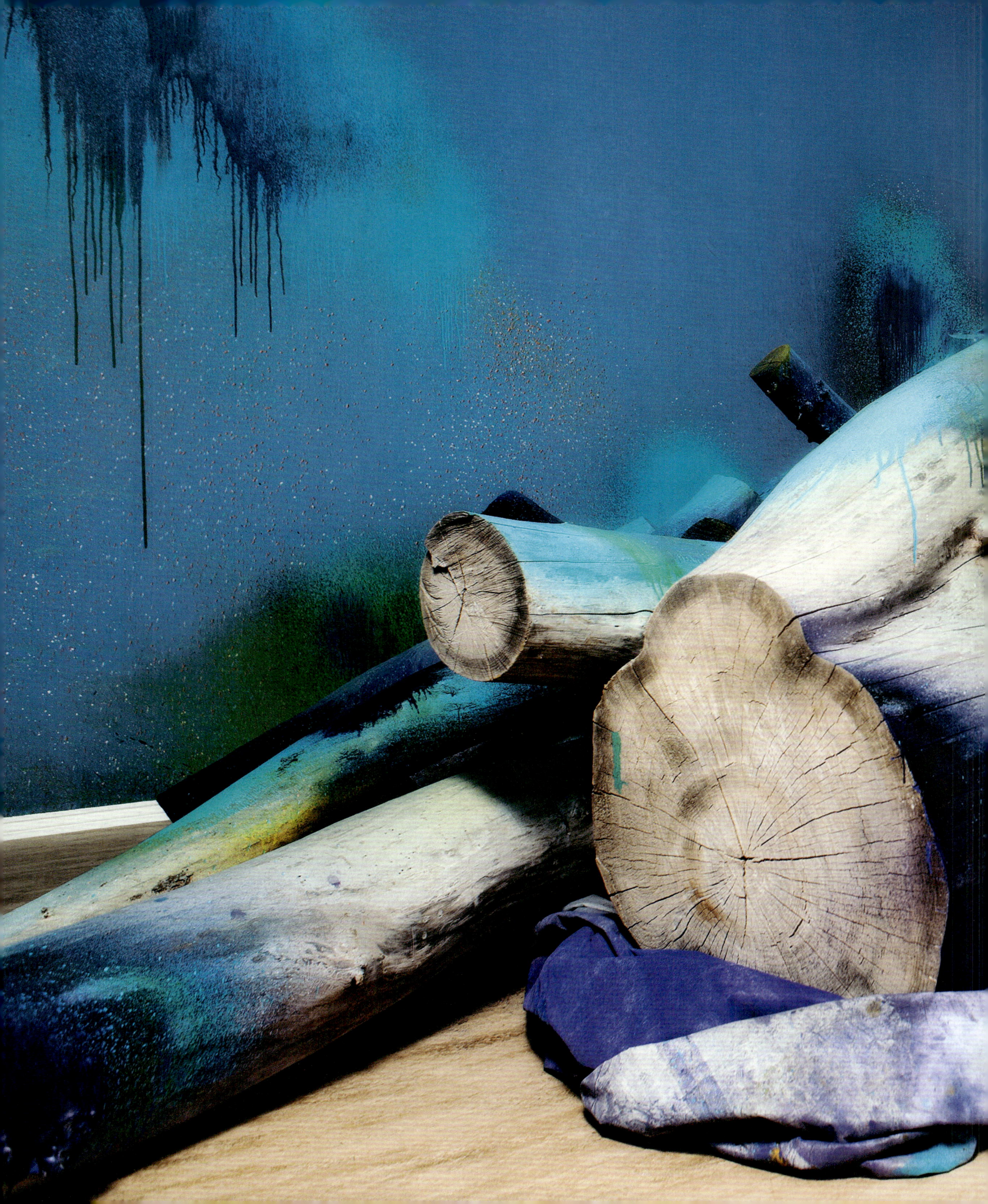

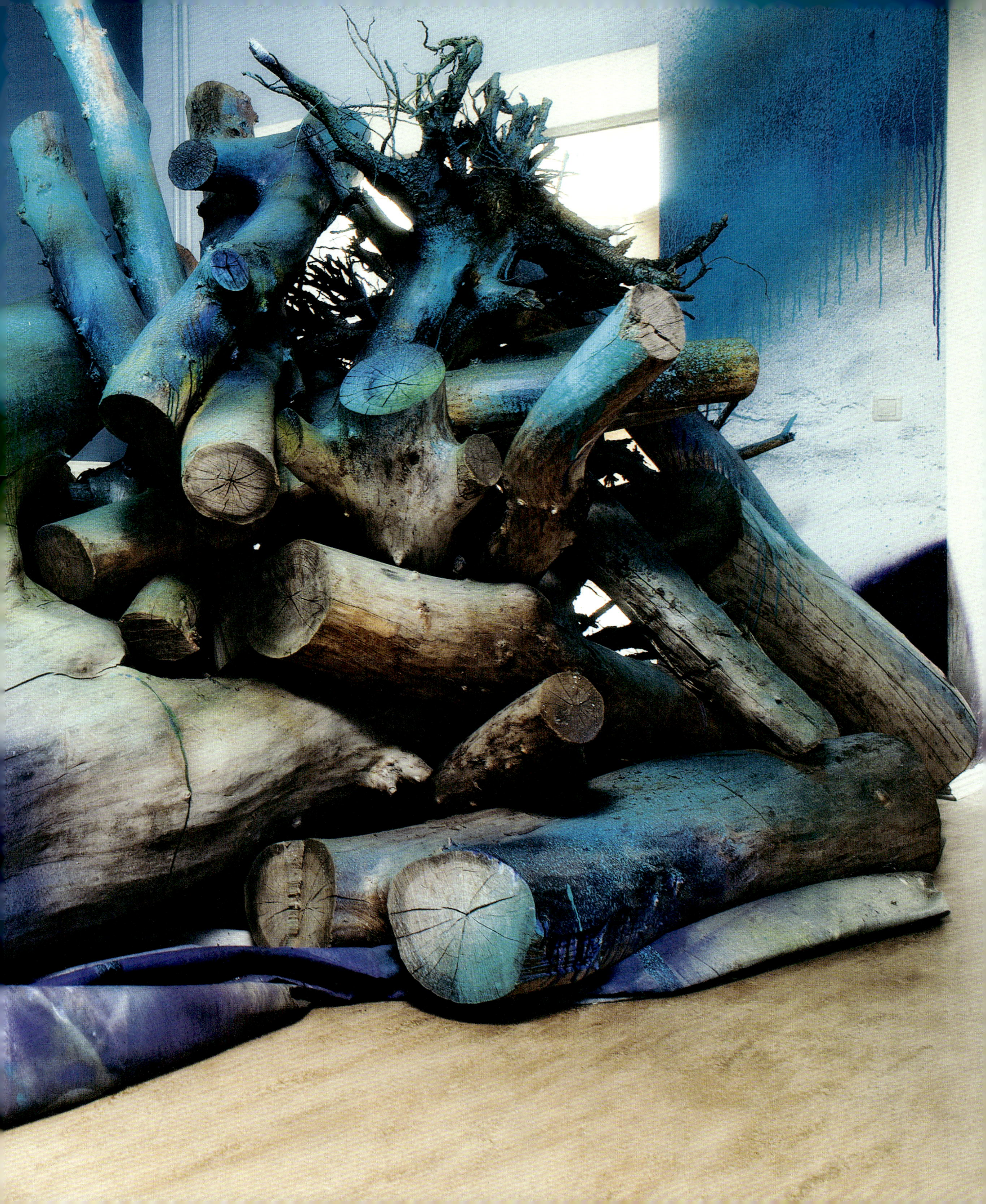

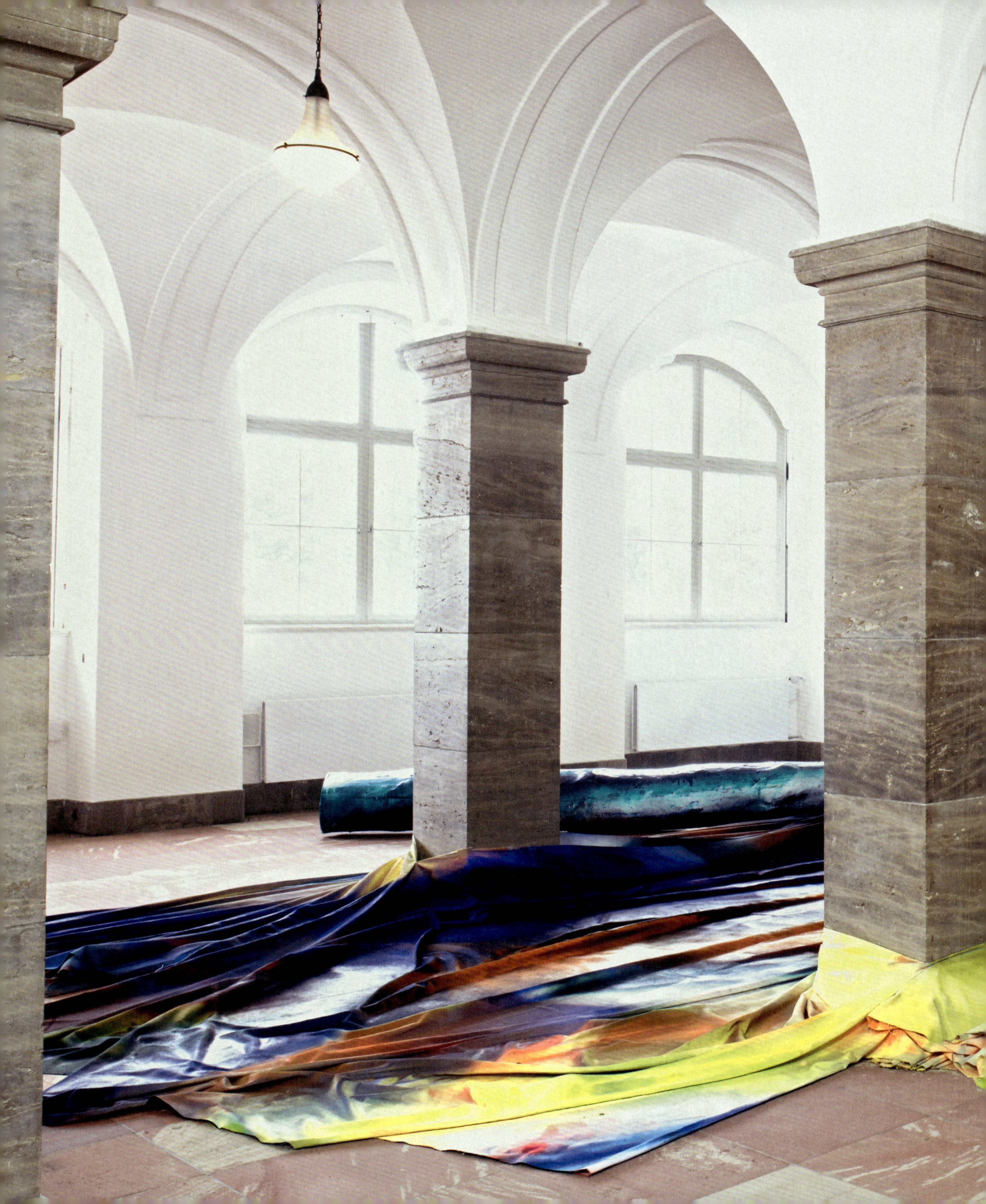

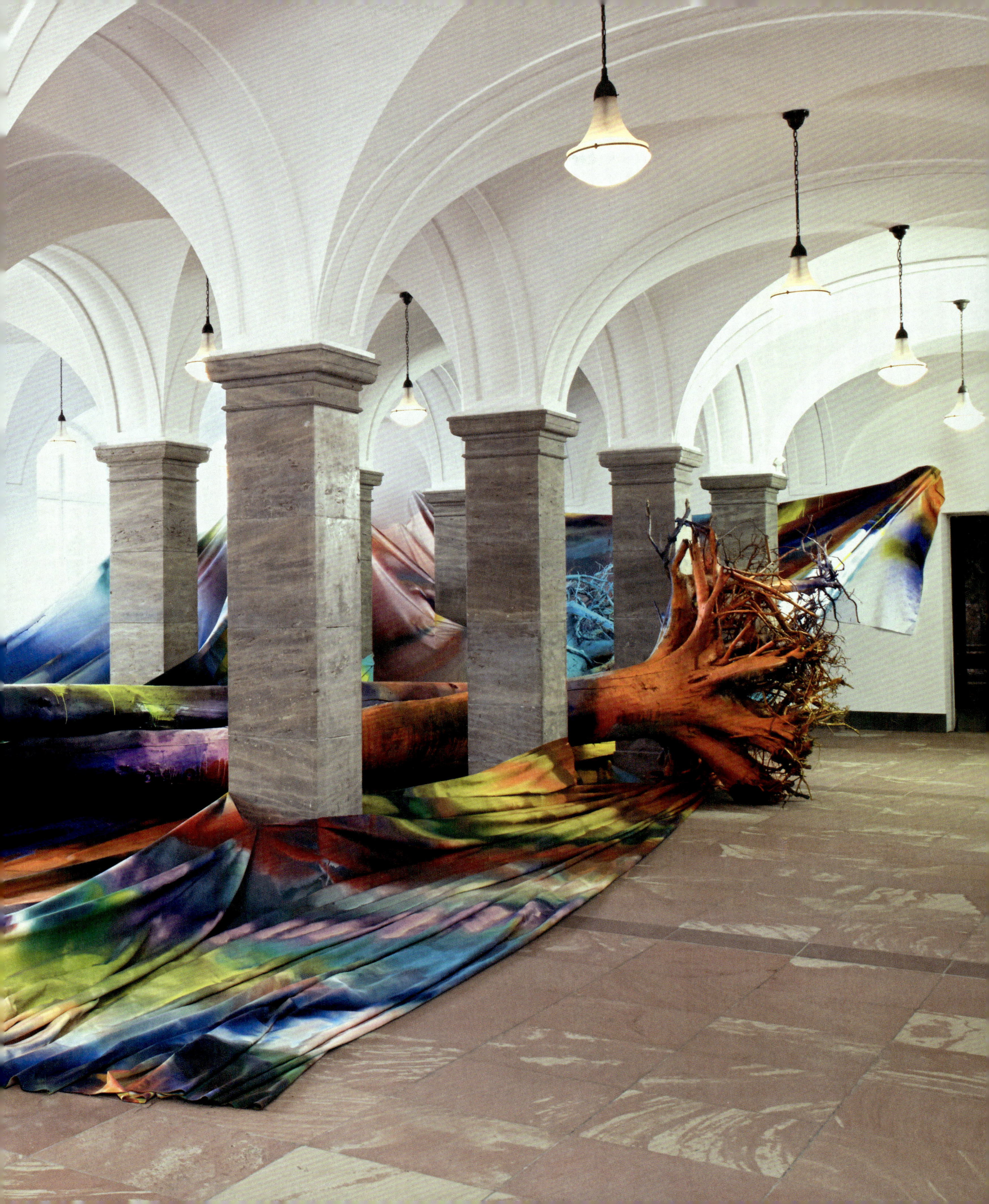

that flow through and around us', which we, according to her, often don't heed or
even detect because of what she calls 'our human hubris and our earth-destroying
fantasies of conquest and consumption' – essentially, our human-centric approach
to the world.[16] Grosse does heed them, however; her work abounds with such 'vital
materialities'. Color, by the way, is one of them, and it very much has 'thing-power'
in her work. 'Vibrant matter' and a profoundly respectful and inquiring engagement
with substances and things are fundamental in Grosse's art. This also fits with the
carnival drive in her work. For Bakhtin, 'carnivalized situations' have everything to do
with the suspension of deep-rooted hierarchies and power-based relationships. In the
Anthropocene, there is no firmer hierarchy than the one placing us, as humans – quite
recent additions to a planet 4.5 billion years old – as somehow separate from, and
dominant over, nature.

Incorporating things allows Grosse to radically expand her aesthetic – paint and
color interacting with myriad objects and textures, materials and shapes. It also allows
her to explore her markedly non-hierarchical and unifying vision, in which easy-to-
ignore parts of a space (stairs, doorways, corners) are suddenly just as important as
the most prominent walls and in which ignoble stuff like scraps of clothing, scattered
soil, and rocks are of equal significance as brilliantly colored paintings on architectural
surfaces or canvases. It especially connects with the carnival and Bakhtin, who wrote
of the 'joyful relativity of all structure and order'. His subsequent passage could also
be a very apt description of one of Grosse's painting installations:

> A free and familiar attitude spreads over everything: over all values, thoughts,
> phenomena, and things. All things that were once self-enclosed, disunified,
> distanced from one another by a noncarnivalistic hierarchical worldview are
> drawn into carnivalistic contacts and combinations. Carnival brings together,
> unifies, weds, and combines the sacred with the profane, the lofty with the low,
> the great with the insignificant, the wise with the stupid.

One Floor Up More Highly (2010) (fig.55) was Katharina Grosse's first large-scale
installation in the US, at MASS MoCA (Massachusetts Museum of Contemporary
Art). She mixed painting, sculpture, and architecture to fashion a visually stunning
and mind-bending landscape of sorts in a cavernous gallery that still retains many
traces of its former identity (MASS MoCA is housed in an imposing complex of
nineteenth-century factory buildings).

At the outset a large stack of white Styrofoam shards, jutting from a pile of
painted soil, towered over the viewer, suggesting an ice jam heaped up by a rushing
river in early spring, a cliff face, magnified crystalline forms, and perhaps also the
icebergs in Caspar David Friedrich's *Das Eismeer* (The Sea of Ice), 1823–4. It also
'gathered' light streaming through the many windows and in front of it were several
ersatz, multicolored boulders. Four sizable mounds of actual soil, dispersed through

previous spread

54. Sieben Stunden, Acht Stimmen, Drei Bäume
(Seven Hours, Eight Voices, Three Trees)   2015
Museum Wiesbaden

Acrylic on fabric and tree
330 × 1400 × 2400 cm (130 × 551 × 945 in)

the space, were spray-painted by Grosse – bright orange, lustrous red, green, magenta, deep purple, orange, greenish-yellow, turquoise, and ultramarine. She also mixed and combined an array of gestures and marks: broad zones, thin bands, curlicue squiggles, arcs, and diagonals.

Faux (yet convincing) boulders, rocks, and stones made from Styrofoam covered with sand, soil, or bark – or from chicken wire and mulch – and also spray-painted, were scattered about on the soil and floor, resulting in a total conflation of real and simulated nature, accentuating a note of theme parks, movie props, and theater. Three jagged stacks of large, white Styrofoam shards nestled against the soil and angled upward; their stark whiteness contrasted with the abundant colors every-where else. A large, white half-disk on the floor, made of glass-fiber-reinforced plastic and streaked with colors, rested atop more painted soil and some discarded clothes; it was like a hyper-inflated piece of cracked pottery, or perhaps a broken-off section of some futuristic machine. A low mound of soil sloped against the wall, rippling with green, red, purple, and blue hues. Licks of paint, especially deep blue, climbed up part of the wall and spread across parts of several windows. You were looking at a painting on the wall and windows but also through and around it toward the sky and the Berkshire mountains in the distance. Grosse's spray-painted marks formed a colorful membrane between inside and outside, architecture and nature, walls and sky.

There were constant shifts in scale in *One Floor Up More Highly*. Sometimes Grosse's work loomed above you, making you feel tiny; at other times it was low on the floor making you feel huge. You could climb up stairs to an exposed balcony where Grosse's title, quite literally, made sense – for you were now actually 'one floor up more highly', surveying the undulating installation below. But the title had additional connotations: heightened consciousness; altered realities; ecstatic encounters not with nature per se, but with an especially hybrid and mediated nature worked into art. You were in the exultant position of an explorer astonished by an enthralling landscape, doing so with upsweep and rapt contemplation, akin to the male figure atop a rocky pinnacle in Friedrich's famous *Der Wanderer über dem Nebelmeer* (Wanderer above the Sea of Fog, *c*.1818). With carnival colors, Styrofoam geology, and concocted rocks, Katharina Grosse had devised a challenging twenty-first-century work that retained a nineteenth-century aura of powerful beauty and the transportive sublime.

At the same time, Grosse's installation had a very rough streak. It suggested rock slides and grinding erosion, abandoned construction sites and entropic ruins, maybe even the aftermath of an environmental catastrophe from which people had fled. Grosse's works are joyful and exuberant. They can also be fractious and unnerving.

Grosse's *Untitled Trumpet* (2015) was situated in the Aperto section of the Venice Biennale exhibition *All the World's Futures*, curated by Okwui Enwezor (fig.56). The Aperto is a protected, historical building; you can't mess with its walls. Grosse devised a novel solution. She installed white fabric as soft walls, mounds of soil on the floor, and various objects – all of which she spray-painted with multiple colors.

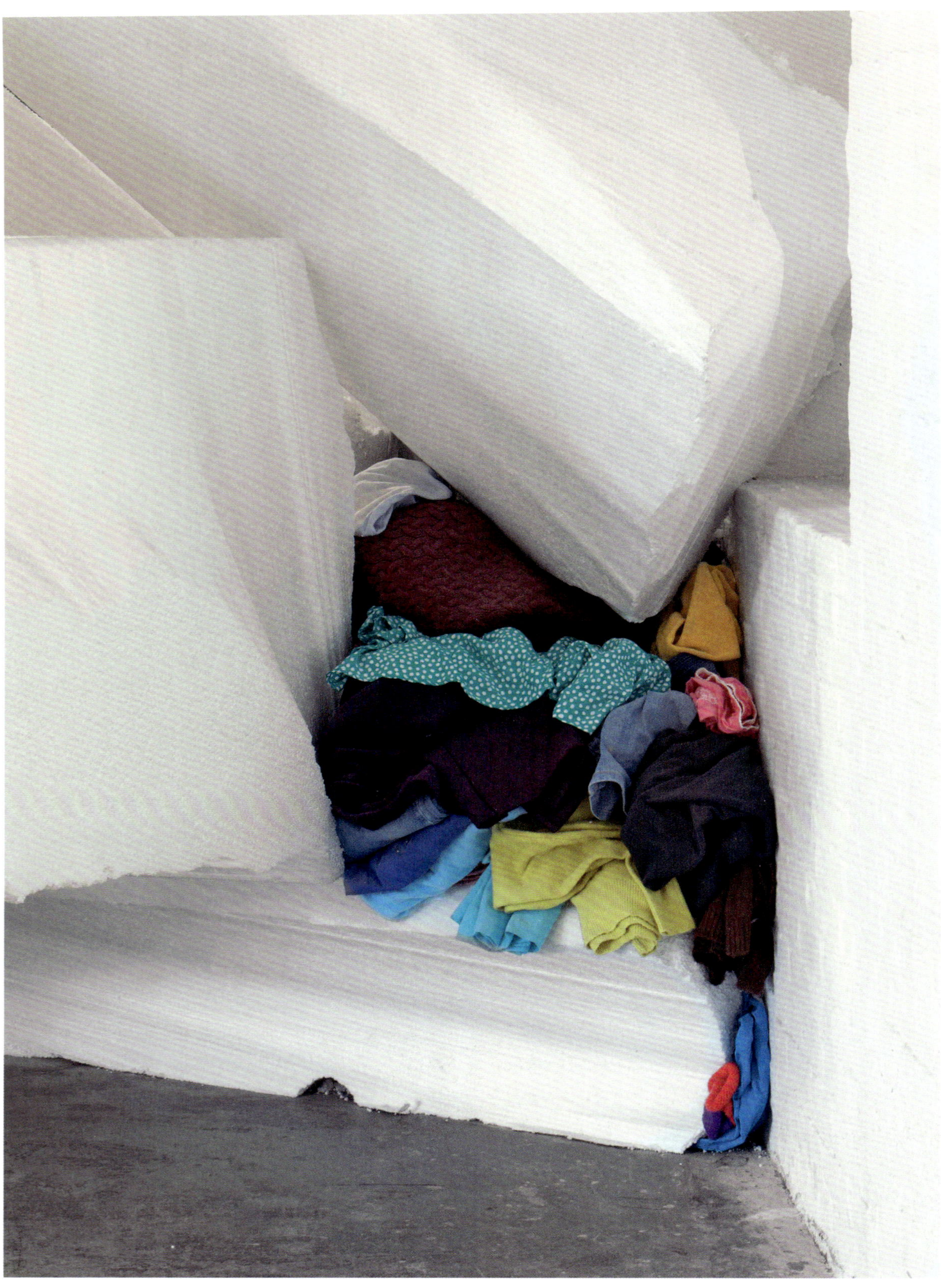

55. One Floor Up More Highly   2010
MASS MoCA, North Adams, Massachusetts

Acrylic on wall, floor, clothing, Styrofoam, and glass-fiber-reinforced plastic
Main exhibition hall work: 780 × 1680 × 8260 cm (307 × 661 × 3252 in)

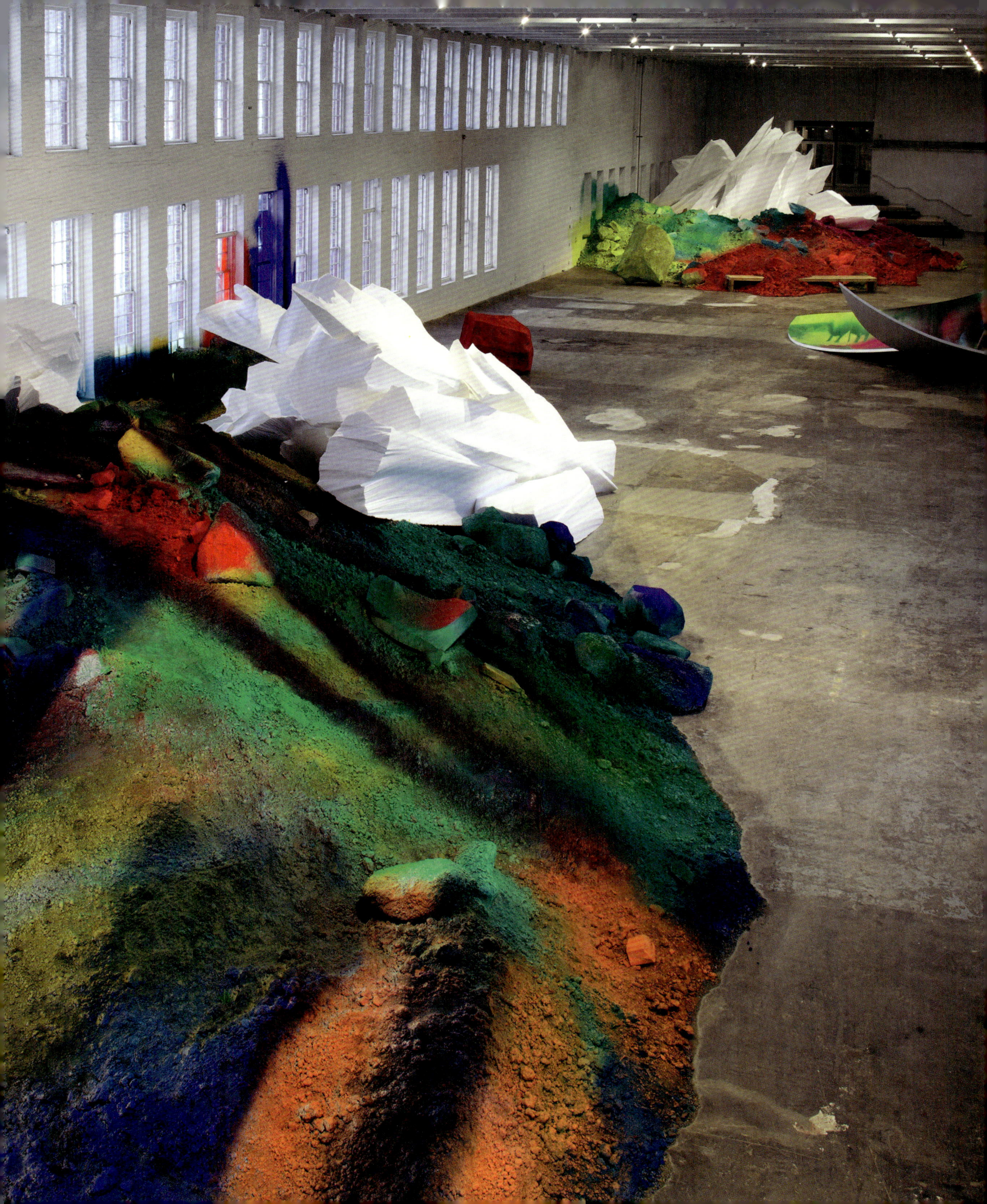

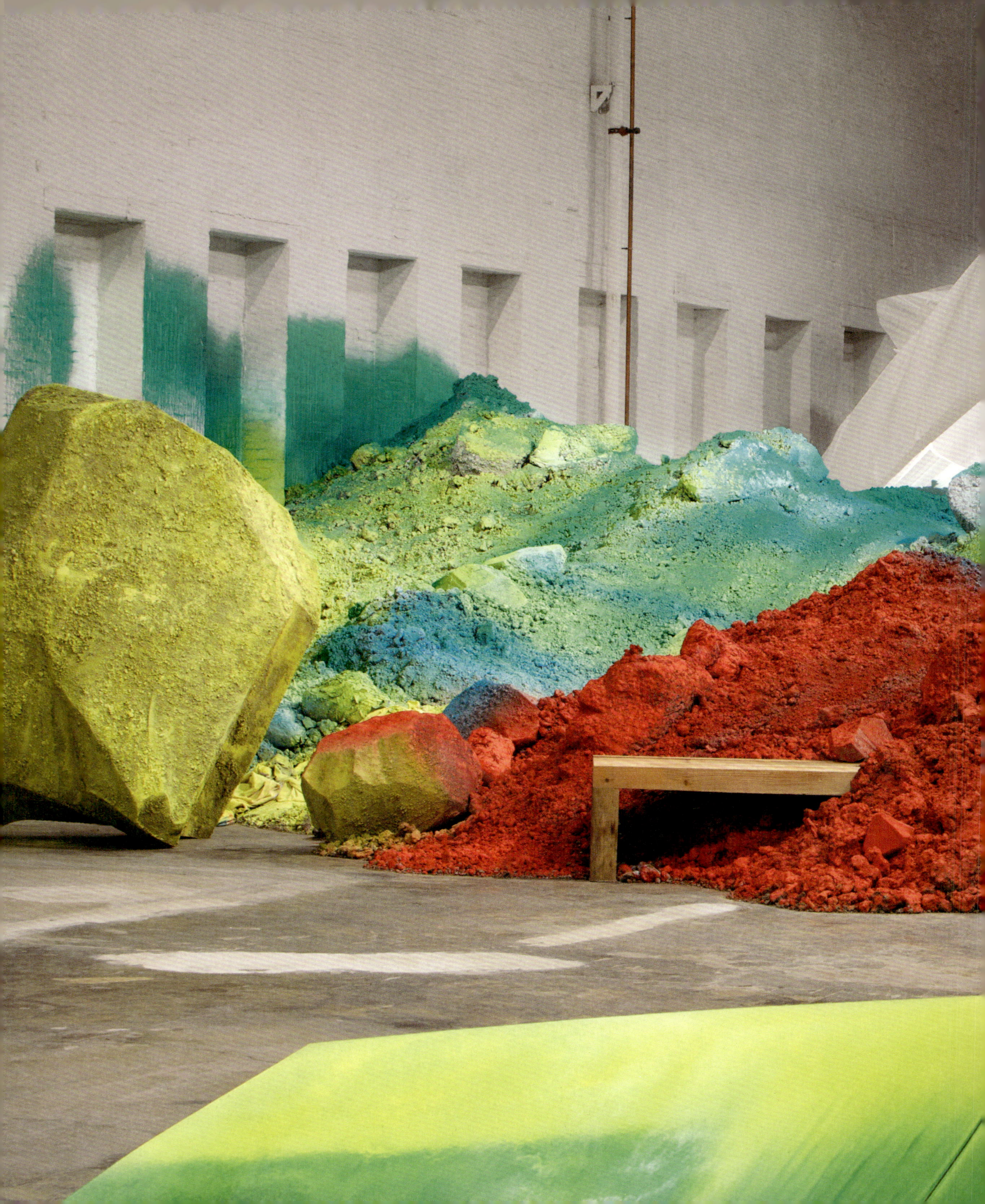

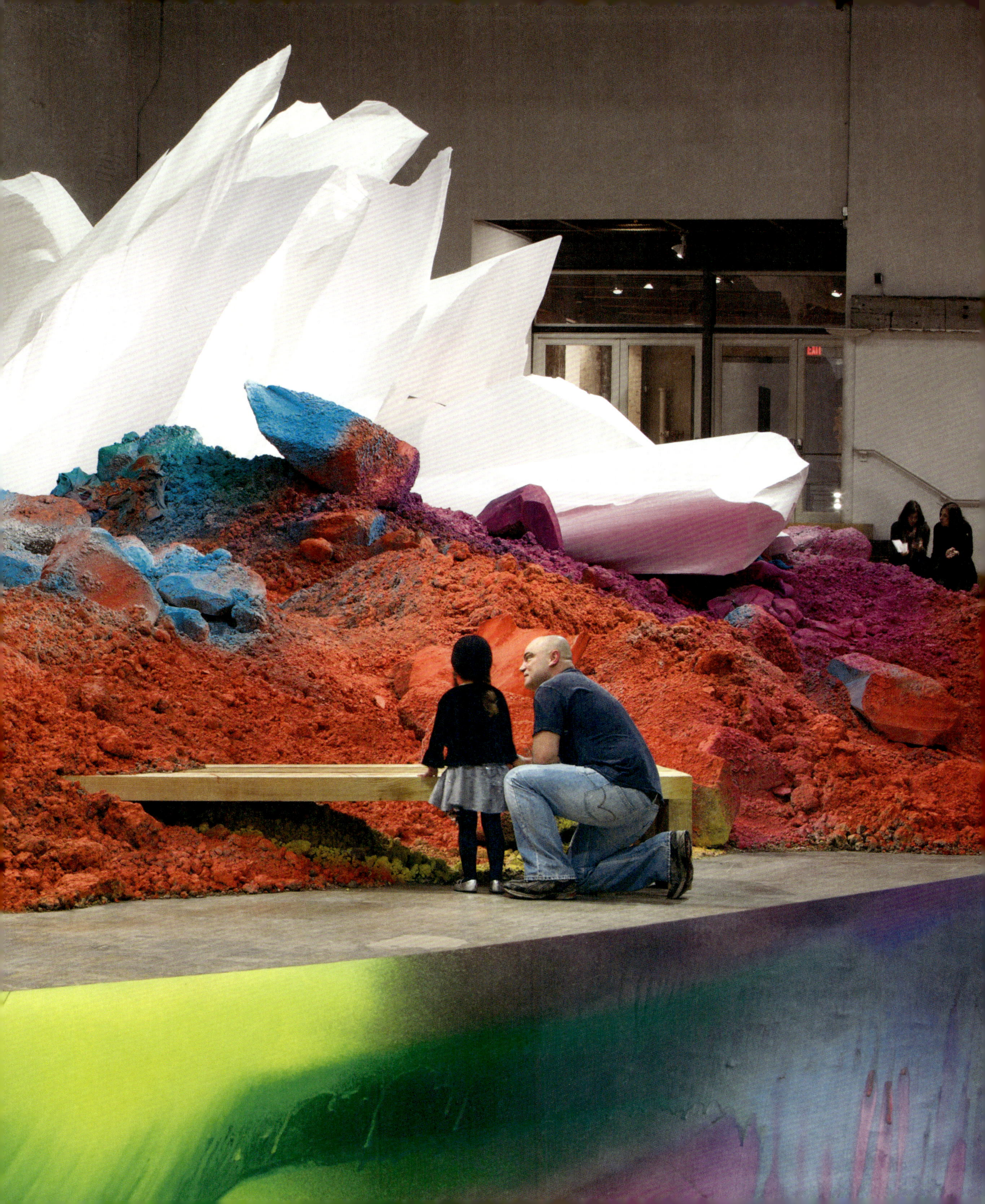

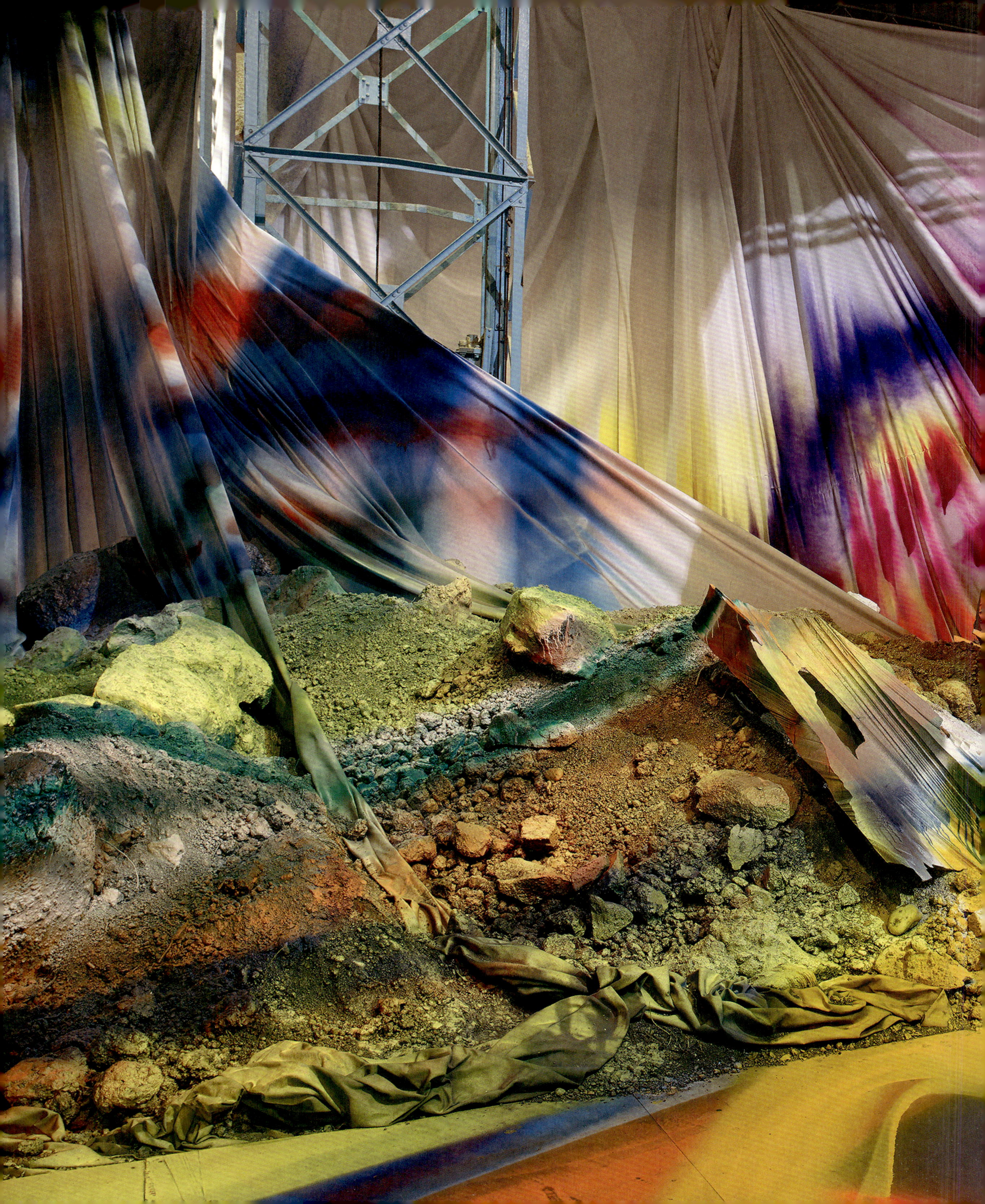

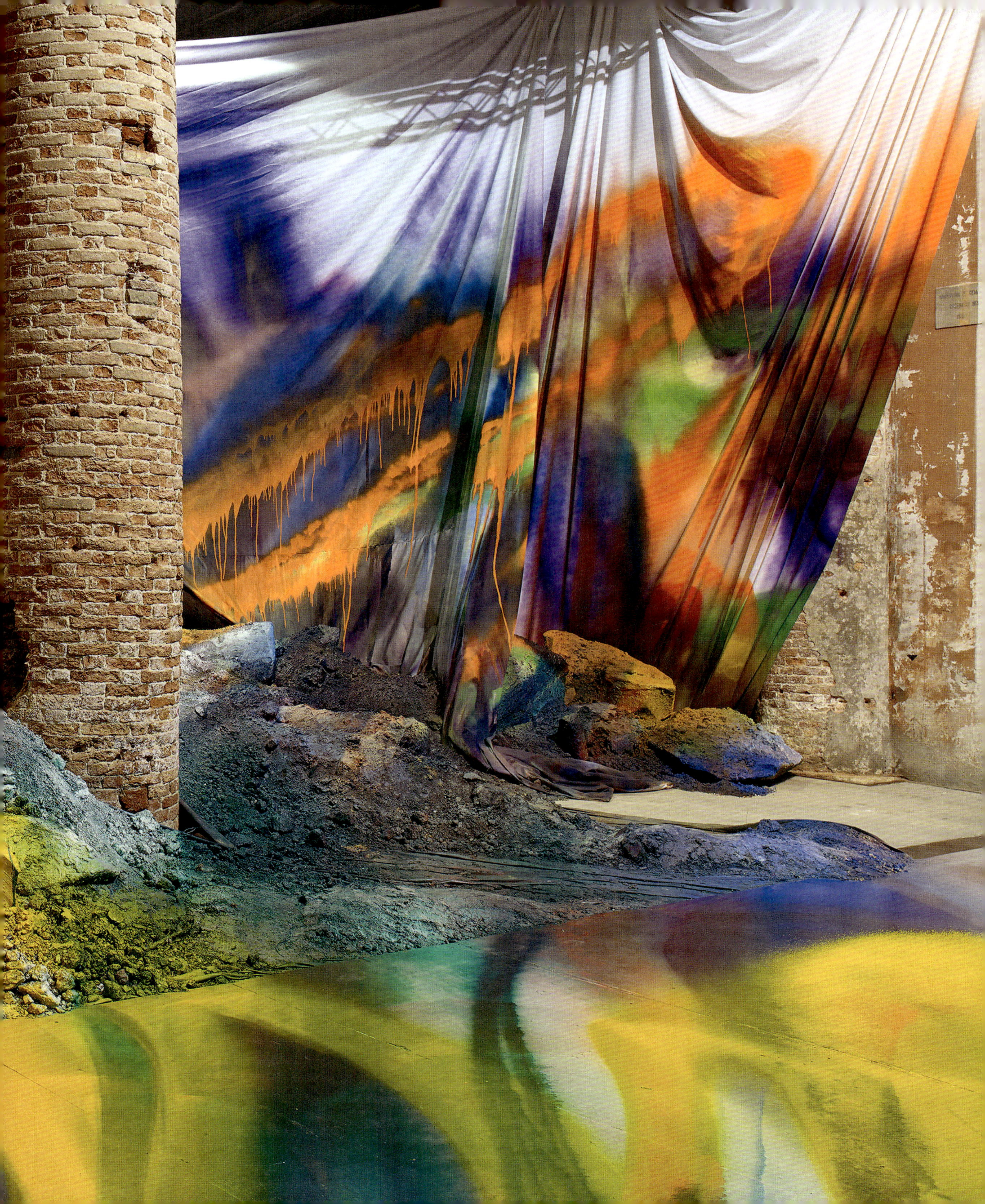

As is usual, there were a lot of artworks in the Aperto: tons of them, seemingly going on for miles and threatening to become a slow, bewildering blur for even the most committed of viewers. Grosse's painting installation didn't just stand out; it was an absolute showstopper. White fabric (with many folds) sloped into the space from on high; a huge mound of dirt, seeded with crumpled fabric, was on the floor; various objects, including rocks and aluminum chunks, were scattered about. Grosse spray-painted everything – or, rather, parts of everything – with giant-size yellow squiggles, twanging green bands, a feathery light yellow-green that seemed to be half-dissolving into the soil, purple half arcs, opulent cobalt blues in different shapes, and orange streaks slanting across the fabric and onto the floor a bit like beams of sunlight. Parts of the extant architecture, including exposed brick columns, were integrated into the piece. An upright metal tower cast shadows on both fabric and walls, which merged with the painted areas. Viewers walked through on a multicolored, spray-painted, wooden boardwalk, seeing and absorbing Grosse's installation on either side. Prominent on the floor was soil – albeit soil transformed by paint.

This painting installation seemed to be coming from all directions at once – from overhead, underfoot, and all around – a swirling, centrifugal painting and an aerial one too. It was exquisite but also exceedingly rough, even semi-apocalyptic. It looked like stellar rubble. It looked like a weirdly joyful and ecstatic construction (or demolition) site or maybe an eccentric theater set displaying itself as a performance – a color, objects, materials, light, and shadow performance that was always occurring,

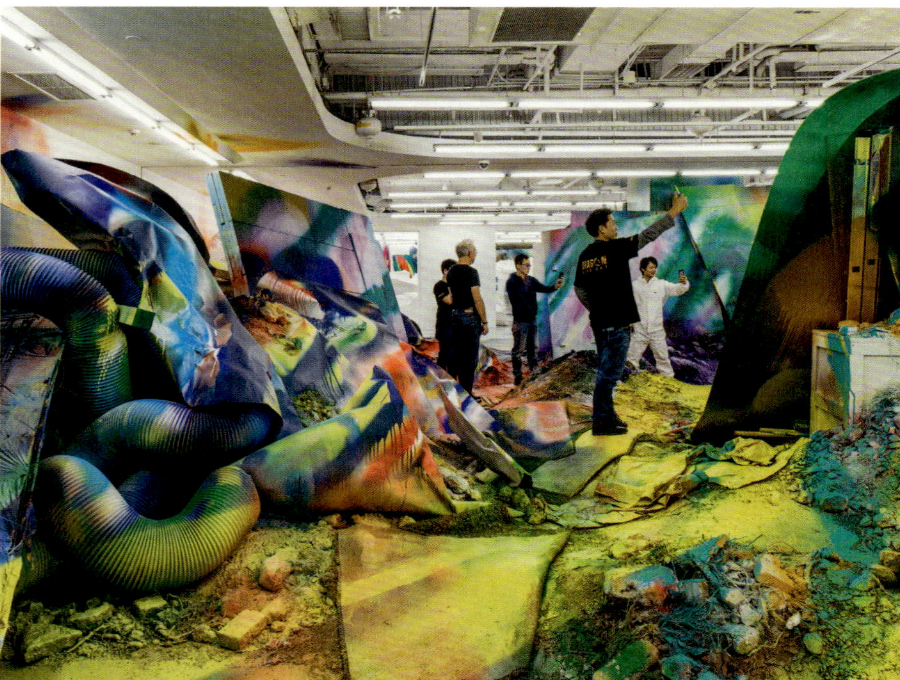

previous spread

56. Untitled Trumpet   2015
All the World's Futures, 56th Venice Biennale

Acrylic on wall, floor, and various objects
660 × 2100 × 1300 cm (260 × 827 × 512 in)

left and following spread

57. Mumbling Mud – Underground   2018
chi K11 art museum, Shanghai

Acrylic on soil and various objects
370 × 1620 × 2400 cm (145 × 637 × 944 in)

always renewing itself, always changing. This was also one of many times when Grosse's works have embraced primal, world-shaping forces: cohesion and entropy, regeneration and decay.

Katharina Grosse's five-part *Mumbling Mud* (2018) was developed on-site at the chi K11 Art Museum in Shanghai (fig.57). This mixed-media installation (actually it was about as mixed as things get) consisted of five distinct yet interrelated zones, each exploring very different ways of making paintings, or quasi-paintings.

Long ago, as I previously noted, during Grosse's student days in Düsseldorf, her professor, Gotthard Graubner, instructed the students that the painting is 'your building site'. Zone 1 (The Underground) in Grosse's installation was a building site for real. Piles of dirt seeded with rocks and stones, crates, stacks of sections of drywall, panels, industrial tubing, the floor, walls, and other materials were spray-painted blue, orange, yellow, purple, and many colors more. While exquisitely constructed it also suggested entropic ruins. In Zone 2 (The Ghost) Grosse's over-the-top colors suddenly vanished. Instead, a large, bright-white sculpture carved from Styrofoam, which loosely suggested an excised chunk of bedrock, seemed almost apparitional, blending with the white floor and walls while cutting into the space and blocking your view. Nearby, large photographs of Grosse's Berlin studio, printed on floor-to-ceiling sections of silk, showed images of sculptures and paintings in process. As viewers passed through the space, Grosse's silk work reacted to their bodies, swaying and undulating slightly. Meanwhile, images of artworks made way over there in Berlin, more than 8000 kilometers (5000 miles) away, interacted with actual artworks in the exhibition – including paintings and sculptures.

It's not that Katharina Grosse was exactly quoting from her past works; each zone in this show was fresh and new. Still, correspondences abounded, and the exhibition was linked to some 20 years of her oeuvre. Zone 4 (Stomach) – with sloping, spray-painted fabric in myriad colors descending from the ceiling to cover the floor – recalled her huge, fabric enclosure at Carriageworks in Sydney (see fig.18) but it behaved very differently, chiefly because the ceiling at chi K11 is so much lower. Viewers didn't just look at this extreme painting. They entered it and were enveloped by it as they wended their way through a maze-like, alternative world full of bright colors coursing every which way. When they finally emerged they were in Zone 5 (Showroom), a carnivalesque transformation of a home-décor showroom with furniture, rugs, a bookcase, a potted plant, a painting, walls, and the floor streaked with muted colors and frosted with white paint (fig.58). This decidedly non-high-end showroom seemed oddly ethereal, partly occluded, half-disappearing into white fog. With its startling diversity and fluxional verve, Grosse's exhibition both challenged and transported viewers – turning the art-viewing experience into an exhilarating voyage of discovery and surprise.

pages 114–115

58. Mumbling Mud – Showroom   2018
chi K11 art museum, Shanghai

Acrylic on furniture, wall and floor, 295 × 1140 × 1,308 cm
(116 × 449 × 515 in)

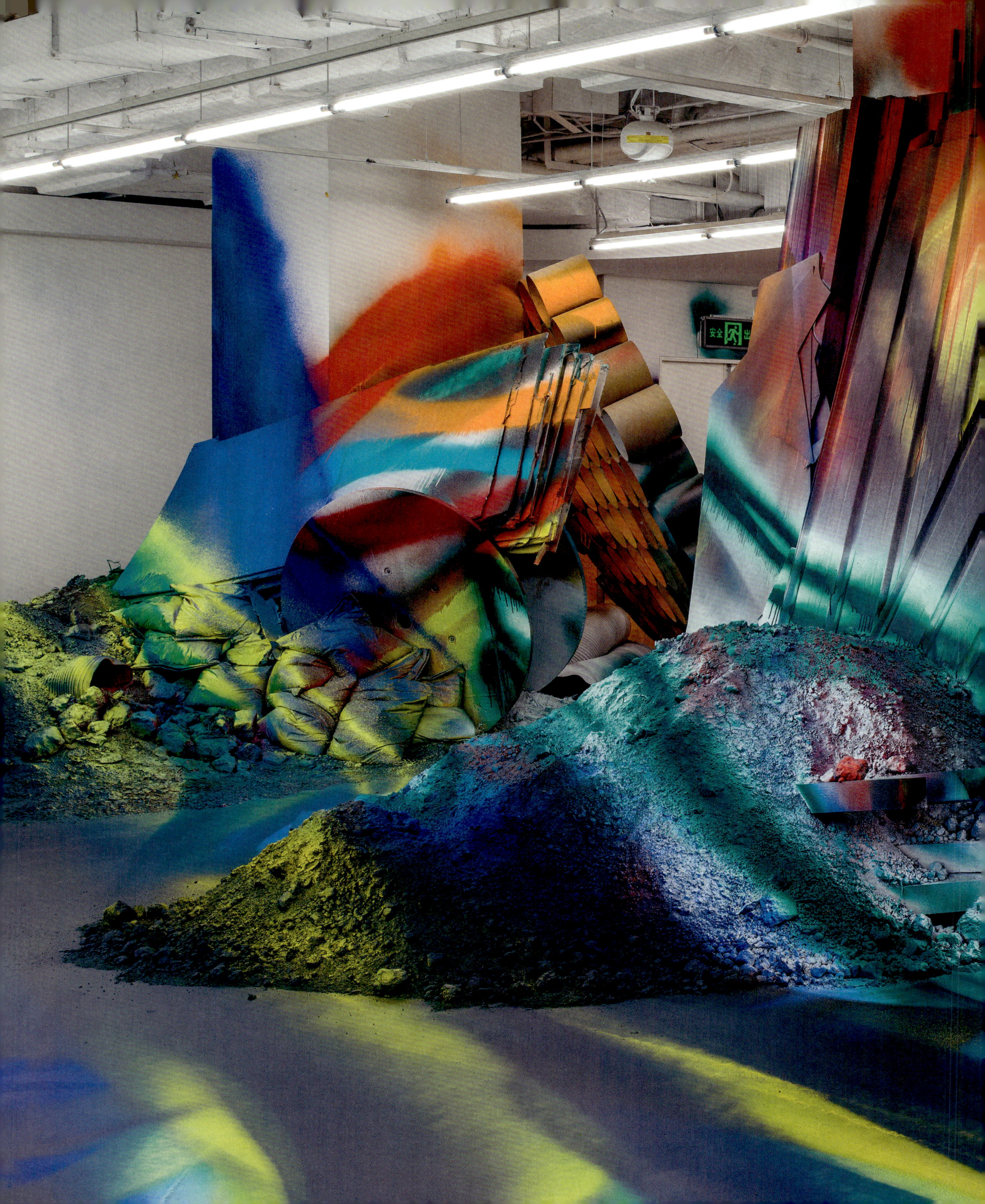

安全出口

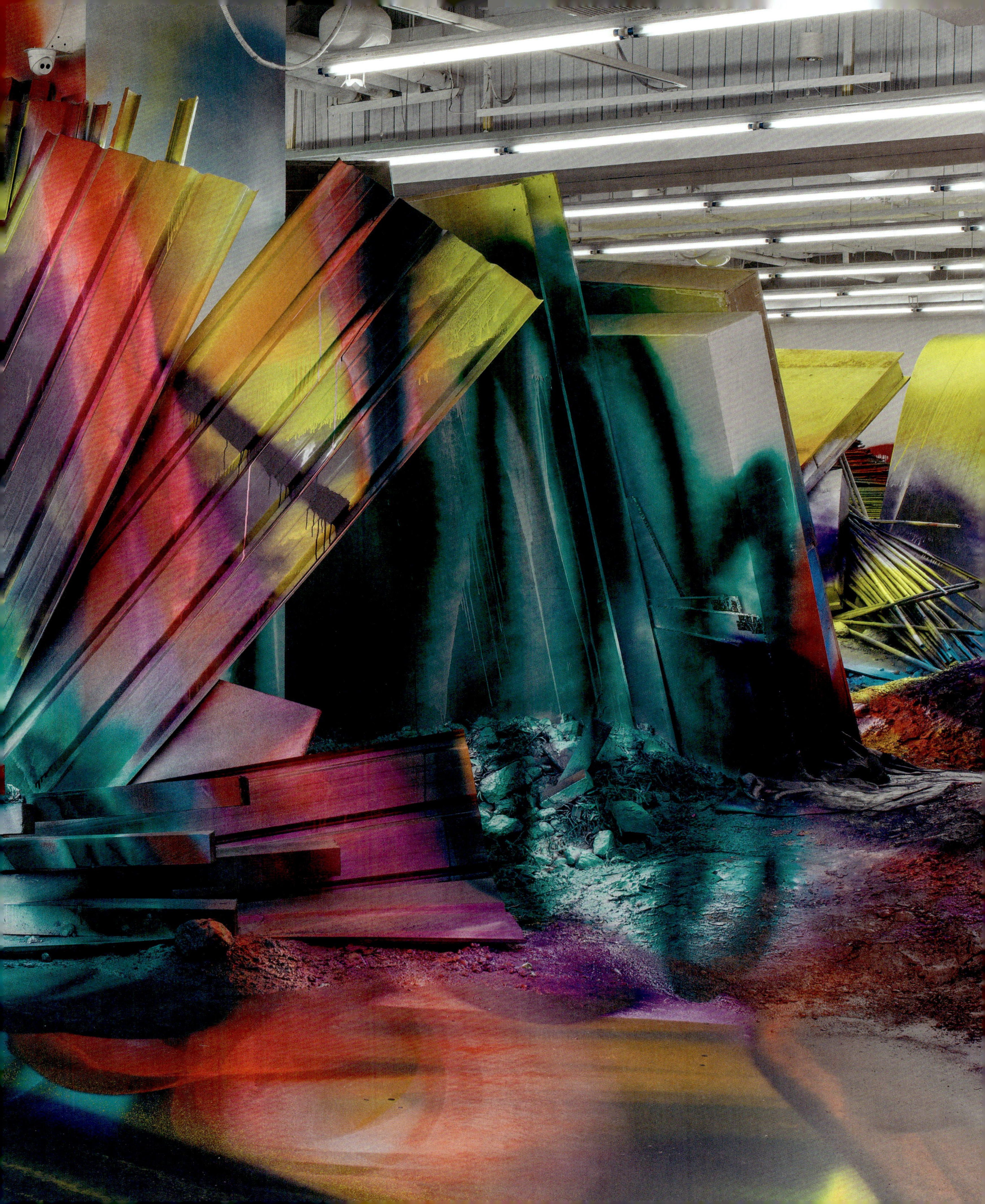

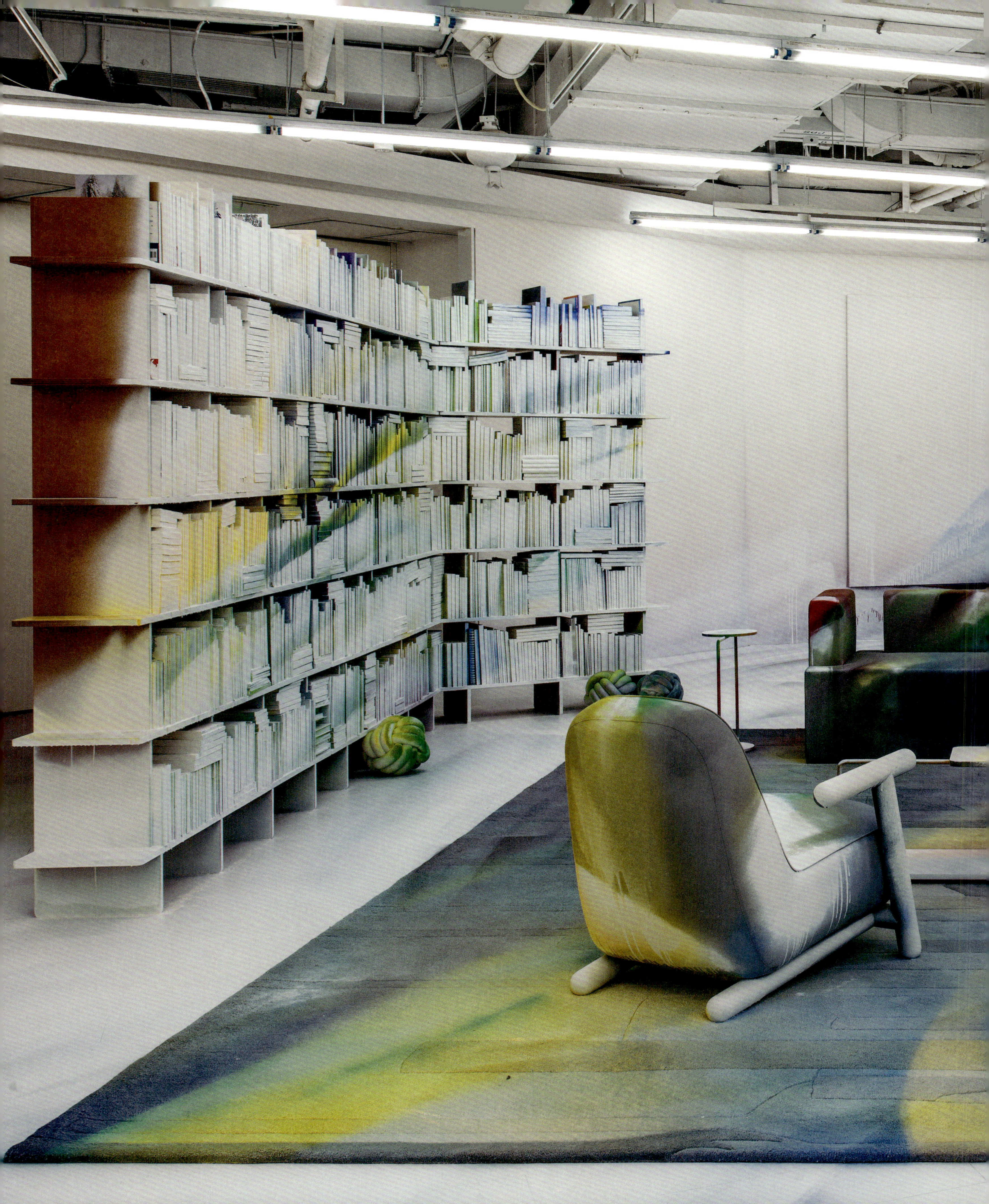

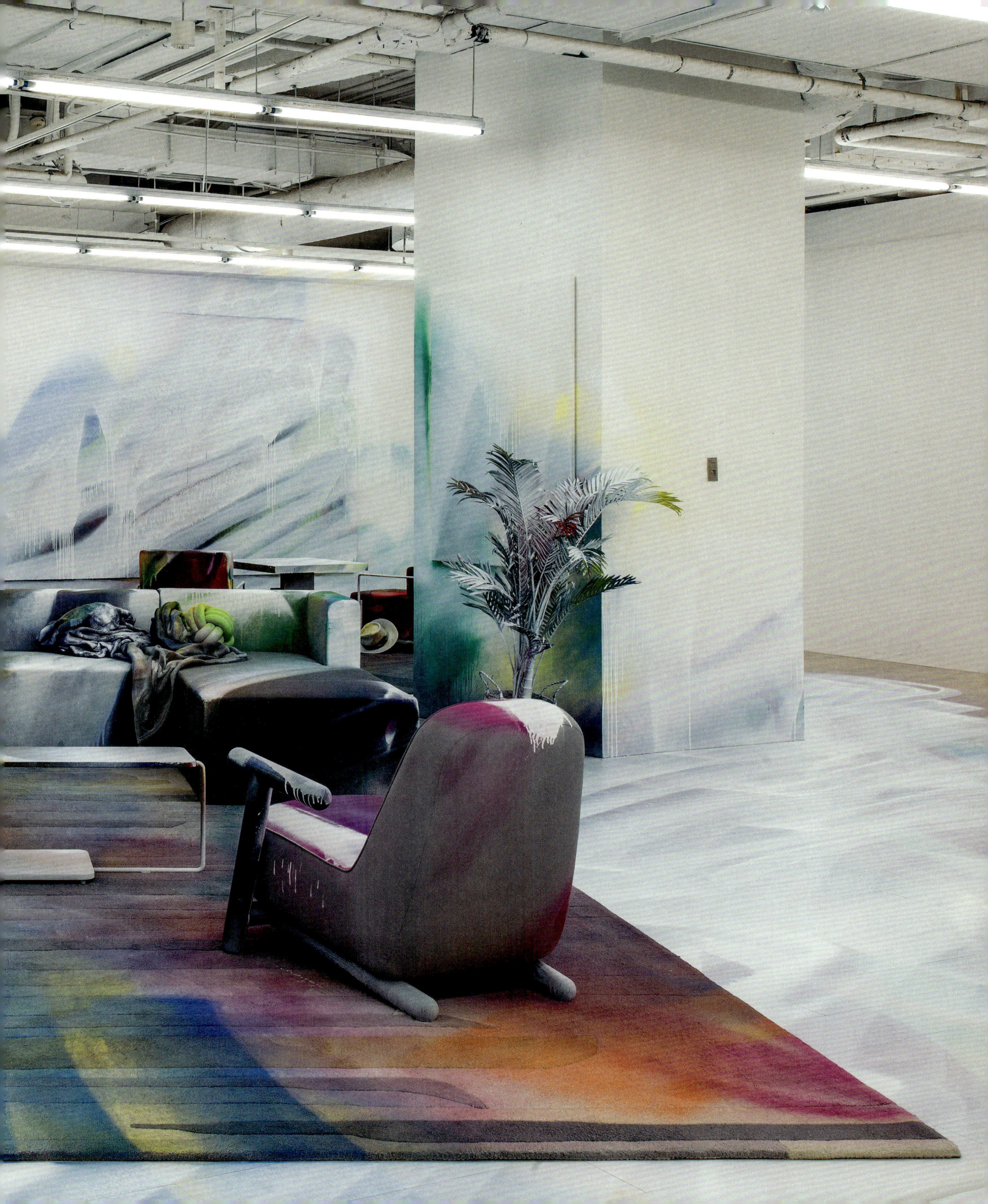

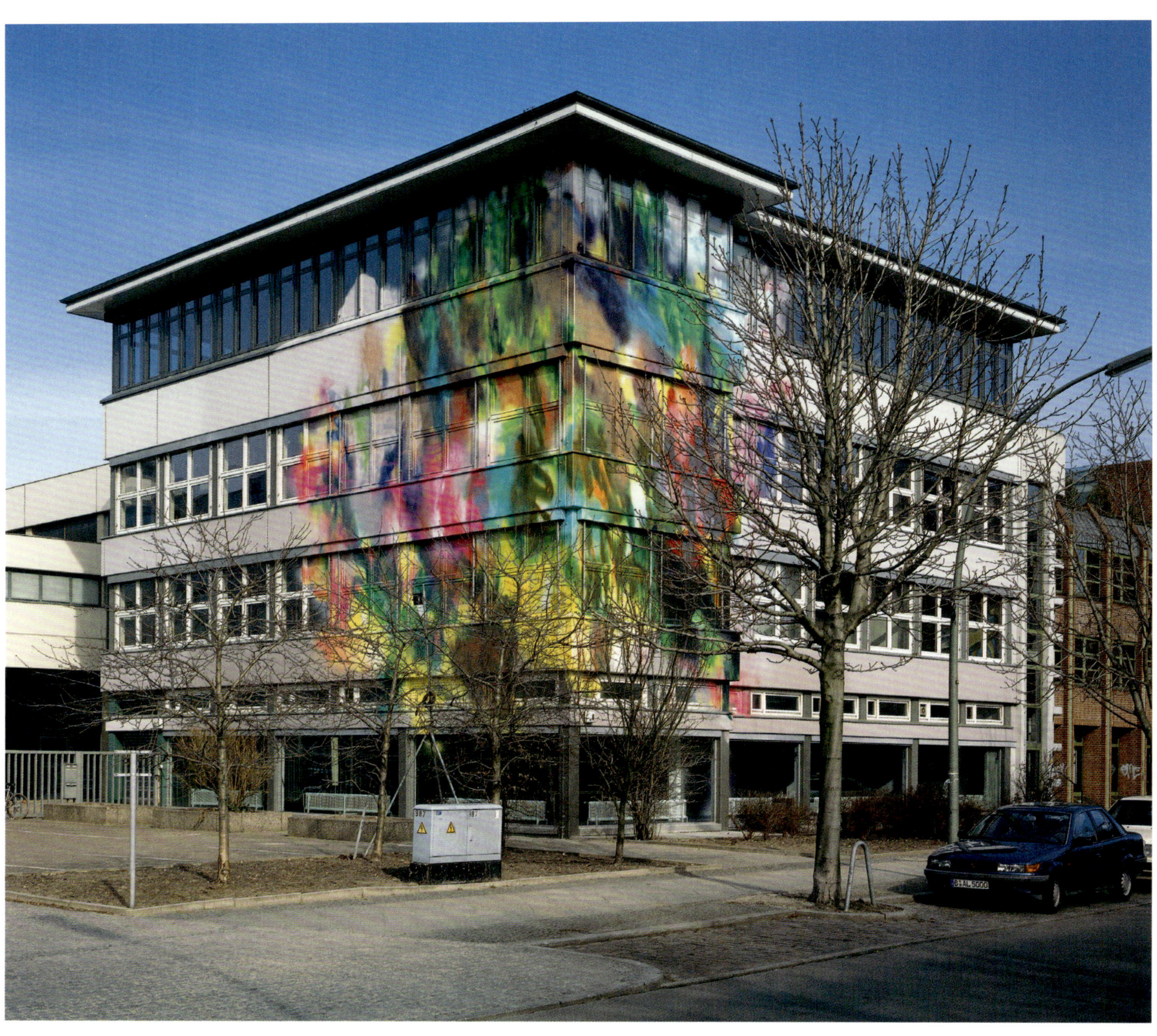

59. Untitled   2003

Berlinische Galerie – Landesmusem für Moderne Kunst,
Fotografie und Architektur, Berlin

Acrylic on aluminum, concrete, glass, and plastic
1300 × 1000 × 1000 cm (512 × 394 × 394 in)

4   The Outdoor Carnival

In the summer after her first year in art school Katharina Grosse went to Sardinia with a friend from school, a young Italian woman. She was on a strange mission that she still can't really explain. She brought with her 'a tiny set of watercolors'. The two friends stayed for weeks in 'a roofless house' that belonged to a percussionist, a friend of Grosse's friend. They bought 38 liters (10 gallons) of white paint and 38 liters (10 gallons) of Mediterranean blue paint to supplement the watercolors, and spent their days painting a large, coastal rock with what Grosse calls 'the movement of colors' while taking photographs of their progress and occasionally fending off Sardinian boys. This was Grosse's first temporary outdoor painting installation, made painstakingly over 'many, many days' with small watercolor brushes. The rock was important, but so too was the setting: an unorthodox painting in relation to, and transformative of, its surroundings. Especially important was moving off the canvas into the world and onto things. Combing through Grosse's archives, we managed to unearth previously unpublished photographs of this work, which has also never been critically addressed. It is striking just how much this painted Sardinian rock anticipates Grosse's painting installations, both outdoor and indoor, that would come many years later.

While Grosse has frequently brought the outside into her work – with all her rocks, soil, and trees, all her evocations of sunlight and clouds – she has also frequently worked outdoors, on buildings and in the land, as a unique, latter-day practitioner of Land Art. Whereas the first generation of artists associated with Land Art was in full flight from painting (as were many of its subsequent practitioners as well), Grosse very much remains a painter and brings a painter's (not a sculptor's) sensibility to her projects; the world, including land and buildings, becomes her 'canvas'.

Unlike some of the more renowned examples of Land Art, Grosse's works have so far never been in remote sites nor are they, in the main, permanent; instead, they have been mostly temporary works in liminal sites where humans and nature meet, where city and landscape converge, where past and present are intertwined: sites that are also fraught with political and ecological import. With their frequently large sizes, abundant colors, and outright showmanship, Grosse's outdoor artworks are among her most distinctly carnivalesque. They arrive to affect change and generate frank excitement, akin to that long-ago circus in Emily Dickinson's hometown. They are not just artworks to be seen, but instead brazen visual, spatial, and architectural forces and events to be deeply experienced.

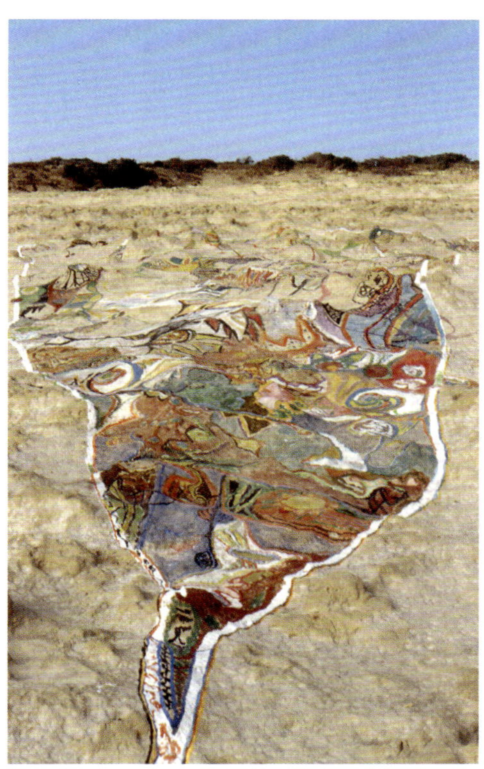

60. Watercolor painting by Katharina Grosse, Kerstin Klöckner and unknown friend, Sardinia, 1982

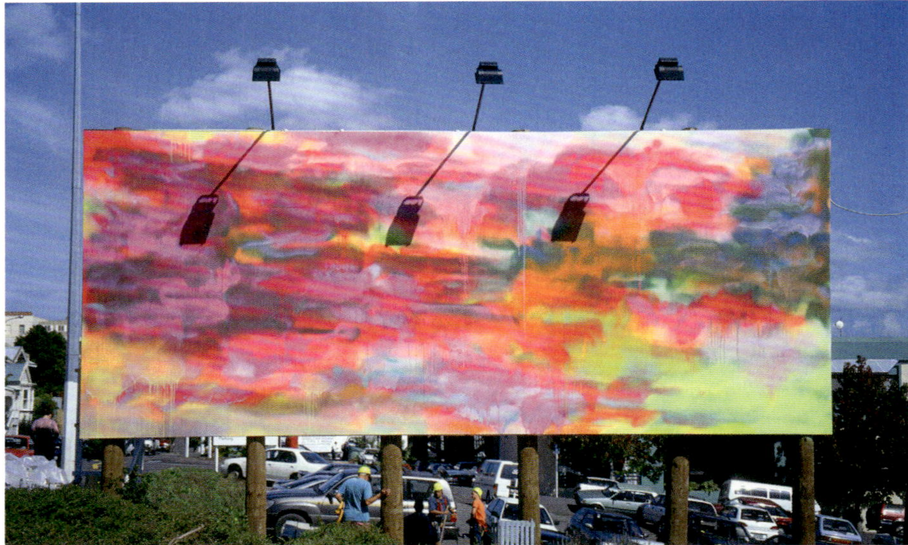

61. Untitled   2001
Upper Queen Street, Auckland

Acrylic on billboard
450 × 1200 cm (177 × 472 in)

By 2001 Grosse had already made many indoor, in situ paintings; her fresh and unorthodox approach to painting was increasingly in demand. In Auckland, New Zealand, instead of making another one she decided to make an outdoor painting on an extra-large billboard, about twice the size of a normal one and supported by six thick, upright logs (*Untitled*, 2001) (fig.61). Nearby were other billboards, doing the usual: hawking products and services, luring customers. This was at one of the busiest intersections in Auckland.

Grosse's work was an exaggerated, carnivalized version of an otherwise routine billboard. With mostly horizontal reds, pinks, oranges, blues, and yellows and with prominent drips visible, it advertised nothing and utterly confounded quite a number of viewers, who couldn't figure out what the heck this strange billboard was up to.

Framed against the sky, it seemed to channel and absorb the blue sky, passing clouds, sunset and sunrise colors, the vicissitudes of daylight. I asked Grosse whether this had been her intention. Her answer: 'A work has to be so open that it can involve any other structure' – in this case, including the sky but also the shadows of the three lights on top of the work. Enthusiastic students helped for days, erecting a tent where they could drink tea. One 'older student' shot '120 rolls of film' chronicling the proceedings. Professors debated (excruciatingly, I imagine) whether Grosse's billboard was art or architecture. While it was on view artists and musicians showed up to stage impromptu performances. Grosse's outdoor works, in part because they are so magnetic and fresh, tend to double as communal experiences and zones of alternative consciousness. People gather at them, 'live' in them – often for a long time – partaking of their surprising energies. At the opening Grosse arranged for celebratory champagne and 500 oysters to be served from a camper van to all the people who had helped.

62. psychylustro – The Drama Wall   2014

Along the tracks of Philadelphia's public transportation

Acrylic on wall, ground and various objects
1250 × 10,000 cm × 450 cm (492 × 3937 × 177 in)

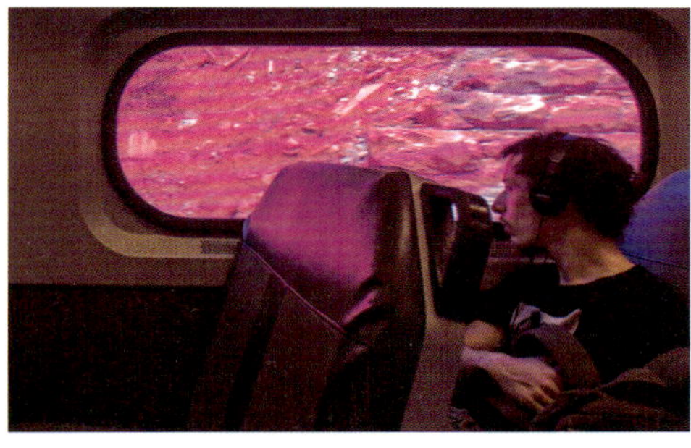

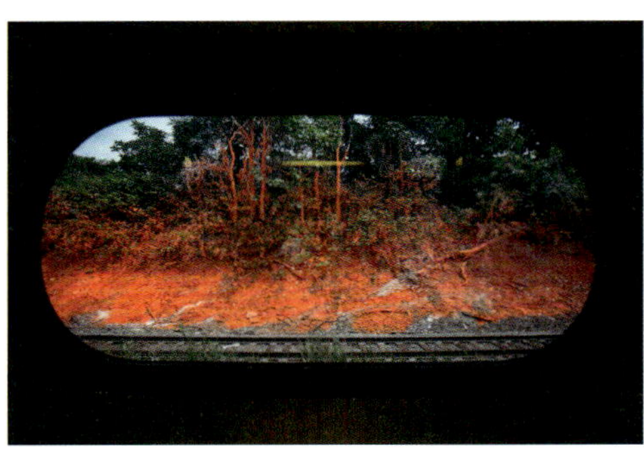

63. psychylustro – The Green Passage   2014

Along the tracks of Philadelphia's public transportation

Latex paint on various objects
670 × 6500 cm (264 × 2560 in)

In 2003 Grosse won an important award, the Berlinische Galerie's Fred Thieler Prize for painting, which involved an exhibition. She decided to not exhibit paintings inside the museum but instead to spray-paint part of the Modernist building's rather uniform facade with twisting and billowing magentas, greens, yellows, purples, and aquas (*Untitled*, 2003) (fig.59). It was as if ecstatic, lambent vapors were climbing up, altering, and subverting this very institutional-looking structure, which was a former glass factory. Most of the rather dour building was left as is; part of it was given this spectacular new 'costume'. Several years ago, Grosse told me, somewhat enigmatically, that her work has a lot to do with 'anarchic sexuality'. It is my instinct that some of this may have been operating here.

Grosse often downplays a specifically feminist understanding of her work and she also evades all attempts to fit her work into this or that camp, this or that ideology. Still, gender implications abound in her work – and especially with this particular painting. That chunky edifice in Berlin was about as 'male' as they come: imposing, all right angles and rigidity, uniform – the architectural equivalent of a typical male business suit. Grosse unleashed her carnival colors on it. They twisted it, subverted it, temporarily changed it (actually becoming a part of it) from something routine that has to be accepted as a matter of course into something colorful, exotic, and impassioned. That stolid building was, in short, yet another bastion of public masculinity. Grosse – a solo female – made it crazily gorgeous and flamboyant. In my opinion, Grosse's work – although she would by no means describe herself as a political artist – is actually extremely political. Rather than commenting on the need for change, her works affect substantial change right here and now. She decisively alters public spaces, as well as how we perceive and behave in such spaces. She enlivens things, intensely so. She makes an often dyed-in-the-wool world fresh and surprising.

Rather than exhibiting paintings in Philadelphia (that would be the normal thing to do, as an artist) Grosse painted Philadelphia (most definitely, the carnival thing to do). Grosse's *psychylustro* (2014) – and you can still see some of its remnants from the train – was sited largely in an urban wasteland of gutted warehouses, crumbling infrastructure, and beleaguered nature (figs 62–5). She spray-painted, on a vast scale, the industrial buildings, some intact and others dilapidated, and urban grounds in this mostly forlorn and uninhabited part of the city, which doubles as a central corridor for trains. People entering or leaving the city by rail passed through a vibrant orange, pink, white, and green wonderland that was at once gritty and gorgeous: a pink railroad trestle; an orange-and-white gutted warehouse; an orange embankment with its colors framed by the surrounding green foliage; green-and-white walls; pink bushes, trees, and ground. Some people perceived this colorful urban painting as wonderful art. Others, no doubt, perceived it as graffiti gone completely amok – or maybe as a toxic disaster. While wondrous and spectacular in a most carnivalesque way, it also highlighted a shocking level of neglect and entropy in this major US city.

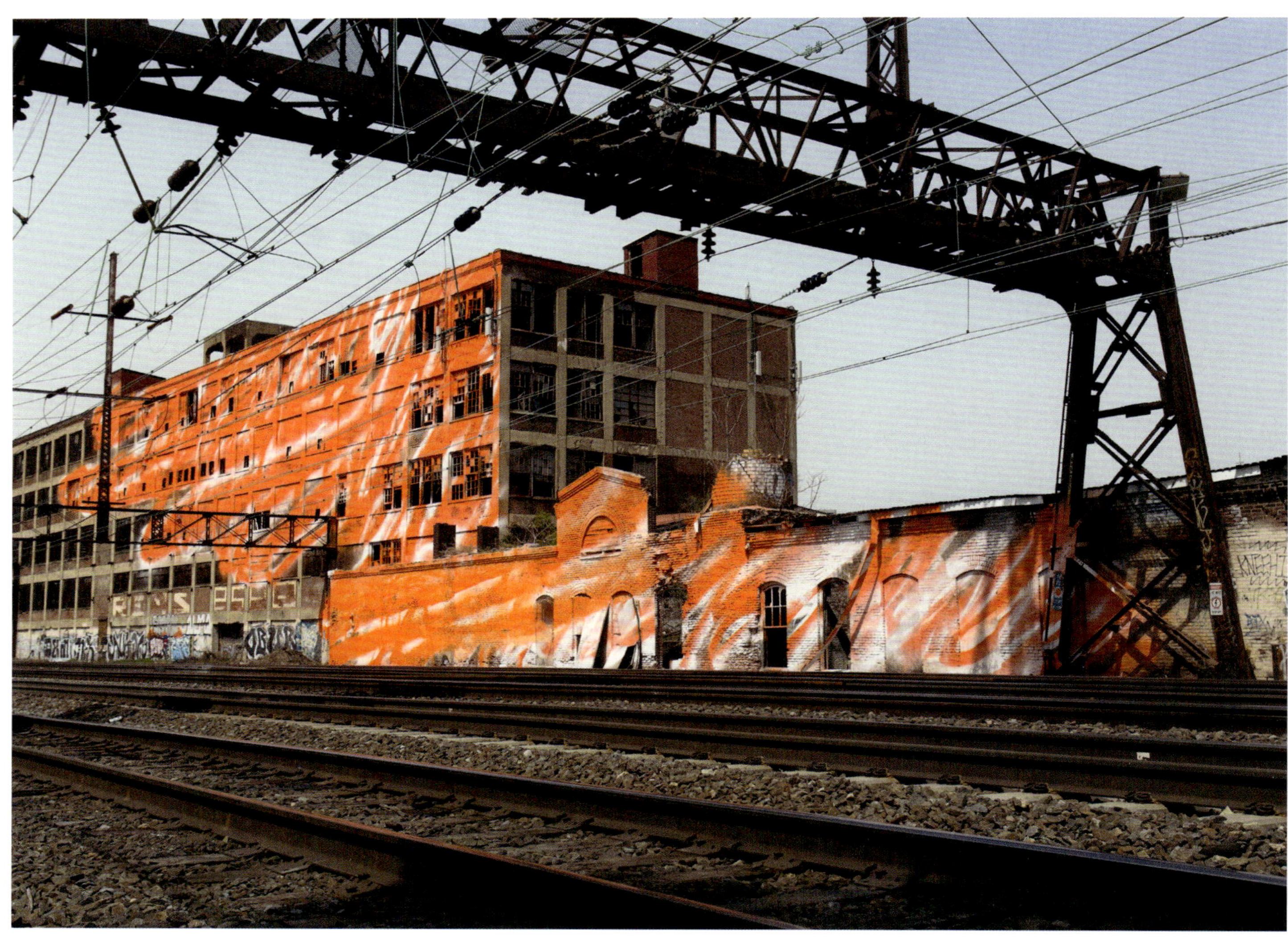

64. psychylustro – The Warehouse   2014
Along the tracks of Philadelphia's public transportation

Acrylic on various objects
2100 × 14,500 cm (826 × 5708 in)

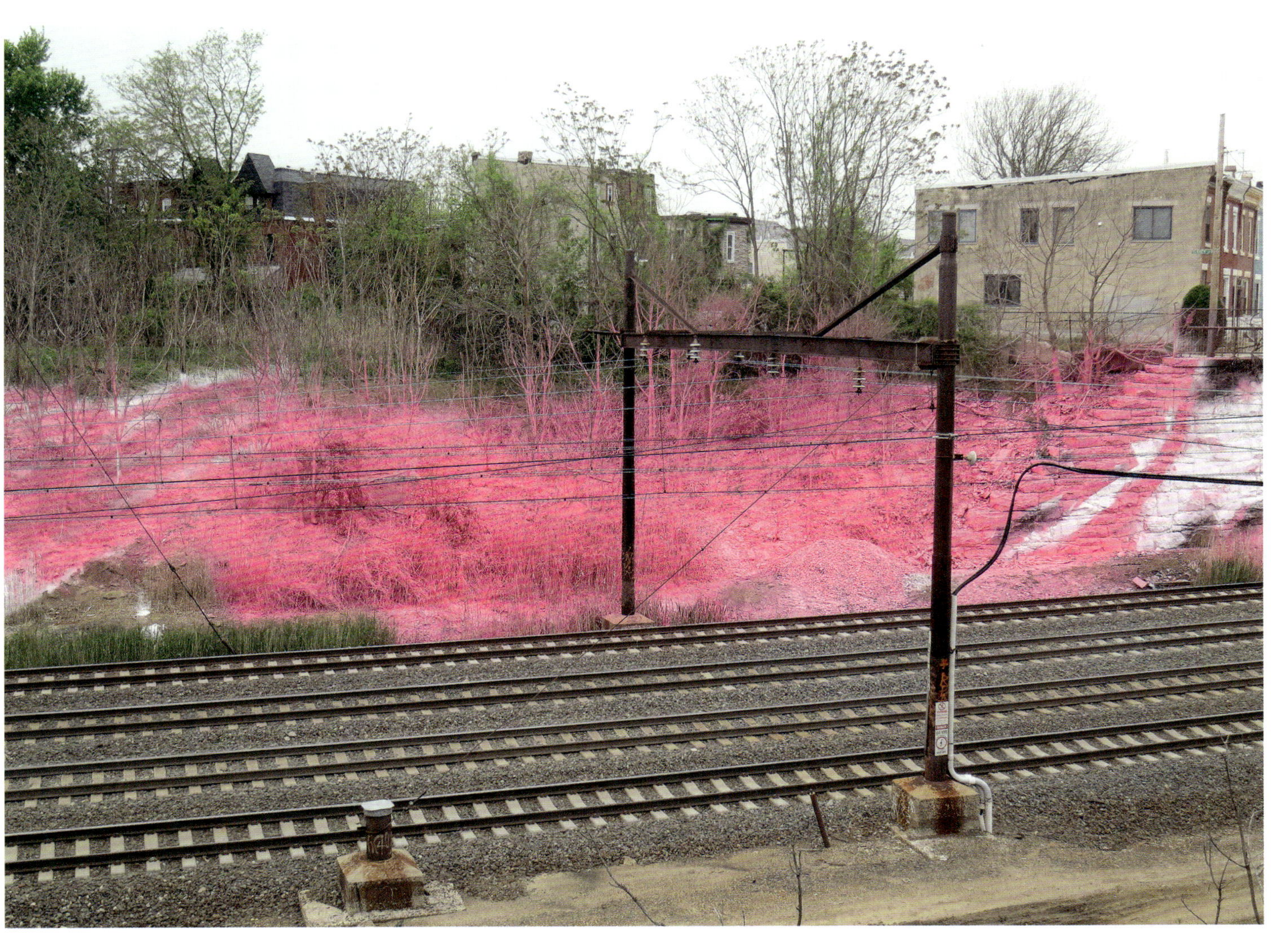

65. psychylustro – The Drama Wall   2014
Along the tracks of Philadelphia's public transportation

Acrylic on various objects
1250 × 10,000 × 450 cm (492 × 3937 × 177 in)

In 2017 for the ecologically minded ARoS Triennial entitled 'THE GARDEN
– End of Times; Beginning of Times' in Aarhus, Denmark, Grosse revisited this
approach: not a landscape painting but a painting made on the land. This resulted in
her most controversial outdoor painting to date, although she hardly intended it to
be so: a work that generated, according to her, an 'incredible shitstorm' in the media,
symposia, and on the streets having to do with 'the destruction of nature'. *Asphalt
Air and Hair* (2017) was an immense, streaky, pink-and-white acrylic painting on
the ground (fig.67). It stretched across a public beach, covered part of a pedestrian
path and bike lane, and angled up a hill toward the grounds of the Royal Garden –
coating trees, grass, and bushes along the way – and was only interrupted by a busy
highway. It was very carnivalesque, with its bright circus colors. It also oozed over the
landscape like a toxic spill. Granted, acrylic paint is hardly good for the environment
– yet whatever damage Grosse did pales in comparison to, say, five minutes of rush-
hour traffic on the highway and all those exhaust-spewing cars. Intense protest was
lodged against her and her artwork but not against the highway, which already mars
the landscape, and not against cars – or, indeed, against Denmark's substantial North
Sea oil production.

The earlier *Just Two of Us* (2013) really looked as if an abstract circus had
temporarily come to town in downtown Brooklyn (fig.66). It consisted of 17 large,
painted objects installed outdoors at the borough's MetroTech Commons, among rows
and rows of trees. These objects, made of glass-fiber-reinforced plastic and painted
with an array of vibrant colors, were real nature–culture hybrids, hinting at rock shards
and quartz chunks but also industrial detritus and architectural remnants – like the
pieces of a demolished bridge or building, some piled atop one another, others on
their own. From a distance this large cluster of weird, refulgent objects was completely
riveting. You could also move among the objects, wending your way through them,
absorbed with parts and details. Installed for one year, this work responded not just to
the physical site but also to the seasons, trees, and changing daylight. In summer when
the trees were full of leaves, when Grosse's work was enmeshed in green, it looked
completely different to how it did in winter, when the trees were bare and there was
snow. I don't think I've ever encountered an artwork more in dialogue with daily and
seasonal changes and with cycles of regeneration and decay.

Two outdoor works by Grosse, both on buildings and the surrounding land, were
in sites devastated by hurricanes (many scientists trace the severity of these storms to
global warming and rising sea levels). In 2005 Hurricane Katrina wreaked havoc on
New Orleans, and especially the predominantly African-American Lower Ninth Ward.
For the Prospect 1 Biennial in 2008, mounted at a time when much of the city was
still struggling to recover from the storm, Grosse spray-painted part of a Lower Ninth
Ward house bright orange and yellow and, for the first time, extended her painting
onto the ground, where it swept across the front lawn toward the street and covered
a rickety fence (*Untitled*, 2008) (fig.68). Grosse's work was carnivalesque – in a city

right and following spread

66. Just Two of Us   2013
MetroTech Commons, Brooklyn, New York

Acrylic on glass-fiber-reinforced plastic
441 × 2956 × 1058 cm (174 × 1164 × 417 in)

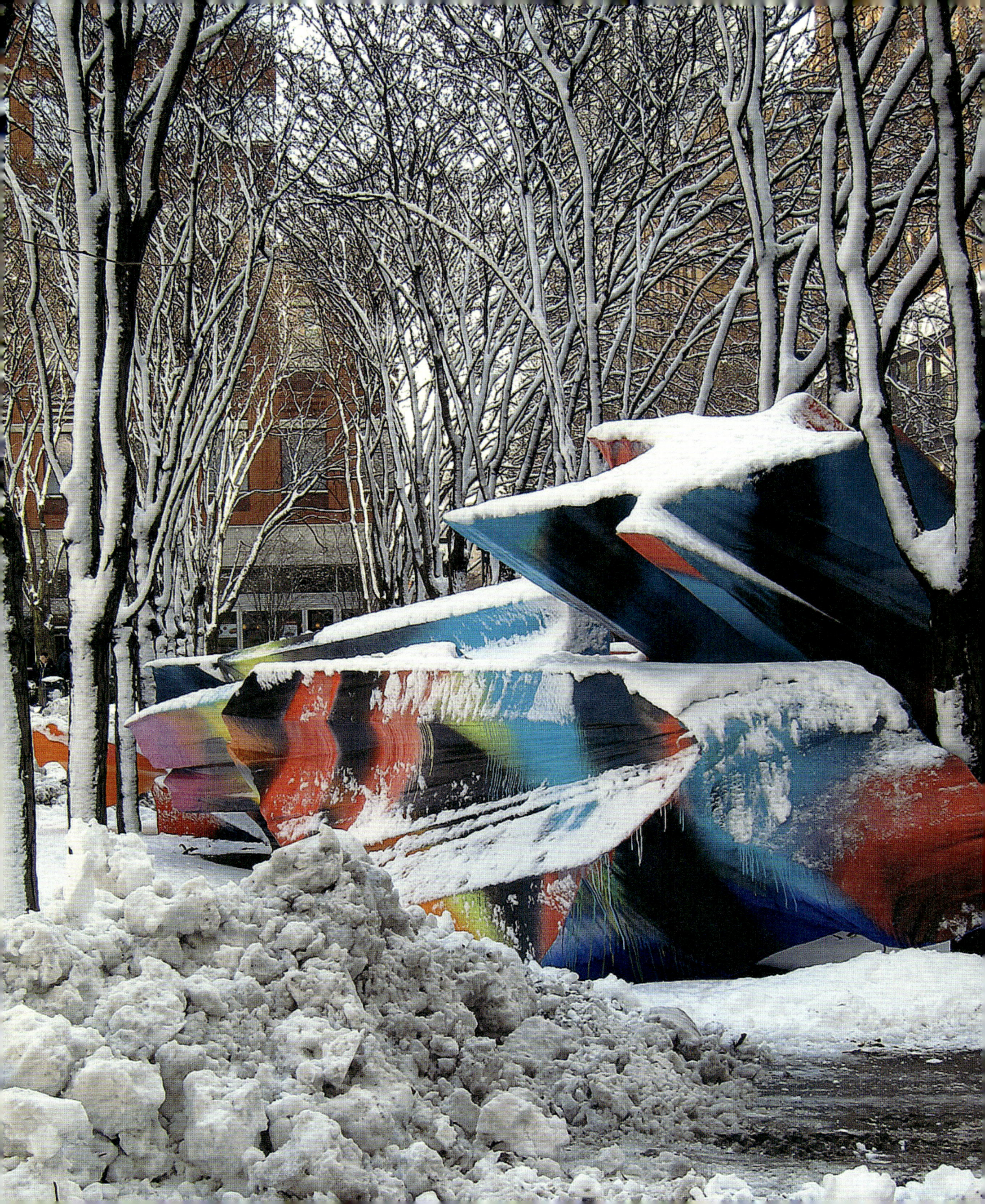

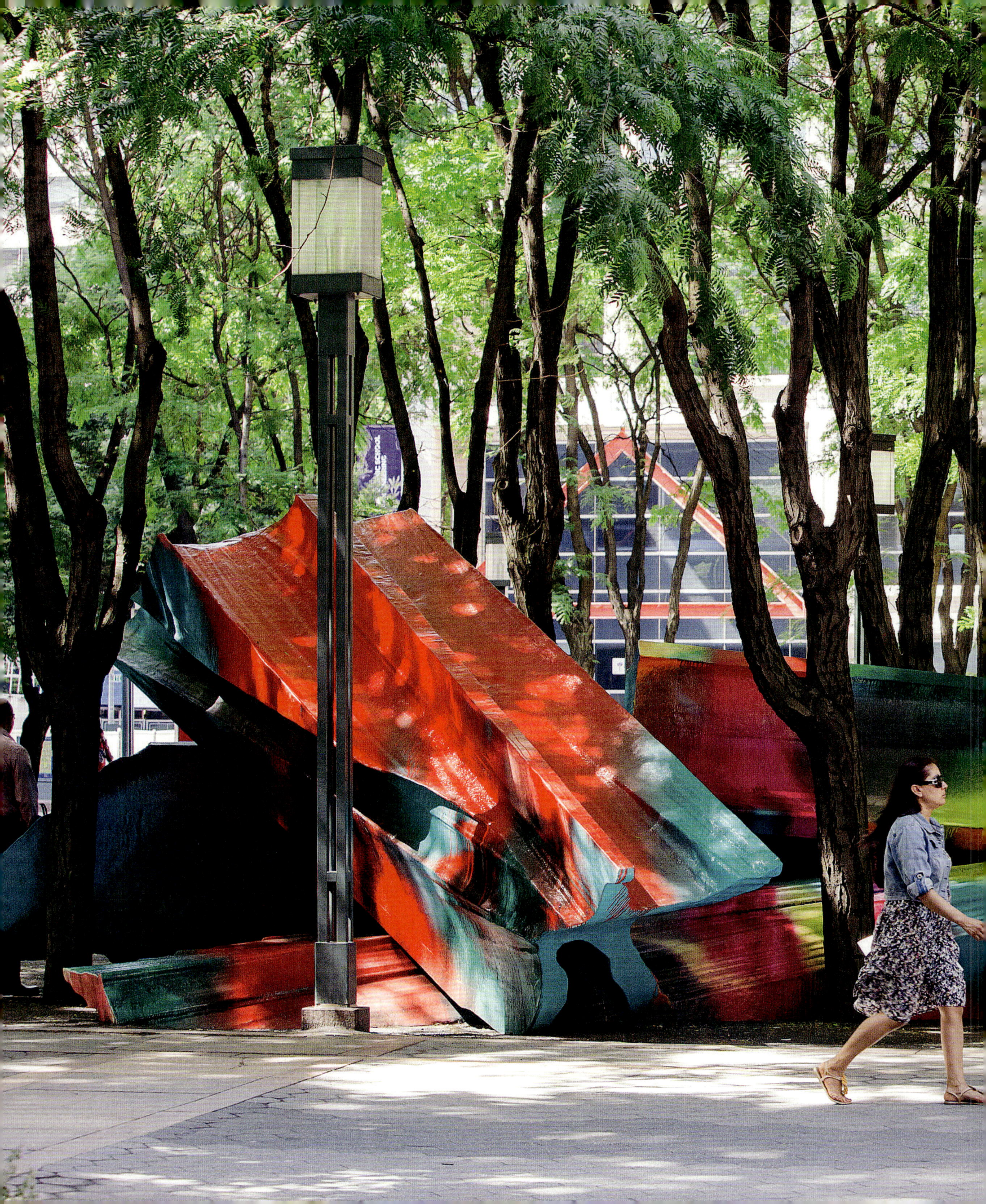

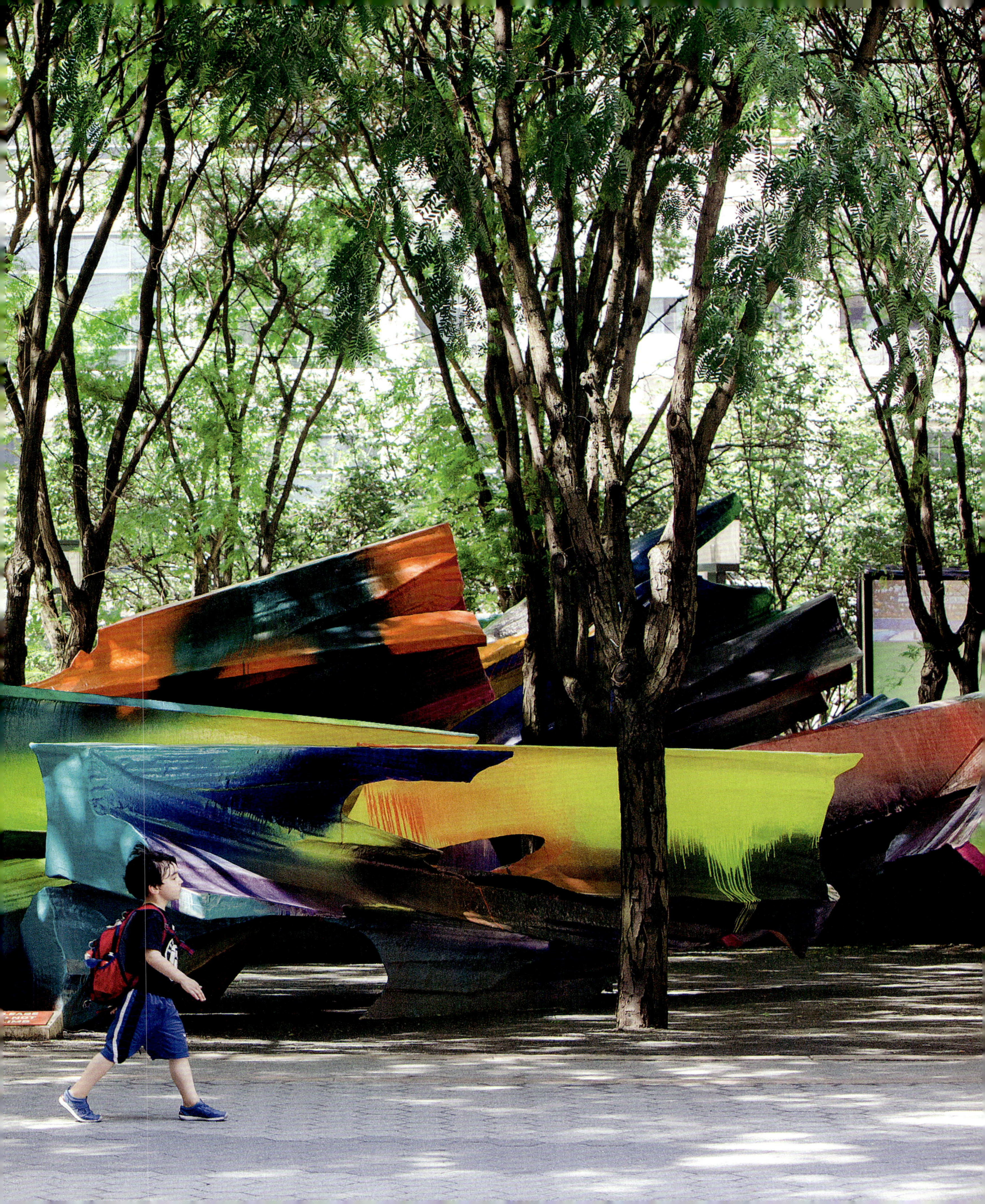

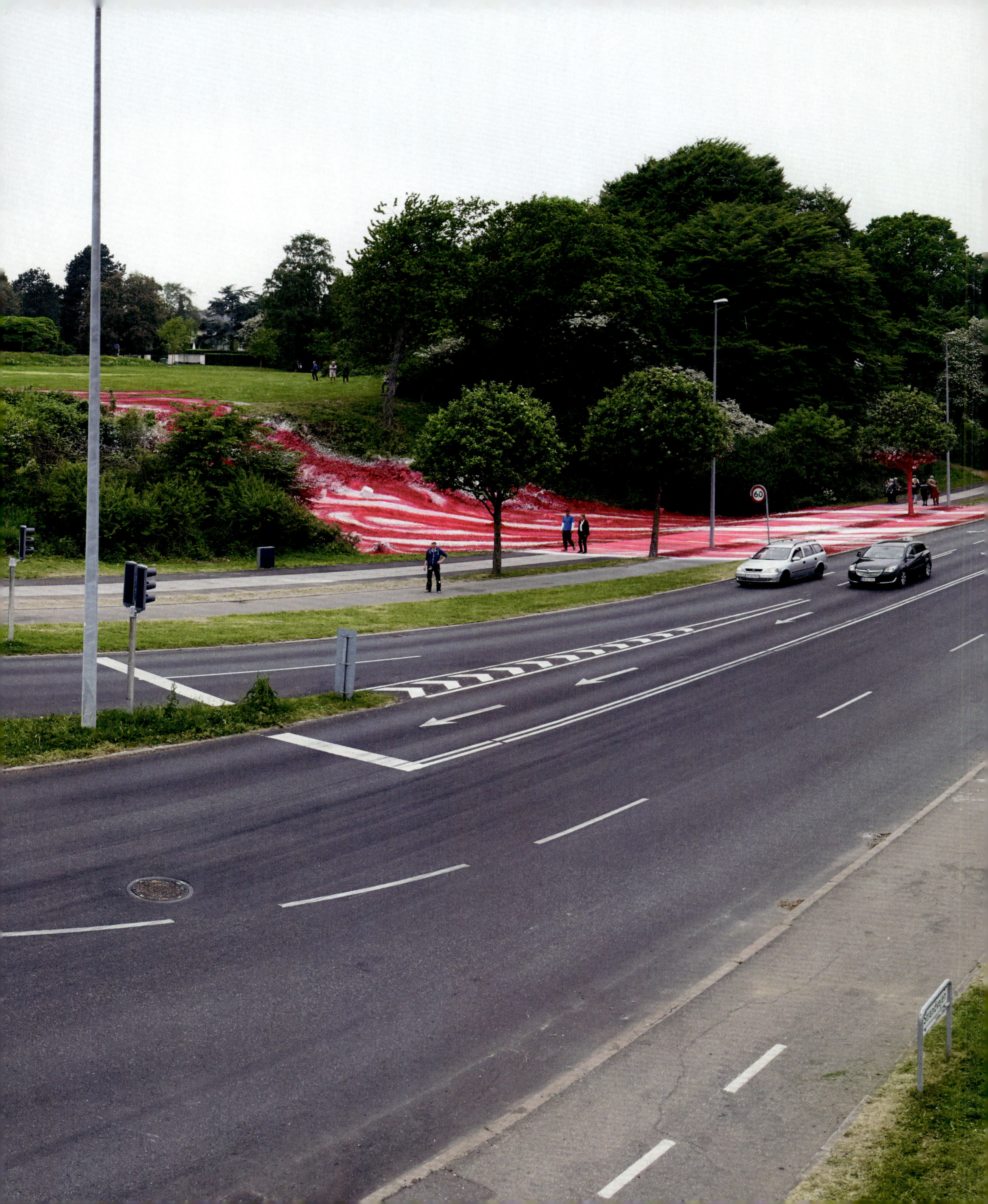

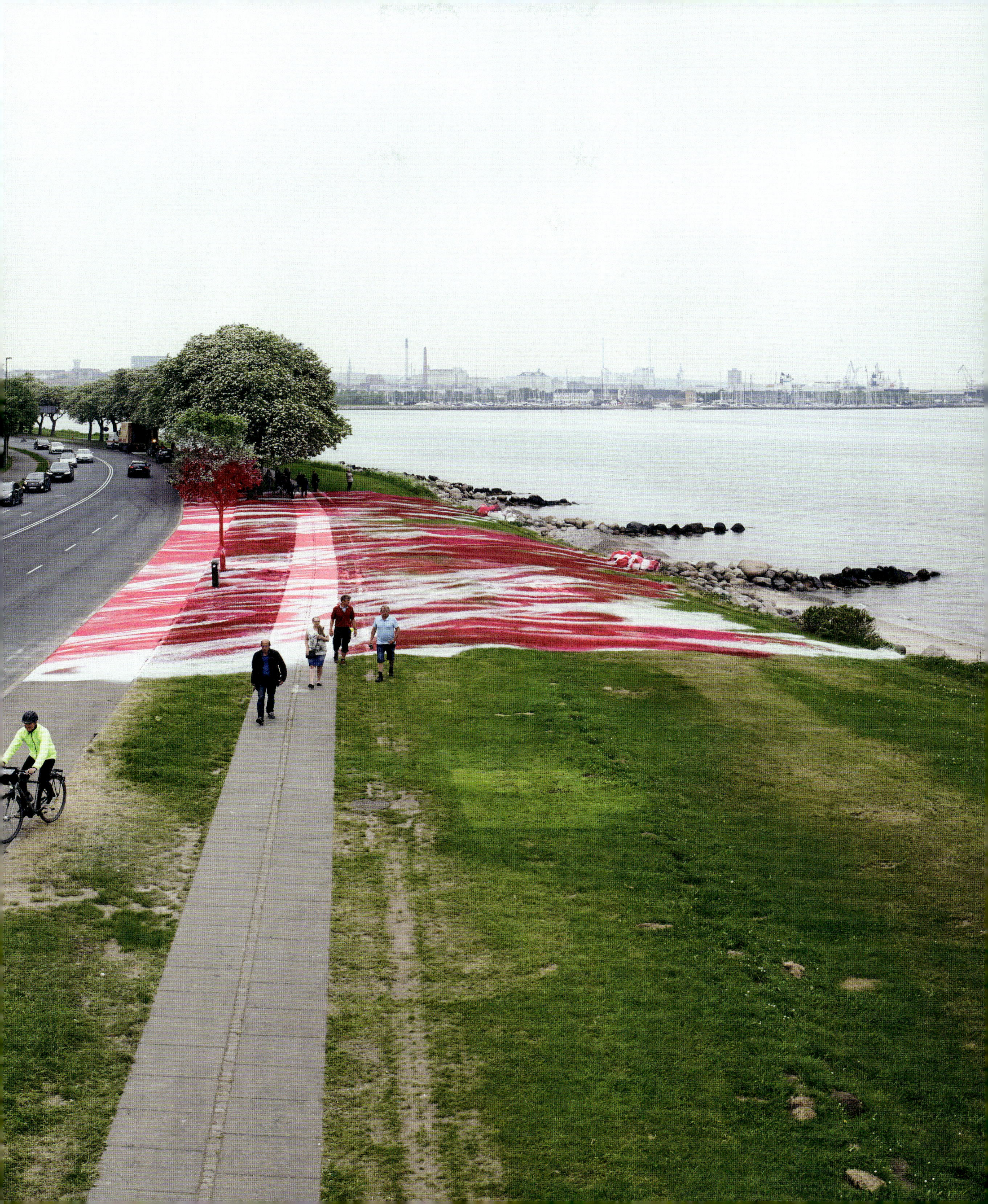

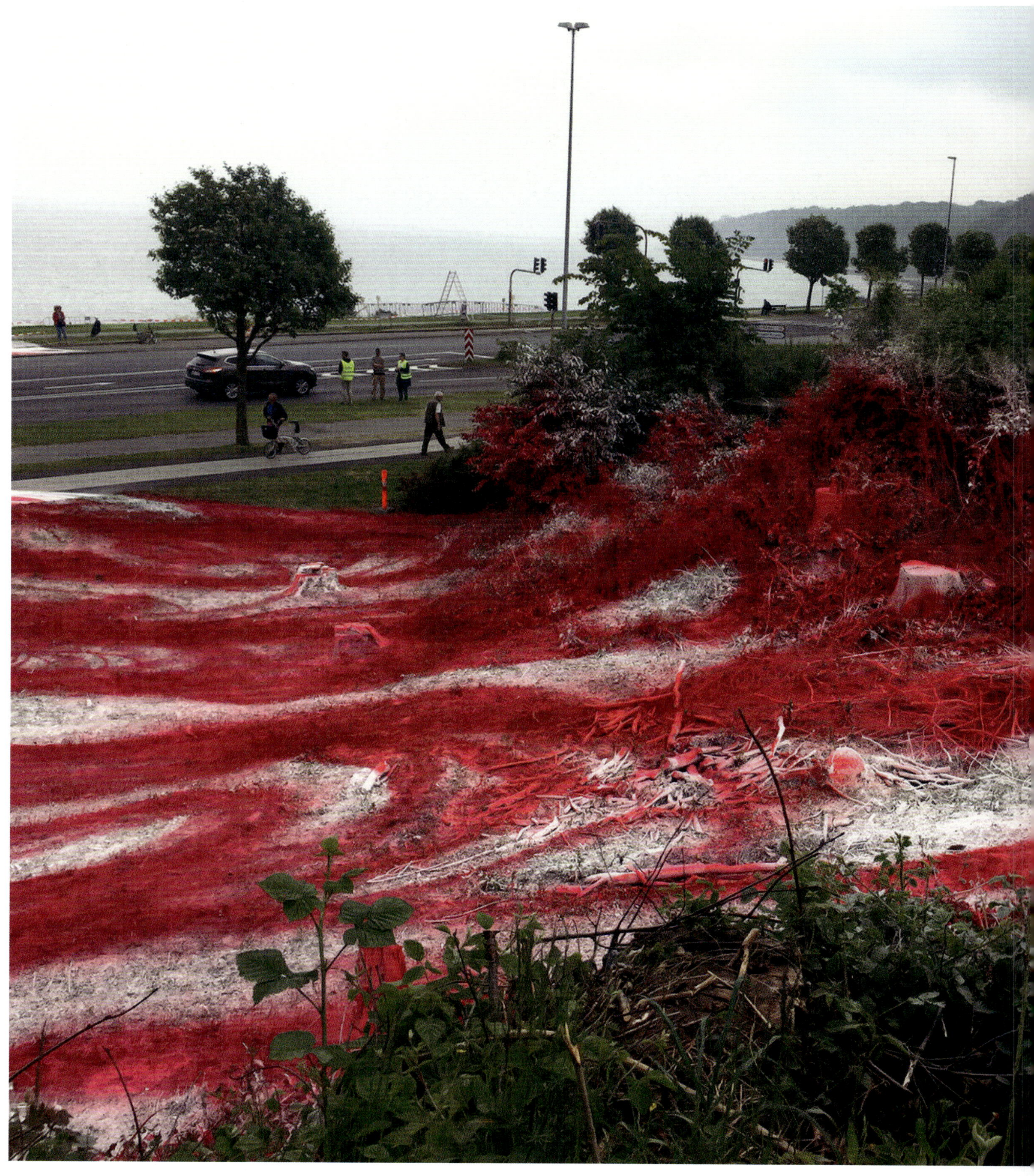

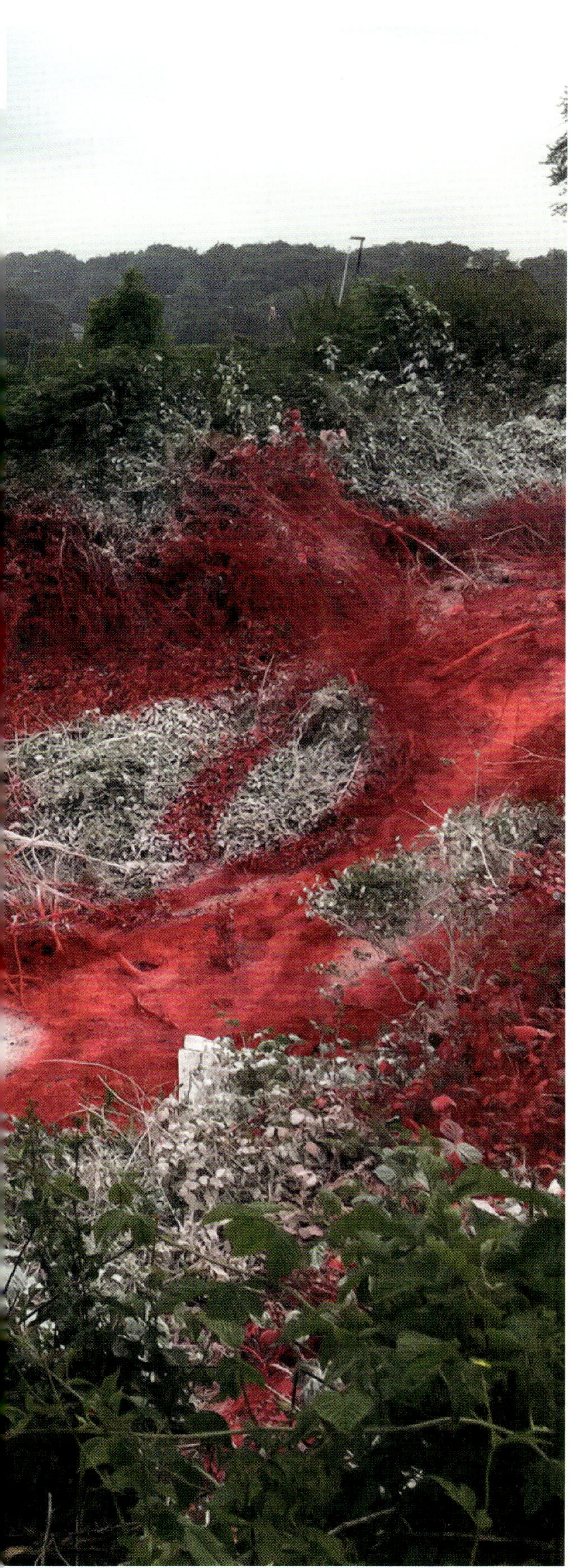

left and previous spread

67. Asphalt Air and Hair   2017
ARoS Triennial, Aarhus

Acrylic on grass, trees, breakwaters, and sidewalks
1200 × 5700 × 10,800 cm (472 × 2244 × 4252 in)

with a rich tradition of 'second line' brass band parades[17] in which performers and participants often wear brilliant colored clothing and costumes – and also profoundly disturbing, evoking gale-force winds, floodwaters, and inundating rain.

In 2012 Hurricane Sandy barreled into New York City with catastrophic damage. Grosse's painting installation *Rockaway* (2016) was installed in, on, and around a largely ruined military building at Fort Tilden in the Gateway National Recreation Area on the Rockaway Peninsula in Queens, the part of New York hardest hit by

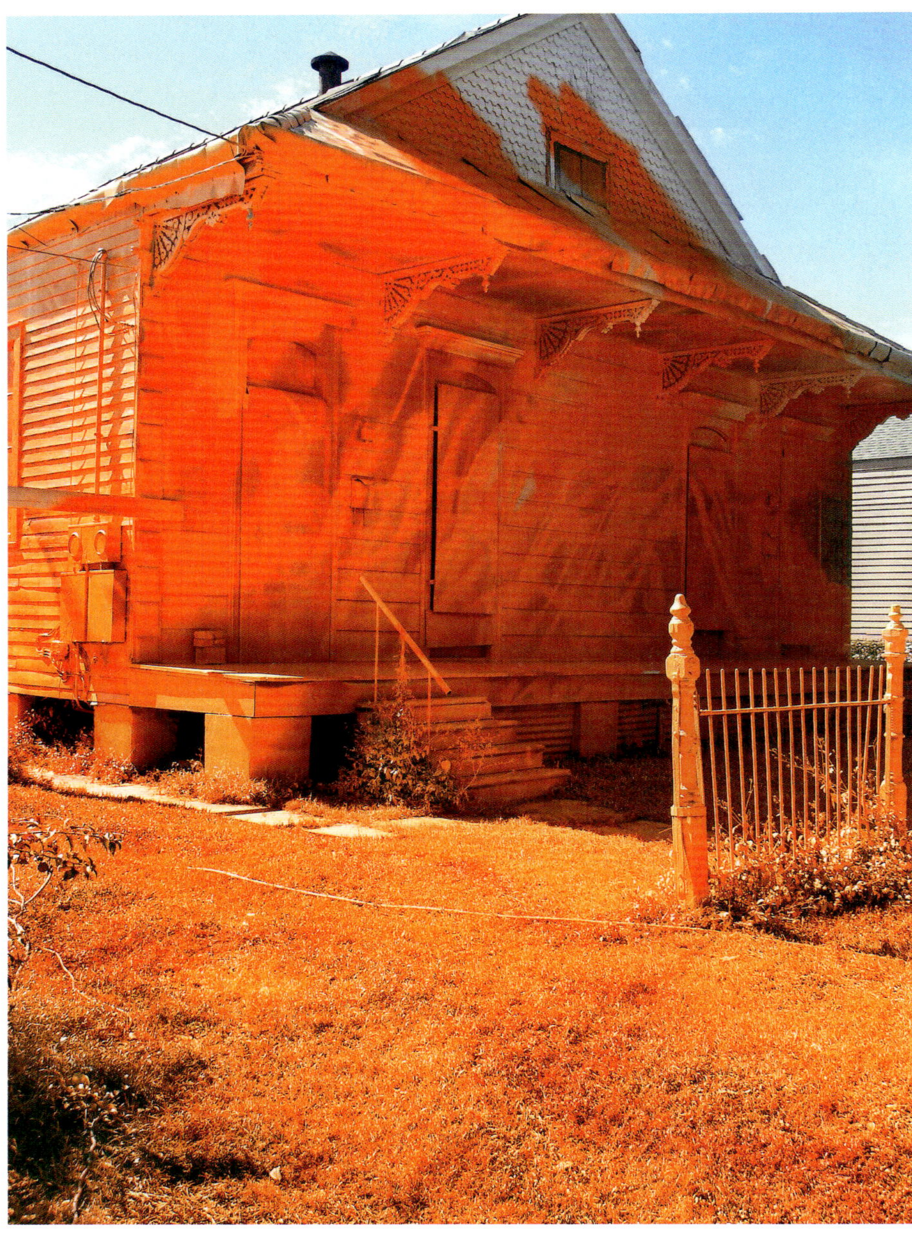

68. Untitled   2008
Prospect 1, New Orleans

Acrylic on various objects
750 × 1200 × 500 cm (295 × 472 × 197 in)

the storm (fig.69). Her project was part of MoMA PS1's ongoing summer series of public-art projects in the Rockaways, meant to celebrate the resurgence of the area in the aftermath of Sandy. Part-time Rockaway resident Klaus Biesenbach – then director of MoMA PS1 and chief curator-at-large at New York's Museum of Modern Art (MoMA), and now director of the Museum of Contemporary Art, Los Angeles (MOCA) – was the curator. What attracted Grosse to this particular site was the way in which 'various histories intertwined, such as the national park, military barracks, the community of the Rockaways, and Hurricane Sandy's traces'.

The structure was a former aquatics building for soldiers stationed at Fort Tilden and their families. Built in 1917, the fort has fallen into disrepair since it was decommissioned in 1974 and absorbed into the Gateway National Recreation Area. Hurricane Sandy walloped the aquatics center, leaving it structurally unsound (it has since been demolished). Grosse revitalized this derelict building on the border between ocean and land – a stark reminder of both Sandy's destruction and the threat of climate change looming over New York City.

With acrylic paint, Grosse transformed this windowless, doorless, damaged shell of a building into a captivating artwork that involved a profound engagement with nature. Its facade, roof, and interior displayed broad streaks; curving shapes; and swirls in red, bright white, and magenta. These colors spread outside across the sand, evoking windswept sand and ocean spray; abundant white forms evoked clouds, whitecaps, and churning sea foam. Especially when viewed from the shore, this work seemed like an abstracted version of a Rockaway sunset – as if Grosse had transmuted the aerial splendor out there above the ocean into a painting right here on the land and the shore. Her installation also suggested waves crashing ashore and lashing at buildings, even the tumultuous waves from Sandy that caused so much damage.

As you took in Grosse's transformative colors from the inside you were always aware of the outside, visible through the many openings where windows and doors had once been: the vast Atlantic, the immense sky, the stretching beach, coastal foliage. This was a flowing exchange between the art and its environment, also between the human and natural worlds. While Grosse spray-painted much of the building she left some parts as they were – including graffiti, evident damage, sections of bare wall, various scraps and tatters, and accumulated branches and leaves. The effect was a dialogue between freshness and oldness, rejuvenation and entropy.

Grosse's painting connected with the yearning for nature and the sea that first brought urban visitors en masse to this once-remote area long ago, and with the dangers of the sea and extreme weather in this time of climate change. It connected as well with the rollicking resort-and-entertainment culture that has flourished in the Rockaways for many years, including amusement parks,[18] hotels, and boardwalk enticements. Grosse's painting installation was a twenty-first-century, sublime, nature-based artwork. It also functioned as garish and alluring seaside attraction, one with a great deal of carnival flair.

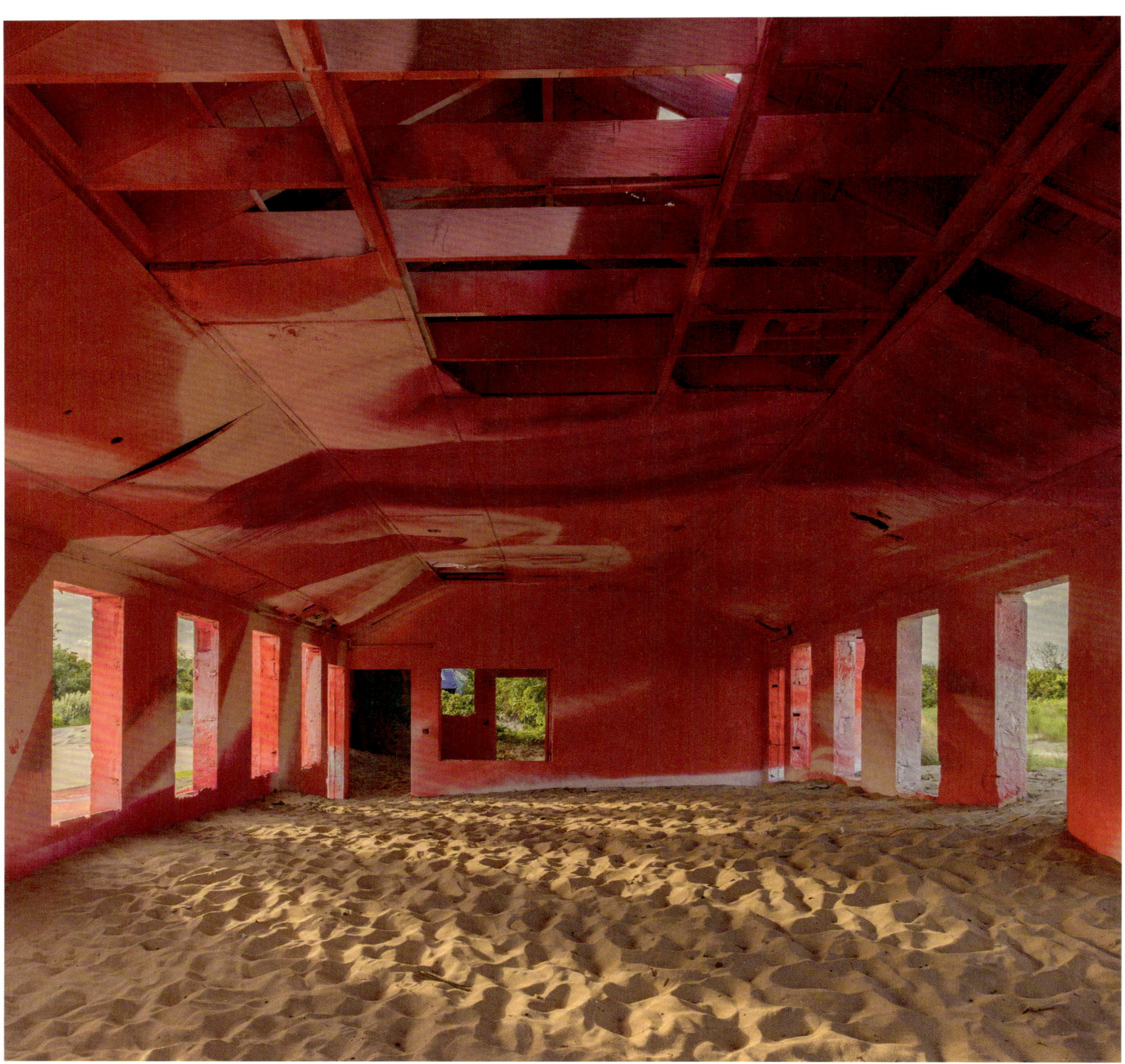

above and right

69. Rockaway   2016
Rockaway! at the Gateway National
Recreation Area at Fort Tilden, New York

Acrylic on various objects
600 × 1500 × 3500 cm (236 × 591 × 1378 in)

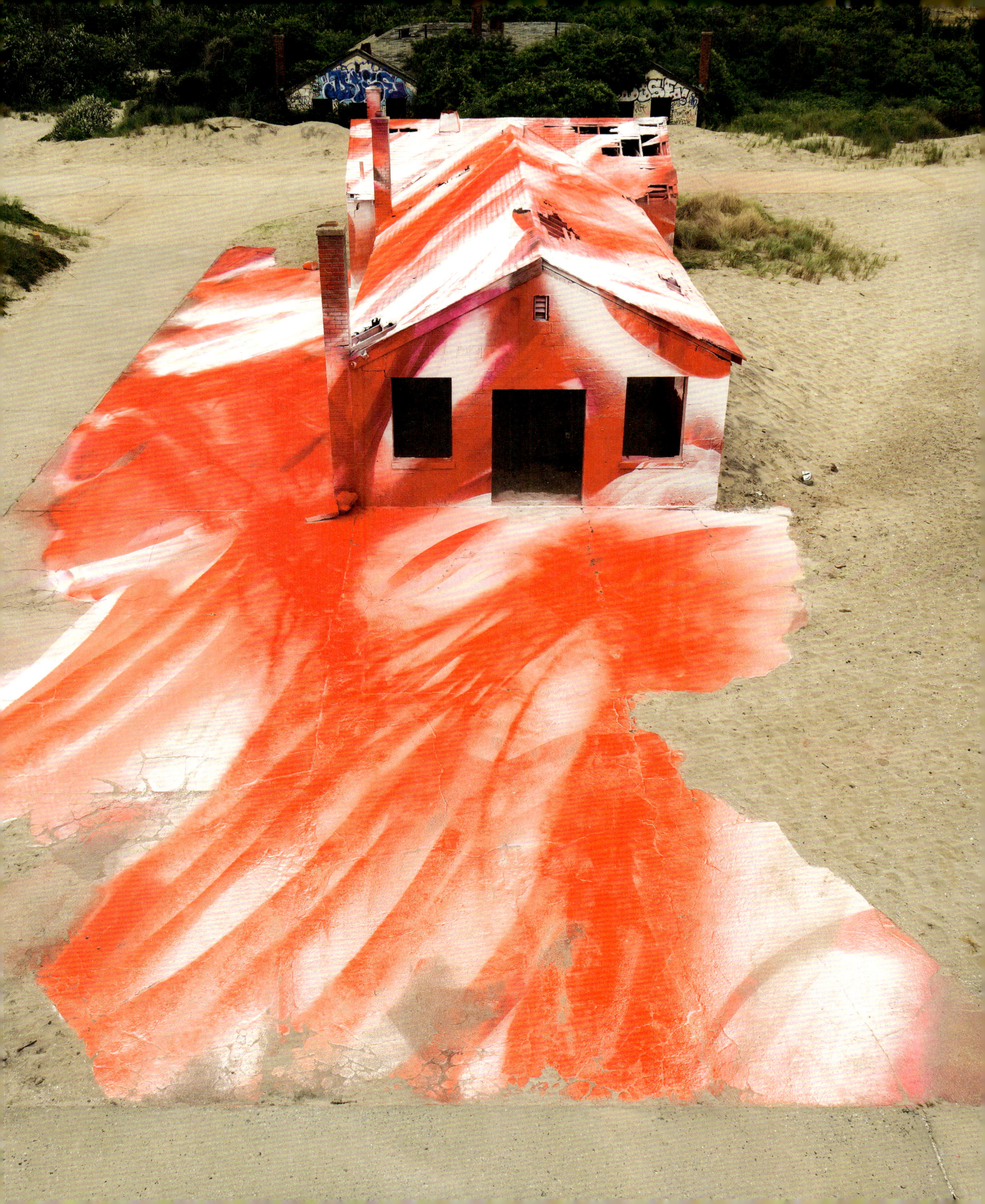

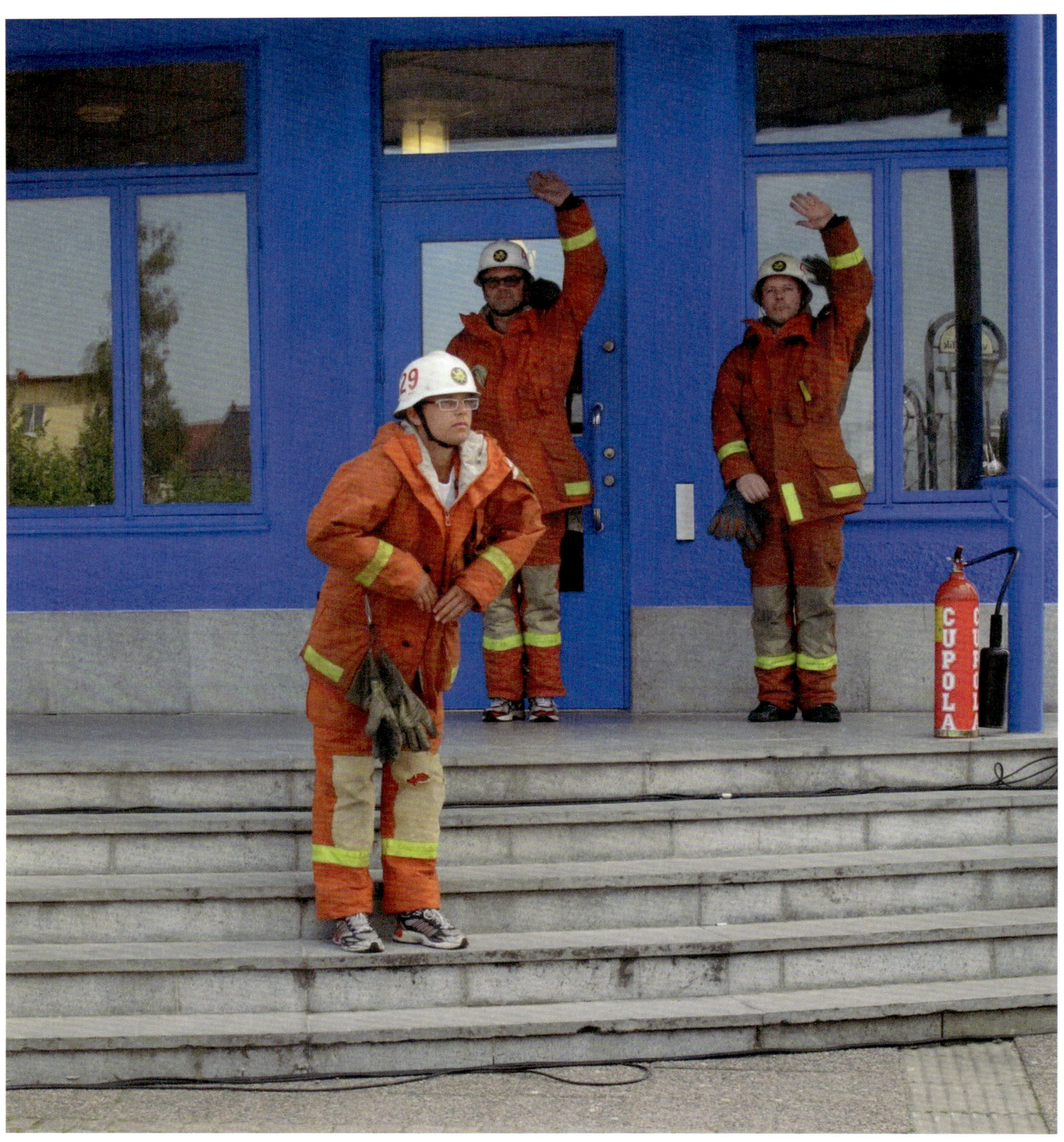

70. Perfomance organised by local firefighters during the inauguration of *The Blue Orange*, 2012.

5   Conclusion

By the final day of my May 2018 meetings with Katharina Grosse in her Berlin studio, we had covered a great deal of territory. But as we were combing through archives, we came across a bright-blue building in Vara, Sweden, a work that I had previously not known.

Vara (incidentally, the verb *vara* means 'to be' in Swedish) is a town of about 4000 inhabitants between Stockholm and Gothenburg. Like many provinical towns it has long been experiencing 'brain drain', with young people leaving for the big city, and needed new cultural attractions to keep young people interested. It had had some success with a concert hall and theater and an additional possibility was the refurbishment of the town's shabby train station. Katharina Grosse was selected as the artist for the job.

For *The Blue Orange* (2012), Grosse instructed that the station be painted a glowing and lustrous blue and that its roof be fitted with special blue tiles (fig.71). She also installed chunky, multicolored sculptures, made of glass-fiber-reinforced plastic and acrylic paint, on the roof, facade and in a nearby park. These sculptures look somewhat like rocks, and also like minerals and crystals, but even more as if resplendent meteorites had fallen from the sky and had stuck, inexplicably and precariously, to just this one building. Grosse wanted to highlight this structure and make it special: to celebrate it as a threshold, as the transitional place where people arrive and depart from the town. She made an excessive, carnivalized version of a building otherwise so familiar and quotidian that most people would have hardly given it a second thought.

Some people in the town were initially furious. An alien artist from faraway Germany had been invited – at taxpayer expense – to not only intervene in but also to disturb, and very possibly ridicule, their little town by making its train station freakish. This opposition would change, over time. Grosse's work would be cherished by many, in part because it put small Vara on a very big cultural map.

At the opening, instead of official speeches Grosse invited townspeople to perform. The fire brigade danced on the train station's roof. A train arrived; people got out and started singing. A little ice cream shop made special blue ice cream and handed it out for free. A bakery made blue muffins. Ropes across the street displayed paintings children had made. One person had composed a pop song about a blue house, and high schoolers performed modern dance to it. There was a podium from which somebody delivered a mock speech, like a mock mayor. A boom lift took dancers and performers up and down. The opening turned into an energetic festival, an ad hoc carnival of sorts.

This joyful and surprising blue building – with its eccentric, multicolored sculptures – is emblematic of the vision and spirit that Katharina Grosse brings to her art and, really, of how far she has propelled what painting is, and can be.

71. The Blue Orange,   2012

Vara train station

Acrylic on wall and glass-fiber-reinforced plastic
1140 × 1295 × 2070 cm (449 × 510 × 815 in)

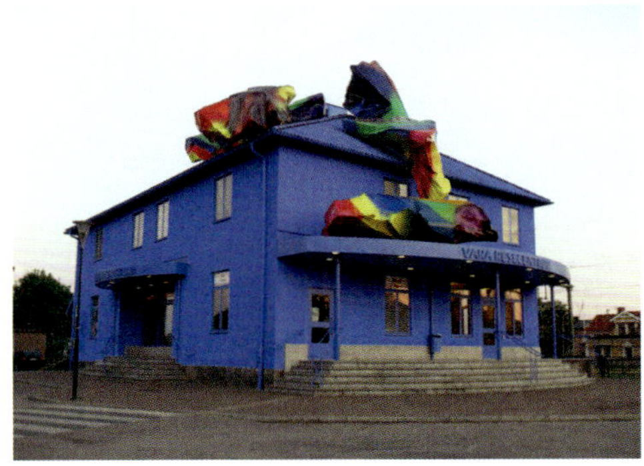

"""

Notes

1. Emily Dickinson Archive, http://archive. emilydickinson.org/correspondence/holland/ l318.html
2. Linda Simon, *The Greatest Shows on Earth: A History of the Circus*, Reaktion Books, London, 2014, p.101.
3. All quotes, unless otherwise noted, are from a series of interviews I conducted with Katharina Grosse in her Berlin studio between 26 and 30 May 2018.
4. Bruce Glaser, 'Questions to Stella and Judd', *ARTnews*, September 1966, pp 58–9.
5. Sigmund Freud, 'Notiz Über den »Wunderblock«' (A Note Upon the 'Mystic Writing Pad'), https://www.academia. edu/8876579/A_Note_Upon_the_Mystic_ Writing_Pad_Freud_1925_
6. *Katharina Grosse – This Drove my Mother up the Wall*, South London Gallery, London, UK, 2017. https://www.southlondongallery.org/ exhibitions/katharina-grosse
7. All quotes from and references to Mikhail Bakhtin are from his *Problems of Dostoevsky's Poetics*, edited and translated by Caryl Emerson, University of Minnesota Press, Minneapolis, MN, 1984, pp 122–4.
8. Andrew Blum, 'ART/ARCHITECTURE; The White Zone is for Loading and Unloading Art', *New York Times*, 28 March 2004.
9. Katharina Grosse note to the author, 27 June 2019.
10. Roman Kurzmeyer, 'Reflexive', *Parkett* 74, 2005, pp 144–5.
11. 'Katharina Grosse with Phong Bui', *Brooklyn Rail*, March 2017.
12. 'Katharina Grosse and Lotta Mossum about The Blue Orange in Vara', National Public Art Council and Vara Municipality, Sweden, 25 May 2012. www.katharinagrosse.com/ blog/katharina_grosse_and_lotta_mossum_ about_the_blue_orange_in_vara
13. Katharina Grosse, 'C.T.S.T. Katharina Grosse reflects on the work of Cy Twombly', *Gagosian Quarterly*, Spring 2017, https:// gagosian.com/quarterly/2017/02/23/ctst
14. Katharina Grosse in conversation with Lothar Frangenberg, 'diskurs. Ein Interview mit Katharina Grosse zu raumbezogenen Sprayarbeiten ihrer letzten Ausstellungen', conducted on 5 October 2004 in her studio in Düsseldorf, quoted and translated in Ulrich Loock et al., (eds), *Katharina Grosse*, Verlag der Buchhandlung Walter König, Cologne, 2013, pp 325–6.
15. For a more detailed exploration of the connections between Katharina Grosse and Land Art, see Philipp Kaiser, 'Expansive Formations', in *Katharina Grosse: Inside the Speaker*, exh.cat., Museum Kunstpalast, Düsseldorf, 2014/2015, pp 73–7.
16. Jane Bennett, *Vibrant Matter: A Political Ecology of Things*, Duke University Press, Durham, NC, 2010.
17. 'Second line' brass band parades are a distinctive New Orleans tradition traced back to nineteenth-century African-American neighborhood organizations, fraternal societies, and funeral processions.
18. The famous Rockaways' Playland – which opened, under a different name, in 1902 (although some sources say 1901 or 1903) and thrived for decades before it ceased operations in 1985 – officially closed in 1987 and was torn down, eventually making way for condominiums.

Select Bibliography

The two primary sources for my text are 25 years of personal experience with Katharina Grosse's art and also with her, and the extremely valuable daily interviews that I conducted with her in her Berlin studio, 26–30 May 2018.

There is voluminous information on Grosse, or relating to her, in catalogues, books, articles, and videos – far too much to cite here. Below is a selection of texts and videos that I found especially helpful and insightful.

Ackermann, Marion, 'Cool Puppen: On Katharina Grosse's Wall Pieces' in, *Katharina Grosse: Cool Puppen*, exh.cat., Ikon Gallery, Birmingham; Städtische Galerie im Lenbachhaus und Kunstbau, Munich; Kunstmuseum St. Gallen; Kunsthalle zu Kiel, Kiel, 2002

Bakhtin, Mikhail, *Problems of Dostoevsky's Poetics*, edited and translated by Caryl Emerson, University of Minnesota Press, Minneapolis, MN, 1984

Bennett, Jane, *Vibrant Matter: A Political Ecology of Things*, Duke University Press, Durham, NC, 2010

Böddeker, Steffen, 'In Marfa' in, Stefan Böddeker, Roman Kurzmeyer, Judy Millar, Angela Schneider, Beat Wismer, and Katharina Grosse, *Katharina Grosse: Location, Location, Location*, Richter Verlag, Düsseldorf, 2002

Brandlhuber, Arno and Katharina Grosse, 'Do You Think Architecture Is . . .' in, *Katharina Grosse: Another Man Who Has Dropped His Paintbrush*, exh.cat., Galleria Civica di Modena, Modena, 2009

Budak, Adam, 'Production of Miracles. Notes On and Around Katharina Grosse's WUNDERBILD' in, *Katharina Grosse: Wunderbild*, exh.cat, National Gallery Prague, Prague, 2018

Burkard, Lene, 'Double Floor Painting' in, *Katharina Grosse: Double Floor Painting*, exh.cat., Kunsthallen Brandts Klædefabrik, Odense, 2004

Cameron, Dan, 'Cascades of Discontinuity' in, *Katharina Grosse*, monograph, edited by Gagosian. Contributions by Dan Cameron, Okwui Enwezor, and Louise Neri. Conversation with Katharina Grosse by Isabelle Graw. Gagosian, New York, 2018

Craft, Catherine, 'Setting the Surface Free' in, *Katharina Grosse: Wunderblock*, exh.cat., Nasher Sculpture Center, Dallas, TX, 2013

Ebony, David, 'Chromatic Theater', *Art in America*, September 2011, pp 96–103

Enwezor, Okwui, 'Katharina Grosse's Festival of Form' in, *Katharina Grosse*, monograph, edited by Gagosian. Contributions by Dan Cameron, Okwui Enwezor, and Louise Neri. Conversation with Katharina Grosse by Isabelle Graw. Gagosian, New York, 2018

Farronato, Milovan, 'Wherever You Are' in, *Katharina Grosse: Another Man Who Has Dropped His Paintbrush*, exh.cat., Galleria Civica di Modena, Modena, 2009

'How to Stop and Start Painting: Jonathan Watkins and Katharina Grosse in Conversation' in, *Katharina Grosse: Cool Puppen*, exh.cat, Ikon Gallery, Birmingham; Städtische Galerie im Lenbachhaus und Kunstbau, Munich; Kunstmuseum St. Gallen; Kunsthalle zu Kiel, Kiel, 2002

Kaiser, Philipp, 'Expansive Formations' in, *Katharina Grosse: Inside the Speaker*, exh.cat., Museum Kunstpalast, Düsseldorf, 2014–15

Katharina Grosse: Shadowbox, exh.cat., texts by Laura Bieger, Katja Blomberg, Uta Degner, Antje Dietze, Alexander Koch, and Gerd G. Kopper, Temporäre Kunsthalle Berlin, Berlin, 2009

'Katharina Grosse and Lotta Mossum about *The Blue Orange* in Vara', National Public Art Council and Vara Municipality, Sweden, 25 May 2012 www.katharinagrosse.com/blog/katharina_grosse_and_lotta_mossum_about_the_blue_orange_in_vara

Katharina Grosse: Sieben Stunden, Acht Stimmen, Drei Bäume / Seven Hours, Eight Voices, Three Trees, exh.cat., texts by Sally McGrane, Jörg Daur, Alexander Klar, Annika Reich, Teresa Präauer, Monika Rinck, Ann Cotton, Dustin Breitenwischer, Museum Wiesbaden, Wiesbaden, 2015

Katharina Grosse: This Drove my Mother up the Wall, South London Gallery, London, 2017, https://www.southlondongallery.org/exhibitions/katharina-grosse

'Katharina Grosse with Phong Bui', *Brooklyn Rail*, March 2017

Katharina Grosse, monograph, edited by Gagosian. Contributions by Dan Cameron, Okwui Enwezor, and Louise Neri. Conversation with Katharina Grosse by Isabelle Graw. Gagosian, New York, 2018

'Katharina Grosse Full Interview', video in conjunction with Grosse's exhibition *The Horse Trotted Another Couple of Metres, Then It Stopped*, Carriageworks, Sydney, 2 April 2018, https://carriageworks.com.au/journal/katharina-grosse-full-interview/

Katharina Grosse: Mumbling Mud, exhibition booklet chi K11 art museum, Shanghai, introductory texts by Venus Lau and Ulrich Loock, conversation between Katharina Grosse, Venus Lau and Ulrich Loock, Shanghai, 2018

Katharina Grosse – Gotthard Graubner. Farbe Absolut – Absolute Color, exh.cat., contribution by Eva Schmidt, interview with Katharina Grosse by Corinne Diserens; MKM Museum Küppersmühle für Moderne Kunst, Duisburg, Cologne, 2019

Katharina Grosse: Knot Book, exh.cat., contributions by Stephen Gilchrist, Kelly McDonald, Katharina Grosse, interviews by Katharina Grosse with Beatrice Gralton, Hayden Fowler, Hans Grosse, Craig Hull, Kelly McDonald, Elisabeth Schuhmann, Glenn Thompson, Romin Walter; Carriageworks, Sydney, 2020.

Kurzmeyer, Roman, 'Reflexive', *Parkett* 74, 2005, pp 140–6

Lebovici, Elisabeth, 'Katharina Grosse. A Stairway to Excess' in, *Katharina Grosse: Wunderbild*, exh.cat, National Gallery Prague, Prague, 2018

Loock, Ulrich, (various texts) in, Ulrich Loock, Annika Reich, and Katharina Grosse (eds), *Katharina Grosse*, Verlag der Buchhandlung Walther König, Cologne, 2013

Loock, Ulrich, 'Invisibility. On Katharina Grosse's WUNDERBILD' in, *Katharina Grosse: Wunderbild*, exh.cat, National Gallery in Prague, Prague, 2018

Millar, Judy, 'Location, Location, Location' in, Stefan Böddeker, Roman Kurzmeyer, Judy Millar, Angela Schneider, Beat Wismer, and Katharina Grosse, *Katharina Grosse: Location, Location, Location*, Richter Verlag, Düsseldorf, 2002

Mouffe, Chantal, 'An Agonistic Conception of the Museum' in, *Katharina Grosse: Wunderbild*, exh. cat, National Gallery Prague, Prague, 2018

Nanoru, Michael, 'Highlights: The Sound and Vision of Katharina Grosse' in, *Katharina Grosse: Wunderbild*, exh.cat, National Gallery in Prague, Prague, 2018

'On Painting: Katharina Grosse in Conversation with Isabelle Graw' in, *Katharina Grosse*, monograph, edited by Gagosian. Contributions by Dan Cameron, Okwui Enwezor, and Louise Neri. Conversation with Katharina Grosse by Isabelle Graw. Gagosian, New York, 2018

Biography

'Public Art Funds Talks at The New School',
The New School and The Public Art Fund,
New York, 19 May 2014, https://www.
katharinagrosse.com/blog/public_art_fund_
talks_at_the_new_school_katharina_grosse_
the_new_school

Simon, Linda, *The Greatest Shows on Earth*,
Reaktion Books, London, 2014

'Under the influence: Katharina Grosse,
Sarah Sze, and Hans Ulrich Obrist', Art
Basel *Artists Talks/Artists' Influencers*, 16
June 2018, https://www.youtube.com/
watch?v=TEi6FmUJoPM&feature=youtu.be

Vettese, Angela, 'Another Man Who Has
Dropped His Paintbrush' in, *Katharina Grosse:
Another Man Who Has Dropped His Paintbrush*,
exh.cat., Galleria Civica di Modena, Modena,
2009

Wäspe, Roland, 'Der Weisse Saal Trifft Sich im
Wald' in, *Katharina Grosse: Cool Puppen*, exh.
cat., Ikon Gallery, Birmingham; Städtische
Galerie im Lenbachhaus und Kunstbau,
Munich; Kunstmuseum St. Gallen; Kunsthalle
zu Kiel, Kiel, 2002

Additionally, I wrote the following texts, which
I occasionally drew on and incorporated in
excerpted and reconstituted forms:

'Uninhibited Thinking in Public Space:
Katharina Grosse's Architectural Paintings',
Parkett, No. 74, 2005, pp 112–18

'Katharina Grosse', *Sculpture*, October 2011,
pp 26–31.

'Sea Change: Katharina Grosse in the
Rockaways', *Art in America*, 4 August 2016,
https://www.artnews.com/art-in-america/
features/sea-change-katharina-grosse-in-the-
rockaways-60006/

1961
Born in Freiburg im Breisgau, Germany
Lives and works in Berlin, Germany and New
Zealand

1981
Studied Art History and English Language
and Literature, Ruhr-Universität Bochum,
Germany

1982–1985
Studied at the University of Fine Arts Münster,
Germany

1985–1990
Studied at the Kunstakademie Düsseldorf,
Germany

2000–2009
Professor at Weißensee Kunsthochschule Berlin,
Germany

2010–2018
Professor at the Kunstakademie Düsseldorf,
Germany

Awards, Fellow- and Scholarships

1992
Villa Romana Prize, Florence, Italy

1993
Schmidt-Rottluff Stipend, Germany

1995
Stiftung Kunstfonds Bonn, Germany

1999
The Chinati Foundation's Artist in Residence
programme, Marfa, TX, USA

2001
Artist in Residence at Elam School of Fine Art
programme, Auckland, New Zealand

2002
Andy Warhol Residency Award, Headlands
Foundation, San Francisco, CA, USA

2003
Fred Thieler Award, Berlin

2014
Oskar Schlemmer Award, Great State Prize for
Visual Arts of Baden-Wuerttemberg

2015
Otto-Ritschl-Kunstpreis, Wiesbaden, Germany

Member of The Akademie der Künste (Academy
of Arts), Berlin
Member of Advisory Board Fine Arts, Goethe-
Institut

Grosse has been selected by the German Federal
Government as a jury member for the 2020–23
stipends at Villa Massimo, Rome; Casa Baldi,
Olevano Romano; and Cité Internationale des
Arts, Paris

Exhibitions

Selected solo exhibitions

2020

It Wasn't Us, Hamburger Bahnhof – Museum für
Gegenwart – Berlin, Germany
Is It You?, Baltimore Museum of Art, MD, USA

2019

*Katharina Grosse x Gotthard Graubner. Absolute
Color*, MKM Museum Küppersmühle für
Moderne Kunst, Duisburg, Germany (two-
person show with Gotthard Graubner)
Mural: Jackson Pollock | Katharina Grosse, Museum
of Fine Arts, Boston, MA, USA (two-person
show with Jackson Pollock)
Mumbling Mud, chi K11 art space, Guangzhou,
China

2018

Mumbling Mud, chi K11 art museum, Shanghai,
China
Prototypes of Imagination, Gagosian, London, UK
Wunderbild, National Gallery in Prague, Czech
Republic
*Le numerose irregolarità: Katharina Grosse / Tatiana
Trouvé*, Villa Medici, Rome, Italy
(two-person show with Tatiana Trouvé)
*The Horse Trotted Another Couple of Metres, Then It
Stopped*, Carriageworks, Sydney, Australia

2017

This Drove my Mother up the Wall, South London
Gallery, London, UK
Katharina Grosse, Galerie nächst St. Stephan
Rosemarie Schwarzwälder, Vienna,
Austria
Katharina Grosse, Gagosian, 555 W 24th St, New
York, NY, USA
Katharina Grosse, König Galerie, Berlin,
Germany

2016

Katharina Grosse, MoMA PS1's *Rockaway!* series,
Queens, NY, USA
Katharina Grosse, Museum Frieder Burda, Baden-
Baden, Germany

2015

Seven Hours, Eight Rooms, Three Trees, Museum
Wiesbaden, Germany (including permanent
indoor installation)

yes no why later, Garage – Museum of
Contemporary Art, Moscow, Russia
The Smoking Kid, König Galerie, Berlin, Germany

2014

psychylustro, City of Philadelphia Mural Arts,
Philadelphia, PA, USA
Who, I? Whom, you?, Kunsthaus Graz, Austria
Inside the Speaker, Kunstpalast, Düsseldorf,
Germany

2013

Two younger women come in and pull out a table, De
Pont Museum, Tilburg, Netherlands
WUNDERBLOCK, Nasher Sculpture Center,
Dallas, TX, USA
Just Two of Us, Public Art Fund, New York, NY,
USA

2012

Third Man Begins Digging Through Her Pockets,
MOCA – Museum of Contemporary Art
Cleveland, OH, USA

2010

One Floor Up More Highly, MASS MoCA, North
Adams, MA, USA

2009

Shadowbox, Temporäre Kunsthalle, Berlin,
Germany
Hello Little Butterfly I Love You What's Your Name,
ARKEN Museum for Moderne Kunst, Ishøj,
Copenhagen, Denmark

2008

Another Man Who Has Dropped His Paintbrush,
Galleria Civica di Modena, Modena, Italy

2007

Atoms Outside Eggs, Museu de Arte
Contemporânea da Fundação de Serralves,
Porto, Portugal
Atoms Inside Ballons, Renaissance Society,
Chicago, IL, USA
Picture Park, Queensland Art Gallery South
Bank, Brisbane, Australia

2006

Holey Residue, De Appel, Amsterdam,
Netherlands

2005

Constructions à *cru*, Palais de Tokyo, Paris, France
Something Leadlight, Bergen Kunsthall, Bergen,
Norway

2004

Infinite Logic Conference, Magasin III Stockholm
Konsthall, Stockholm, Sweden
Double Floor Painting, Kunsthallen Brandts
Klædefabrik, Odense, Denmark
Perspectives 143: Katharina Grosse, CAMH –
Contemporary Arts Museum Houston, TX,
USA

2002

Der weisse Saal trifft sich im Wald, Kunstmuseum
St. Gallen, St. Gallen, Switzerland
Cool Puppen, Städtische Galerie im Lenbachhaus,
Munich, Germany
Cool Puppen, Ikon Gallery, Birmingham, UK

2001

Katharina Grosse, UCLA Hammer Museum, Los
Angeles, CA, USA

1998

Katharina Grosse, Project Space, Kunsthalle Bern,
Bern, Switzerland

Selected Group Exhibitions

2019

*Frozen Gesture: Gesture in Painting from Roy
Lichtenstein to Katharina Grosse*, Kunst
Museum Winterthur, Winterthur, Switzerland

2017

*ARoS Triennial: 'THE GARDEN – End of
Times; Beginning of Times'*, Aarhus, Denmark

2015

All the World's Futures, Fifty-sixth International Art
Exhibition – La Biennale di Venezia, Venice,
Italy

2014

Wizz Eyelashes – Walter De Maria, Katharina
Grosse, Sol LeWitt, Magasin 3 Stockholm
Konsthall, Sweden

2013
At Work – Studio and Production as a Subject of Today's Art, Museum für Gegenwartskunst Siegen, Siegen, Germany
Wall Works, Hamburger Bahnhof – Museum für Gegenwart, Berlin, Germany
Sixth Bienal de Curitiba, Curitiba, Brazil

2011
The Indiscipline of Painting, Tate St. Ives, Cornwall, UK

2009
Embrace!, Denver Art Museum, Denver, CO, USA
Space as Medium, Pérez Art Museum Miami, Miami, FL, USA

2008
Shake Before Using, Artium – Basque Museum-Center Of Contemporary Art, Vitoria-Gasteiz, Spain
Prospect.1, New Orleans Biennial, New Orleans, LA, USA

2007
Franchise, Stichting VHDG, Leeuwarden, Netherlands

2006
Berlin–Tokyo/Tokyo–Berlin: The Art of Two Cities, Mori Art Museum, Tokyo, Japan
Deutsche Wandstücke – Sette scene di nuova pittura germanica, Museion, Bolzano, Italy
Taipei Biennial: 'Dirty Yoga', Taipei, Taiwan
Der Blaue Reiter im 21. Jahrhundert, Städtische Galerie im Lenbachhaus, Munich, Germany

2005
Extreme Abstraction, Albright-Knox Art Gallery, Buffalo, NY, USA

2003
Contemporary Art of Germany, Busan Museum of Art, Busan, South Korea
Process, Kiasma – Museum of Contemporary Art, Helsinki, Finland

2002
Twenty-fifth Bienal de São Paulo, São Paulo, Brazil
Urgent Painting, Musée d'Art Moderne de la Ville de Paris, Paris, France

2001
'Casino 2001': first Quadrennial, S.M.A.K., Ghent, Belgium

1998
'Every day': eleventh Biennale of Sydney, Sydney, Australia

Selected Public Collections

Albertina Museum, Vienna, Austria
Albright-Knox Art Gallery, Buffalo, NY, USA
ARKEN Museum for Moderne Kunst, Copenhagen, Denmark
Centre Georges Pompidou, Paris, France
De Pont Museum, Tilburg, The Netherlands
Istanbul Modern, Istanbul, Turkey
Kunsthaus Zürich, Zürich, Switzerland
Kunstmuseum Bern, Bern, Switzerland
Kunstmuseum Bonn, Bonn, Germany
Kunstmuseum Liechtenstein, Vaduz, Liechtenstein
Kunstsammlung NRW, Düsseldorf, Germany
Kunstmuseum Stuttgart, Germany
Lenbachhaus, Munich, Germany
Mildred Lane Kemper Art Museum, St. Louis, MO, USA
Magasin 3 Stockholm Konsthall, Stockholm, Sweden
MAXXI – Museo nazionale delle arti del XXI secolo, Rome, Italy
Museum of Modern Art, graphic collection, NY, New York, USA
Museum Kunstpalast, Düsseldorf, Germany
Museum Folkwang, Essen, Germany
Museum Wiesbaden, Wiesbaden, Germany
Nasher Sculpture Center, Dallas, TX, USA
Neues Museum, Nuremberg, Germany
Pérez Art Museum Miami, Miami, FL, USA
The Serralves Foundation - Museu de Arte Contemporânea, Porto, Portugal
Staatliche Museen zu Berlin, Berlin, Germany
Sprengel Museum, Hanover, Germany
QAGOMA (Queensland Art Gallery and Gallery of Modern Art), Brisbane, Australia

Acknowledgments

I first wish to thank Katharina Grosse. We have been friends and colleagues for 25 years (and counting), during which time I have been privileged to witness the development of her extraordinary art and vision. Her attentiveness, generosity, keen insights, and forthright feedback helped shape my text and make this book possible. I am also indebted to Katharina Grosse's excellent team in Berlin. Kristin Rieber and Natalija Martinovic, in particular, were invaluable in terms of facilitating my research, providing me with information and images, and patiently answering my innumerable questions.

Heartfelt thanks to Barry Schwabsky, an art critic and poet that I (and a great many others) have long held in the very highest esteem. He recommended me for this project and provided crucial editing and suggestions at different stages of the writing process. I am honored that he placed his trust in me.

I am grateful for travel-related financial support from The Dean's Office of Virginia Commonwealth University School of the Arts, the Gagosian, Galerie nächst St. Stephan Rosemarie Schwarzwälder, and König Galerie. My research involved trips to Rome, Sydney, and Prague to see and absorb Katharina Grosse's painting installations, and to Berlin to interview her over five days. The support I received was of fundamental importance.

I am deeply grateful to those at Lund Humphries with whom I worked so fruitfully: Lucy Myers for her support, thoughtful guidance, and wise editing; Sarah Thorowgood for her masterly involvement with so many aspects of publishing this book; Rochelle Roberts for her thorough attention to images and layout; and Ian McDonald for his skillful copyediting. All are extremely talented. All bring dedication and expertise to their work.

Finally, I wish to thank my son Max Volk, who went from 16 and a sophomore in high school, when I began this project, to 18 and a college-bound senior at its conclusion. He often inquired how my writing was going and how the book was progressing, and gave me welcome encouragement – including at times (there were many) when my spirit was flagging. He also accompanied me on my final research trip to Prague, where he had the opportunity to experience Katharina Grosse's marvelous and immersive painting installation *Wunderbild* in person.

Photography credits

All works © Katharina Grosse and VG Bild-Kunst, Bonn, 2020 unless otherwise stated below. Numbers refer to pages.

Courtesy National Gallery in Prague, Galerie nächst St. Stephan Rosemarie Schwarzwälder, Vienna, Gagosian, and KÖNIG GALERIE, Berlin, London, Tokyo. Photography by Jens Ziehe: 6, 12-13; Photography by Jens Ziehe: 8; Studio Katharina Grosse: 11; Courtesy Nationalgalerie, Staatliche Museen zu Berlin. Photography © Christian Gahl: 15; Courtesy Kunsthaus Graz and Galerie Nächst St. Stephan Rosemarie Schwarzwälder, Vienna. Photography by Nicolas UMJ Lackner: 16-17; Courtesy Fundação Bienal de São Paulo. Photography by Juan Guerra: 18-19; Courtesy Magasin III Museum & Foundation for Contemporary Art and Galerie Nächst St. Stephan Rosemarie Schwarzwälder, Vienna. Photograph by Christian Saltas: 21; Courtesy South London Gallery and Gagosian. Photography by Andy Keate: 22; Courtesy The Renaissance Society, Chicago. Photography by Tom von Eynde: 24; Courtesy Queensland Art Gallery, Brisbane. Photography by Natasha Harth: 25; Courtesy The Renaissance Society, Chicago. Photography by Tom von Eynde: 26-27; © Katharina Grosse and VG Bild-Kunst, Bonn, 2020 / Nic Tenwiggenhorn and VG Bild-Kunst, Bonn, 2020; Courtesy Temporäre Kunsthalle Berlin. Photography by Nic Tenwiggenhorn © DACS 2020: 28; © Katharina Grosse and VG Bild-Kunst, Bonn, 2020 / © Nic Tenwiggenhorn and VG Bild-Kunst, Bonn, 2020; Courtesy KÖNIG GALERIE, Berlin, London, Tokyo. Photography Nic Tenwiggenhorn © DACS 2020: 47, 48-49; © Katharina Grosse and VG Bild-Kunst, Bonn, 2020 / Nic Tenwiggenhorn and VG Bild-Kunst, Bonn, 2020. Photography by Nic Tenwiggenhorn © DACS 2020: 82; © Katharina Grosse and VG Bild-Kunst, Bonn, 2020 / Nic Tenwiggenhorn and VG Bild-Kunst, Bonn, 2020; Courtesy Kunsthalle Düsseldorf. Photography by Nic Tenwiggenhorn © DACS 2020: 87; © Katharina Grosse and VG Bild-Kunst, Bonn, 2020 / Nic Tenwiggenhorn and VG Bild-Kunst, Bonn, 2020; Courtesy Museum Wiesbaden and KÖNIG GALERIE, Berlin, London, Tokyo. Photography Nic Tenwiggenhorn © DACS 2020: 100-101; © Katharina Grosse and VG Bild-Kunst, Bonn, 2020 / Nic Tenwiggenhorn and VG Bild-Kunst, Bonn, 2020; Courtesy La Biennale di Venezia, Barbara Gross, Munich, Galerie nächst St. Stephan Rosemarie Schwarzwälder, Vienna, KÖNIG GALERIE, Berlin, London, Tokyo and Mark Müller, Zurich. Photography by Nic Tenwiggenhorn © DACS 2020: 108-109; © Katharina Grosse and VG Bild-Kunst, Bonn, 2020 / Nic Tenwiggenhorn and VG Bild-Kunst, Bonn; Courtesy ARoS Kunstmuseum, Aarhus, and KÖNIG GALERIE, Berlin, London, Tokyo. Photograph by Nic Tenwiggenhorn © DACS 2020: 126-127; Courtesy Temporäre Kunsthalle Berlin. Photograph by Jens Ziehe: 29; Courtesy Pearson International Airport, Toronto. Photography by Isaac Applebaum: 30; Courtesy of KÖNIG GALERIE, Berlin, London, Tokyo and Facebook. Photography by John Barnett: 31; Courtesy Kunstmuseum Bonn and Galerie nächst St. Stephan Rosemarie Schwarzwälder, Wien. Photography by David Ertl: 33t; Courtesy Villa Medici, Rome, Gagosian and KÖNIG GALERIE, Berlin, London, Tokyo. Photography by Alessandro Vasari: 34; Commissioned by Carriageworks, Sydney; Courtesy Gagosian. Photography Zan Wimberley: 37t, 37b, 38-39; Courtesy Kunsthalle Bern. Photograph by Michael Fontana: 40; Collection of Museum für Gegenwartskunst Siegen. Photograph by Sabine Reitmaier: 41; Collection of Kunstmuseum Stuttgart; Photograph by Olaf Bergmann: 54; Photograph by Sebastian Schobbert: 55; Photograph by Studio Katharina Grosse: 57; Photograph by Olaf Bergmann: 58, 60-61, 62; Courtesy Gallery Mark Müller. Photograph by Olaf Bergmann: 59; Deutsche Bank Collection; Photograph by Olaf Bergmann: 63; Courtesy The Drawing Center, New York, NY. Photograph by Cathy Carver: 64; Photograph by Katharina Grosse: 65; Courtesy Chinati Foundation, Marfa, TX, photography by Rob Johannesma: 67; Courtesy Chinati Foundation, Marfa, TX, photography by Rob Johannesma: 66; Courtesy Atelier Amden and Kunsthaus Glarus. Photography by Christoph Kern: 68t, 68b; Courtesy Y8 / International Sivananda Yoga Vedanta Center, Hamburg. Photography by Frank Bergmann: 69, 70; Courtesy Kiasma - Museum of Contemporary Art, Helsinki. Photography by Yehia Ewels: 72, 73; Courtesy Ikon Gallery, Birmingham. Photography by Olaf Bergmann: 75, 76, 77; Courtesy CAMH - Contemporary Arts Museum Houston. Photography by Lisa Hardaway: 78-79; Courtesy CAMH - Contemporary Arts Museum Houston. Photography by Katharina Grosse: 80; Courtesy Magasin III Museum & Foundation for Contemporary Art, Stockholm. Photography by Mattias and Elisabeth Givell: 84, 85; Courtesy Kunsthallen Brandts Klaedefabrik, Odense. Photography by Torben Eskerod © DACS 2020: 88-89; Courtesy Palais de Tokyo, Paris. Photography by Florian Kleinefenn: 90-91; Courtesy Taipei Biennial. Photograph by Katharina Grosse: 92; Courtesy Nasher Sculpture Center, Dallas, and Galerie nächst St. Stephan Rosemarie Schwarzwälder, Vienna. Photography by Kevin Todora: 93, 94-95, 96; Courtesy Pierogi: 96; Courtesy Kurt-Kurt, Berlin. Photograph by Pfelder: 97; Courtesy Kurt-Kurt, Berlin. Photograph by Sebastian Schobbert: 98-99; Courtesy MASS MocA, North Adams, Christopher Grimes Gallery, Santa Monica, and Galerie nächst St. Stephan Rosemarie Schwarzwälder, Vienna. Photography by Art Evans: 105; Courtesy MASS MocA, North Adams, Christopher Grimes Gallery, Santa Monica, and Galerie nächst St. Stephan Rosemarie Schwarzwälder, Vienna. Photography by Art Evans: 104, 106-107; Courtesy of chi K11 art museum, Shanghai, Galerie nächst St. Stephan Rosemarie Schwarzwälder, Vienna. Photography by JJYPHOTO: 110, 112-113; Courtesy Gow Langsford Gallery. Photograph by Katharina Grosse: 118; Courtesy Berlinische Galerie – Landesmuseum für Moderne Kunst, Fotografie und Architektur, Berlin. Photograph by Olaf Bergmann: 116; Commissioned by the City of Philadelphia Mural Arts Program, USA. Photography by Steve Weinik: 119t, 119b, 120, 121; Commissioned by Public Art Fund, New York; Courtesy Collection of Christian and Sonia Zugel, KÖNIG GALERIE, Berlin, London, Tokyo. Photograph by Deniz Pekerman: 122; Commissioned by Public Art Fund, New York; Courtesy Collection of Christian and Sonia Zugel, KÖNIG GALERIE, Berlin, London, Tokyo. Photograph by Liz Ligon: 124-125; Courtesy ARoS Kunstmuseum, Aarhus, and KÖNIG GALERIE, Berlin, London, Tokyo. Photograph by Katharina Grosse: 128-129; Courtesy Prospect New Orleans. Photograph by Studio Katharina Grosse: 130; Commissioned by MoMA PS1. Image courtesy MoMA PS1. Photography by Pablo Enriquez: 132, 133; Commissioned by Vara Municipality and Public Art Agency Sweden, Vara, Sweden. Photograph by Katharina Grosse: 134; Commissioned by Vara Municipality and Public Art Agency Sweden, Vara, Sweden. Photograph by Staffan Sävenfjord: 135

Index

Page numbers in *italics* refer to illustrations

First published in 2020 by Lund Humphries

Lund Humphries
Office 3, Book House
261a City Road
London
ECIV IJX

www.lundhumphries.com

Unless otherwise stated illustrations are © Katharina Grosse and
VG Bild-Kunst, 2020

ISBN: 978–1–84822–323–3

A Cataloguing-in-Publication record for this book is available
from the British Library.

Copy-edited by Ian McDonald
Designed by Mark Thomson
Set in Custodia (Fred Smeijers)
Printed in Italy

Frontispiece: Katharina Grosse in 2017, photo by Max Vadukul
Cover: *Sieben Stunden, Acht Stimmen, Drei Bäume /Seven Hours, Eight Voices, Three
Trees* (detail), 2015. © Katharina Grosse and VG Bild-Kunst, Bonn, 2020 / Nic
Tenwiggenhorn and VG Bild-Kunst, Bonn; Courtesy Museum Wiesbaden and
KÖNIG GALERIE, Berlin, London, Tokyo. Photography Nic Tenwiggenhorn

This book was made possible with the support of Gagosian, Galerie Nächst St.
Stephan Rosemarie Schwarzwälder and König Galerie.